# KITCHEN LIBRARY
# PUDDINGS & DESSERTS

# KITCHEN LIBRARY
# PUDDINGS & DESSERTS

CHANCELLOR
PRESS

Front cover shows, clockwise from top left:
Blackcurrant cheesecake (33), Meringue croquembouches (93),
Redcurrant sorbet (161), Figs with lemon cream (1)

Title page shows, clockwise from top left:
Peach gateau (221), Brandy fruit soufflé (65),
Summer puddings (256), Minty chocolate chip ice (177)

Back cover shows, clockwise from top left:
Apricot fritters in brandy (145), Chocolate boxes (121),
Apple shortcake (249), Apricot toasts (193)

First published in Great Britain in 1990 as
*Hamlyn All Colour Puddings and Desserts*

This edition published in 1994 by Chancellor Press
an imprint of Reed Consumer Books Limited
Michelin House, 81 Fulham Road, London SW3 6RB
and Auckland, Melbourne, Singapore and Toronto

Copyright © 1990 Reed International Books Limited

Photographs from Reed Consumer Books Picture Library
Line drawings by Will Giles and Sandra Pond

ISBN 1 85152 639 0

A CIP catalogue record for this book is available
from the British Library

Produced by Mandarin Offset
Printed and bound in Hong Kong

# Contents

# Useful Facts and Figures

## Notes on metrication
In this book quantities are given in metric and Imperial measures. Exact conversion from Imperial to metric measures does not usually give very convenient working quantities and so the metric measures have been rounded off into units of 25 grams. The table below shows the recommended equivalents.

| Ounces | Approx g to nearest whole figure | Recommended conversion to nearest unit of 25 | Ounces | Approx g to nearest whole figure | Recommended conversion to nearest unit of 25 |
|---|---|---|---|---|---|
| 1 | 28 | 25 | 9 | 255 | 250 |
| 2 | 57 | 50 | 10 | 283 | 275 |
| 3 | 85 | 75 | 11 | 312 | 300 |
| 4 | 113 | 100 | 12 | 340 | 350 |
| 5 | 142 | 150 | 13 | 368 | 375 |
| 6 | 170 | 175 | 14 | 396 | 400 |
| 7 | 198 | 200 | 15 | 425 | 425 |
| 8 | 227 | 225 | 16 (1 lb) | 454 | 450 |

**Note:** When converting quantities over 16 oz first add the appropriate figures in the centre column, then adjust to the nearest unit of 25. As a general guide, 1 kg (1000 g) equals 2.2 lb or about 2 lb 3 oz. This method of conversion gives good results in nearly all cases, although in certain pastry and cake recipes a more accurate conversion is necessary to produce a balanced recipe.

**Liquid measures** The millilitre has been used in this book and the following table gives a few examples.

| Imperial | Approx ml to nearest whole figure | Recommended ml | Imperial | Approx ml to nearest whole figure | Recommended ml |
|---|---|---|---|---|---|
| $\frac{1}{4}$ | 142 | 150 ml | 1 pint | 567 | 600 ml |
| $\frac{1}{2}$ | 283 | 300 ml | 1½ pints | 851 | 900 ml |
| $\frac{3}{4}$ | 425 | 450 ml | 1¾ pints | 992 | 1000 ml (1 litre) |

**Spoon measures** All spoon measures given in this book are level unless otherwise stated.

**Can sizes** At present, cans are marked with the exact (usually to the nearest whole number) metric equivalent of the Imperial weight of the contents, so we have followed this practice when giving can sizes.

## Oven temperatures
The table below gives recommended equivalents.

| | °C | °F | Gas Mark | | °C | °F | Gas Mark |
|---|---|---|---|---|---|---|---|
| Very cool | 110 | 225 | ¼ | Moderately hot | 190 | 375 | 5 |
| | 120 | 250 | ½ | | 200 | 400 | 6 |
| Cool | 140 | 275 | 1 | Hot | 220 | 425 | 7 |
| | 150 | 300 | 2 | | 230 | 450 | 8 |
| Moderate | 160 | 325 | 3 | Very Hot | 240 | 475 | 9 |
| | 180 | 350 | 4 | | | | |

## Notes for American and Australian users
In America the 8-fl oz measuring cup is used. In Australia metric measures are now used in conjunction with the standard 250-ml measuring cup. The Imperial pint, used in Britain and Australia, is 20 fl oz, while the American pint is 16 fl oz. It is important to remember that the Australian tablespoon differs from both the British and American tablespoons; the table below gives a comparison. The British standard tablespoon, which has been used throughout this book, holds 17.7 ml, the American 14.2 ml, and the Australian 20 ml. A teaspoon holds approximately 5 ml in all three countries.

| British | American | Australian |
|---|---|---|
| 1 teaspoon | 1 teaspoon | 1 teaspoon |
| 1 tablespoon | 1 tablespoon | 1 tablespoon |
| 2 tablespoons | 3 tablespoons | 2 tablespoons |
| 3½ tablespoons | 4 tablespoons | 3 tablespoons |
| 4 tablespoons | 5 tablespoons | 3½ tablespoons |

## An Imperial/American guide to solid and liquid measures

| Imperial | American | Imperial | American |
|---|---|---|---|
| **Solid measures** | | **Liquid measures** | |
| 1 lb butter or margarine | 2 cups | ¼ pint liquid | ⅔ cup liquid |
| 1 lb flour | 4 cups | ½ pint | 1¼ cups |
| 1 lb granulated or caster sugar | 2 cups | ¾ pint | 2 cups |
| 1 lb icing sugar | 3 cups | 1 pint | 2½ cups |
| 8 oz rice | 1 cup | 1½ pints | 3¾ cups |
| | | 2 pints | 5 cups (2½ pints) |

**Note: When making any of the recipes in this book, only follow one set of measures as they are not interchangeable.**

# Introduction

Fresh and fruity, creamy and light, sizzling hot and crisp or frozen and scooped high, here is a dazzling array or irresistible desserts, bewitching to the eye and very tempting to the palate.

Hamlyn All Colour Puddings and Desserts is a celebration of desserts in all their guises from hot and cold puddings for all the family to stylish and sumptuous creations for party fare. The variety on offer means there is a recipe for every occasion, to suit every pocket, match the skills of novice and experienced cook alike and to ring the seasonal changes.

There are recipes for flaming crêpes, sugar-crusted fritters, light and fluffy mousses, steaming sponge and suet puddings, unforgettable, palate-sticking cheesecakes, crispy, fruit-laden pies, velvety-smooth ice creams and sorbets and light, layered cakes and gâteaux, to name just a few.

A colour photograph illustrates each and every recipe, so that you can see the result you are aiming for and those important decorating and finishing touches can be seen at first hand. When these are complicated they are covered further in the Cook's Tips which appear below each recipe. In addition these may also cover a speedy short-cut, cook-ahead pointers, food ingredient explanations or further ideas for authentic or dazzling decorations.

Attractive colour coding identifies individual chapters so that you can find your way easily through the book and each recipe is numbered so that you can turn to it in double-quick time.

For those who are watching their weight each recipe also gives a calorie-counted assessment of a portion size so that you can plan recipes around a calorie-controlled diet.

Preparation and cooking times, given at the beginning of each recipe will also give you at-a-glance information as to how much time to allow for cooking, chilling and decorating your chosen dessert.

The selection of recipes given is wide and diverse, you'll find many traditional and nursery favourites; yet more new ideas on familiar themes; many new and interesting recipes all the better for trying; and a whole host of foreign favourites collected from around the world.

Choose from over 270 tempting recipes to find the right one for every occasion – many are sure to become your own personal favourites. But remember, for a dessert to be highly-rated it must complement the dishes that go before it. Choose light, fluffy desserts likes soufflés, mousses and ice creams when the starter or main course is on the hefty side or serve richer desserts in wafer-thin portions. However, if they are meagre or light then go to town with a more substantial or rich pudding to satisfy hungry or man-sized appetites.

# Fresh Fruit Desserts

Fresh and fruity, here is the pick of the crop of tempting desserts using the best of spring, summer, autumn and imported winter fruits. Calorie counters can opt for simple yet imaginative fruit salads while those with no such worries can indulge in assemblies of fruit with cream, chocolate, nuts, liqueurs and praline.

## 1 | Figs with Lemon Cream

**Preparation time**
20 minutes, plus 1 hour to chill

**Serves 4**

**Calories**
225 per portion

**You will need**
8 fresh, ripe figs
1 teaspoon caster sugar
juice of 1 lemon
175 ml/ 6 fl oz double cream
8 sprigs of mint to decorate

Peel the figs if preferred, and cut a cross on the top of each one. Press gently to open the cross. Arrange the figs on a serving dish and chill for 1 hour.

Dissolve the sugar in the lemon juice and slowly stir in the cream. Adding the cream slowly to the sweetened lemon juice will thicken the cream. Spoon the cream into the figs, and decorate with sprigs of mint.

## 2 | Pickled Pears in Spiced Vinegar

**Preparation time**
15 minutes, plus 1 hour to chill

**Cooking time**
about 45 minutes

**Serves 4**

**Calories**
238 per portion

**You will need**
200 g/7 oz sugar
250 ml/8 fl oz water
50 ml /2 fl oz red wine
50 ml /2 fl oz red wine vinegar
3 cloves
1 blade of mace
5 black peppercorns
4 pears, peeled, halved and cored and sprinkled with lemon juice

Put the sugar and water in a pan and bring to the boil, stirring until the sugar dissolves. Add the wine, wine vinegar, cloves, mace and peppercorns. Lower the heat and place the pears in the syrup. Poach for about 30 minutes, until completely tender.

Lift the pears out with a slotted spoon and arrange them in a serving dish. Bring the syrup back to the boil until it is reduced to a thick syrup. Pour it over the pears. Leave to cool, then chill for an hour. Serve with whipped double cream with a little of the cold syrup added, and shortbread fingers.

## Cook's Tip

**Rub sugar lumps over the skin of a lemon until well coloured, then use the flavoured lumps whole or crushed in iced drinks.**

## Cook's Tip

**Keep a supply of both whole and ground cloves in your store cupboard, since cloves are difficult to grind yourself. Whole ones are used in recipes such as this, while ground cloves are useful when making fruit cakes.**

# 3 | Summer Salad

**Preparation time**
10 minutes, plus 1 hour
to chill

**Serves 6-8**

**Calories**
53 per portion

**You will need**
1 pineapple
2 oranges, segmented
100 g/4 oz strawberries, halved
100 g/4 oz black grapes, halved
    and seeded
120 ml/4 fl oz white wine
1 tablespoon clear honey
1 ripe pear
1 large banana
lemon balm leaves to decorate
    (optional)

Cut the pineapple in half lengthways, remove the flesh and cut into pieces, discarding the centre core; reserve the pineapple shells. Place the pineapple flesh in a bowl with the oranges, strawberries and grapes. Mix the wine and honey together and pour over the fruit.

Core and slice the pear into the bowl; slice the banana and add to the bowl. Toss the fruit with the wine until well coated. Turn into the pineapple shells and chill for about an hour. Decorate with lemon balm if available, and serve with whipped cream.

# 4 | Apricot and Orange Cream

**Preparation time**
15 minutes, plus
overnight soaking

**Serves 6**

**Calories**
256 per portion

**You will need**
225 g/8 oz dried apricots, roughly
    chopped
300 ml/½ pint orange juice
2 bananas
2 tablespoons Grand Marnier
1 orange
150 ml/¼ pint double cream
2 teaspoons clear honey
150 g/5.2 oz carton natural yogurt

Place the apricots and orange juice in a bowl and leave to soak overnight.

Slice the bananas and add to the bowl with the Grand Marnier. Mix well, then transfer to a serving bowl. Using a potato peeler, peel the rind off half the orange, cut into fine strips and set aside. Grate the remaining rind and mix with the juice of half the orange. Stir this into the cream with the honey, then whip until it stands in stiff peaks. Stir in the yogurt. Spoon over the fruit and sprinkle with the orange rind strips to serve.

## Cook's Tip

**Use the tip of a sharp knife to remove the seeds from halved grapes.**

## Cook's Tip

**Natural yogurt can form the basis of many quick and simple desserts. Stir in some fruit purée, honey, jam, praline (recipe 22), or chopped nuts, diced apple or sliced banana for a speedy and nourishing dessert.**

# 5 | Elderberry and Apple Purée

**Preparation time**
30-40 minutes

**Cooking time**
15-20 minutes

**Serves 6**

**Calories**
128 per portion

**You will need**
1 kg/2 lb cooking apples, peeled
  and cored
juice of 1 lemon
15 g/½ oz butter
50 ml/2 fl oz water
caster sugar to sweeten
225 g/8 oz elderberries

To make the apple purée, slice the apples thinly into a bowl with the lemon juice to prevent discoloration. Melt the butter in a thick saucepan and add the apples and water. Cover and cook gently for about 10 minutes until the apple slices are pulpy. Remove the lid and continue to cook, stirring, until all the liquid has evaporated.

Beat the apple into a thick, smooth purée or blend in a liquidiser for a really smooth result. Add sugar to taste and stir in the elderberries. Spoon into a serving dish and leave to cool. Serve with whipped cream flavoured with a little grated lemon rind and sugar, if desired.

# 6 | Cox's Orange Slices

**Preparation time**
20 minutes

**Cooking time**
20 minutes

**Serves 4**

**Calories**
525 per portion

**You will need**
200 g/7 oz unsalted butter
4 small Cox's apples, peeled,
  cored and cut into 8 segments
65 g/2½ oz soft dark brown sugar
juice of ¼ lemon
juice of 1 orange
2 cloves
25 g/1 oz raisins
4 large slices brown bread

Heat 65 g/2½ oz of the butter in a pan. Fry the apple segments until they start to brown. Add the sugar, lemon and orange juice, cloves and raisins. Simmer gently until the apple is cooked through.

Trim the slices of bread with a knife so they are circular or use a plain round cutter. Heat the remaining butter in a large frying pan and fry the bread until crisp. Place the slices of bread on a serving dish. Arrange eight apple segments on each one in a neat pattern and spoon over the syrup and raisins. Serve hot.

## Cook's Tip

**Elderberries, blackberries and loganberries can be found growing in the hedgerows in August and September. Elderberries add a wonderful flavour to fruit purées, especially apple.**

## Cook's Tip

**As an alternative to frying the bread, brush all over with melted butter, place on a baking tray and cook in a preheated oven, 200C, 400F, gas 6, for 10 minutes until golden brown and crisp.**

# 7 | *Fruit Brûlée*

**Preparation time**
30 minutes, plus 30
minutes to chill

**Cooking time**
about 3 minutes

**Serves 4**

**Calories**
580 per portion

**You will need**
1 egg
1 egg yolk
25 g/1 oz caster sugar
1 teaspoon plain flour
200 ml/⅓ pint double cream
1 dessert apple, peeled, cored and
　sliced
1 nectarine, stoned and sliced
1 orange, peeled, segmented and
　pith and skin removed
1 banana, peeled and sliced on the
　slant
225 g/8 oz sugar
65 ml/2½ fl oz water

Put four freezerproof dessert plates in the freezer for 30
minutes to chill.

Meanwhile, beat the egg, egg yolk, sugar and flour together in a bowl. Scald the cream in a small saucepan.
Pour it into the mixture, stirring constantly to combine
the ingredients thoroughly.
Pour the custard into a clean pan and heat gently, stirring
constantly, until it thickens. Pour the custard on to the
cold plates. Divide the sliced fruit equally between the
plates, arranging them decoratively on top of the custard.
Make a golden caramel with the sugar and water. Spoon
over the fruit and custard.

# 8 | *Bondepige Med Slör*

**Preparation time**
20 minutes

**Cooking time**
15 minutes

**Serves 4**

**Calories**
360 per portion

**You will need**
500 g/1 lb cooking apples, peeled,
　cored and chopped
120 g/4½ oz soft light brown sugar
50 g/2 oz unsalted butter
100 g/4 oz brown breadcrumbs
150 ml /¼ pint double cream
2 tablespoons raspberry jam
　(optional)

Put the apples in a pan with a tablespoon of water and
simmer until tender. Press them through a sieve. Add
90 g/3½ oz of the soft brown sugar.

Heat the butter in a small pan and fry the breadcrumbs
until they are crisp. Remove from the heat and combine
the crumbs with the remaining brown sugar. Put one-
third of the sweetened crumbs in a trifle dish. Spoon half
the apple on top. Repeat these layers, then cover with
the remaining crumbs.

Whip the cream until it holds its shape on the whisk
and spread it on top. Warm the jam slightly, if using, and
spoon it over the cream.

## Cook's Tip

**The method of chilling the
plates quickly in the freezer
can be applied to foods that
you want to cool in a hurry,
such as jellies, chocolate for
decorating and so on.**

## Cook's Tip

**To make breadcrumbs quickly,
use a blender or food
processor. Cut the bread into
cubes and drop them into the
running machine through a
hole in the lid or a tube.**

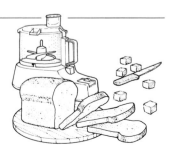

# 9 | *Guava Passion*

**Preparation time**
10 minutes

**Serves 6**

**Calories**
75 per portion

**You will need**
2 oranges
1 (411 g/14½ oz) can guavas
2 bananas (optional)
100 g/4 oz black grapes, halved
    and seeded
2 passion fruit

Peel the oranges, removing all pith, and cut into segments. Place in a serving bowl with the juice from the guavas. Slice the guavas and bananas, if using, and add to the bowl with the grapes. Halve the passion fruit, scoop out the flesh and mix with the other fruit. Serve with whipped cream.

# 10 | *Winter Fruit Salad*

**Preparation time**
5 minutes, plus
overnight soaking

**Cooking time**
15 minutes

**Serves 6**

**Calories**
178 per portion

**You will need**
175 g/6 oz dried apricots
100 g/4 oz dried prunes
100 g/4 oz dried figs
600 ml/1 pint water
2 tablespoons clear honey
2.5 cm/1 in piece of cinnamon
    stick
2 cloves
juice of ½ lemon
50 g/2 oz raisins
25 g/1 oz walnut halves, coarsely
    chopped
25 g/1 oz flaked almonds, toasted

Soak the apricots, prunes and figs overnight. Place the water, honey, cinnamon and cloves in a pan and bring to the boil. Add the lemon juice. Drain the dried fruits and add to the pan. Cover and simmer gently for 10 minutes.

Add the raisins and simmer for 2-3 minutes. Discard the cinnamon and cloves. Spoon into individual serving dishes and sprinkle with the walnuts and almonds. Serve hot or cold, with cream if liked.

## Cook's Tip

*Store oranges at a cool room temperature and they will keep for 1-2 weeks.*

## Cook's Tip

*Remove the stalks and absorb excess surface oil on raisins by rubbing them in a sieve with a little flour.*

## 11 | Peaches in Blackcurrant Sauce

**Preparation time**
*5 minutes, plus 1 hour to chill*

**Cooking time**
*about 10 minutes*

**Serves 6**

**Calories**
*125 per portion*

**You will need**
*500 g/1 lb blackcurrants*
*100 g/4 oz caster sugar*
*250 ml/8 fl oz water*
*grated rind and juice of 1 orange*
*6 ripe peaches, peeled*

Put the blackcurrants, sugar and water in a pan and cook gently, stirring occasionally, for about 10 minutes or until soft. Sieve, pressing as much pulp through as possible. Add the orange rind and juice.

Place the peaches in a serving bowl and pour over the blackcurrant purée. Chill for at least an hour. Serve with cream if liked.

## 12 | Apple and Blackberry Fool

**Preparation time**
*5-10 minutes, plus 1 hour to chill*

**Cooking time**
*15 minutes*

**Serves 6**

**Calories**
*289 per portion*

**You will need**
*500 g/1 lb cooking apples, peeled, cored and sliced*
*225 g/8 oz blackberries*
*50 g/2 oz soft brown sugar*
*300 ml/½ pint double cream, whipped*

Place the apples, blackberries and sugar in a heavy-based pan. Cover and simmer gently for 15 minutes, until soft. Allow to cool, then blend in a liquidiser or food processor to make a purée. Sieve to remove the seeds. Fold the cream into the purée. Spoon into individual dishes and chill for at least an hour.

## Cook's Tip

*Skin peaches in the same way as tomatoes. Place in a bowl and cover with boiling water, leave for a minute, then drain and simply slip off the skin using a sharp, pointed knife.*

## Cook's Tip

*If you are trying to cut down on the fat content of your diet, simply replace the double cream with natural yogurt instead.*

## 13 | Kumquats in Grenadine

**Preparation time**
10 minutes, plus 1 hour
to chill

**Oven temperature**
200C, 400F, gas 6

**Serves 4-6**

**Calories**
146 per portion

**You will need**
750 g/1½ lb kumquats
25 g/1 oz caster sugar
150 ml/¼ pint grenadine

For the langues de chat
75 g/3 oz butter
75 g/3 oz caster sugar
3 egg whites
75 g/3 oz plain flour, sifted
few drops vanilla essence

Wash the kumquats, and cut each one into about four slices. Arrange in individual dishes. Sprinkle with the sugar and pour over the grenadine. Chill for an hour.

Meanwhile, make the langues de chat biscuits. Cream the butter and sugar together until light and fluffy. Lightly whisk the egg whites and gradually beat into the creamed mixture with the flour and vanilla essence. Spoon into a piping bag fitted with a 1 cm/½ in plain nozzle and pipe thirty 7.5 cm/3 in lengths on to greased and floured baking sheets. Bake for 10 minutes, then cool on a wire rack.

Serve the kumquats with cream and the biscuits handed separately.

## 14 | Green Fruit Salad

**Preparation time**
10 minutes, plus 1 hour
to macerate

**Serves 4-6**

**Calories**
87 per portion

**You will need**
150 ml/¼ pint apple juice
1 tablespoon clear honey
3 tablespoons Kirsch or
    Chartreuse
1 green dessert apple, quartered
    and cored
1 pear, quartered and cored
1 Honeydew melon, halved and
    seeded
100 g/4 oz seedless grapes
2 kiwi fruit, peeled and sliced
few lemon balm leaves, chopped

Mix the apple juice, honey and Kirsch or Chartreuse together in a bowl. Slice the apple and pear thinly into the juice and stir to coat completely. Cut the melon flesh into cubes, add to the bowl with the grapes and kiwi fruit and leave for 1 hour, stirring occasionally.

Turn into a serving dish and sprinkle with the lemon balm to serve.

## Cook's Tip

**Kumquats are eaten whole, including the skin. They are also useful for garnishing dishes, especially duck, and are delicious as a preserve.**

## Cook's Tip

**Lemon balm imparts a delicate flavour to cakes if you sprinkle a little of it on to the greaseproof paper lining the tin before adding the cake mixture.**

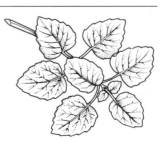

# 15 | *Banana Celestes*

**Preparation time**
*10 minutes*

**Cooking time**
*30-40 minutes*

**Oven temperature**
*180C, 350F, gas 4*

**Serves 4-6**

**Calories**
*415 per portion*

**You will need**
*225 g/8 oz full-fat soft cheese*
*65 g/2½ oz light soft sugar*
*½ teaspoon powdered cinnamon*
*50 g/2 oz unsalted butter*
*6 large firm bananas, peeled,*
  *halved across and sliced*
  *lengthways*
*4 tablespoons double cream*

Beat the cheese, sugar and half the cinnamon together until light and fluffy. Melt the butter in a large frying pan and, when it stops foaming, add the bananas and cook a few at a time until lightly browned. Turn them over gently so that they colour on both sides.

Place half of the bananas, cut-side down, in an oven-proof dish. Spread about half the cheese mixture on top. Cover with the remainder of the bananas and cheese mixture. Pour the cream over the top and bake for 20-30 minutes until the bananas are tender and the cream is a light golden brown colour. Sprinkle with the remaining cinnamon and serve immediately.

# 16 | *Pears in Grenadine*

**Preparation time**
*15 minutes, plus*
*overnight soaking*

**Cooking time**
*30 minutes*

**Serves 6**

**Calories**
*175 per portion*

**You will need**
*6 firm pears, peeled and left*
  *whole*
*450 ml/¾ pint grenadine syrup*
*750 ml/1¼ pints water*
*1 teaspoon ground cloves*
*1 teaspoon ground cinnamon*
*1 teaspoon ground nutmeg*
*juice of 1 lemon*
*225 g/8 oz sugar*

Place the pears in a pan large enough for them all to rest on the base. Mix together with the grenadine and water and pour over the pears. Add the cloves, cinnamon, nutmeg and lemon juice, then bring slowly to the boil. Simmer for 2-3 minutes, then remove from the heat and leave overnight to allow the pears to macerate.

Remove the pears and arrange on a serving dish. Strain the soaking juices into a clean saucepan, and cook rapidly until the liquid has reduced by half.

Add the sugar and stir over a gentle heat until it has dissolved then boil again until a syrup is obtain. (A sugar thermometer should register 107C/225F, or the syrup will form a fine, thin thread if allowed to fall from a spoon on to a dish.) Cool the syrup and pour over the pears. Allow to cool before serving with vanilla ice cream, or cream, if liked.

## Cook's Tip

*Slice bananas as close as possible to the time you serve them. To prevent discoloration, sprinkle or soak them in fresh lemon, lime or orange juice.*

## Cook's Tip

*Grenadine is a syrup made from pomegranates. It is non-alcoholic and is generally used as a base for cocktails – the best known of these being Tequila Sunrise.*

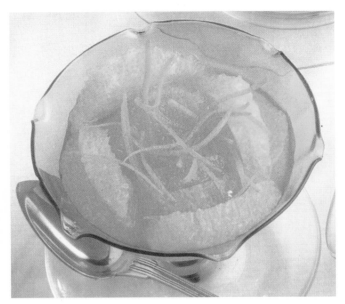

# 17 | Peppermint Pears

**Preparation time**
15 minutes, plus 2-3
hours to chill

**Cooking time**
30-35 minutes

**Serves 4**

**Calories**
99 per portion

**You will need**
100 g/4 oz sugar
300 ml/½ pint water
1 tablespoon lemon juice
8 small Conference pears
3 tablespoons crème de menthe
few drops green food colouring
sprigs of mint to decorate

Place the sugar, water and lemon juice in a pan and cook over a gentle heat until the sugar dissolves.

Peel the pears, leaving the stalks intact. Cut a slice from the base of each pear so they stand upright. Using a small pointed knife, carefully scoop out the pips, starting from the base so that the pears remain whole.

Add the crème de menthe and green food colouring to the sugar syrup and bring to the boil. Place the pears, standing upright, in the saucepan. Cover and simmer for 20-25 minutes until tender.

Transfer the pears to a serving dish. Boil the syrup rapidly until fairly thick, then spoon over the pears. Chill for several hours, spooning the syrup over them from time to time. Decorate with sprigs of mint.

# 18 | Orange and Grapefruit in Caramel

**Preparation time**
40 minutes, plus 3-4
hours to chill

**Cooking time**
10 minutes

**Serves 8**

**Calories**
157 per portion

**You will need**
4 seedless oranges
4 grapefruits
225 g/8 oz sugar
250 ml/8 fl oz water
3 tablespoons Grand Marnier

Pare the rind from 1 orange and half a grapefruit and shred finely. Put the rind in a small pan and cover with boiling water. Bring to the boil and simmer for 2 minutes, then drain. Peel the oranges and grapefruit, removing all the pith. Cut the fruit into segments and arrange in a dish. Put the sugar and 120 ml/ 4 fl oz of the water in a heavy saucepan. Heat gently without letting it boil until all the sugar has dissolved. Increase the heat and boil until it is a rich golden caramel.

Bring the remaining water to the boil in a pan. Remove the caramel from the heat and quickly pour in the hot water. Take great care as the water will splutter over the pan. Stir until the caramel has melted, returning to the heat briefly if necessary. Leave to cool. Add the Grand Marnier. Sprinkle the segments with the prepared peel and pour the syrup over the top. Chill for several hours before serving with langues de chat biscuits (recipe 13).

## Cook's Tip

**Either use plain sprigs of mint to decorate, or make sugared mint leaves. Brush them lightly with egg white and dredge thoroughly with caster sugar. Dry and use on the same day.**

## Cook's Tip

**Avoid the loss of vitamin C content by adding orange juice after cooking rather than before.**

# 19 | *Strawberry Shortcake*

**Preparation time**
20 minutes

**Cooking time**
20 minutes

**Oven temperature**
180C, 350F, gas 4

**Serves 6**

**Calories**
501 per portion

**You will need**
100 g/4 oz butter
50 g/2 oz caster sugar
100 g/4 oz plain flour, sifted
50 g/2 oz cornflour, sifted
225 g/8 oz strawberries
300 ml/½ pint double cream, whipped
sifted icing sugar to dredge

Cream the butter and sugar together until soft and fluffy, then stir in the flour and cornflour. Mix to a firm dough, then turn on to a floured surface and knead lightly.

Divide the mixture in half and roll each piece into a 20 cm/8 in round on a baking tray. Bake for 20 minutes. Leave for a few minutes, then mark one round into six sections. Carefully slide both rounds on to a wire rack to cool.

Slice the strawberries lengthways. Set aside six slices for decoration. Mix three-quarters of the cream with the strawberries and spread over the plain round of shortcake. Break the other round into six sections and place on top. Sprinkle with icing sugar. Pipe a cream rosette on each section and decorate with the reserved strawberry slices.

# 20 | *Pineapple Flambé*

**Preparation time**
10 minutes

**Cooking time**
10 minutes

**Serves 4**

**Calories**
229 per portion

**You will need**
90 g/3½ oz caster sugar
grated rind and juice of 1 orange
juice of ½ lemon
40 g/1½ oz unsalted butter
4 thick slices fresh pineapple
2 tablespoons Kirsch (or rum)

Put the sugar, grated rind and juices in a frying pan. Bring to the boil, stirring until the sugar has dissolved and the mixture thickens to a syrup. Lower the heat and add the butter. Swirl it around the pan until melted.

Add the pineapple slices and cook gently until heated through, basting them regularly with the syrup. Lift each slice out of the pan with a slotted spoon on to warmed individual serving dishes. Pour the Kirsch or rum into the pan. Carefully set the syrup alight and pour it, still flaming, over the pineapple slices.

## Cook's Tip

*For an alternative method of decorating cakes and shortcake, place a paper doyley on top and dredge lightly with icing sugar then remove. This creates a delicate lacy effect.*

## Cook's Tip

*To make banana flambé, replace the caster sugar with soft brown sugar, and use 4 bananas, peeled and halved lengthways, instead of the pineapple. Use rum in place of the Kirsch.*

## 21 | Summer Fruit Whirl

**Preparation time**
15 minutes, plus 1 hour to chill

**Cooking time**
3 hours

**Oven temperature**
110C, 225F, gas ¼

**Serves 6**

**Calories**
316 per portion

**You will need**
175 g/6 oz strawberries, halved
175 g/6oz raspberries
1 tablespoon caster sugar
2 tablespoons brandy
300 ml/½ pint double cream, whipped

**For the meringues**
4 egg whites
225 g/8 oz caster sugar
1 teaspoon lemon juice

To make the meringues, whisk the egg whites until very stiff and dry. Carefully add the sugar 1 tablespoon at a time, whisking very thoroughly between each addition. Whisk in the lemon juice. The meringue should be smooth, glossy and form soft peaks. Place the mixture in a piping bag fitted with a large rose nozzle and pipe eight rounds on to a baking tray lined with silicone paper. Bake for about 3 hours or until the meringues are firm to the touch. Leave on the baking tray until cold.

Meanwhile, place the strawberries and raspberries in a bowl and sprinkle with the sugar and brandy. Leave to soak for 1 hour.

Break the meringues into small pieces and fold into the cream. Spoon one-third of the fruit into six glasses. Cover with half of the cream mixture. Repeat the layers, finishing off with a layer of fruit. Chill for at least an hour before serving.

## Cook's Tip

*To keep meringues fresh and crisp for up to a week, store in an airtight container.*

## 22 | Praline Pears

**Preparation time**
30 minutes, plus 30 minutes to cool

**Cooking time**
about 25 minutes

**Serves 4**

**Calories**
709 per portion

**You will need**
4 ripe, even-sized Comice pears
225 g/8 oz sugar
600 ml/1 pint water
few strips of lemon rind
300 ml/½ pint double cream

**For the praline**
50 g/2 oz sugar
50 g/2 oz whole almonds

To make the praline, put the sugar in a heavy-based pan, moisten with water and boil for 3 minutes. Test as instructed below (see Cook's Tip). Add the almonds and remove from the heat. Stir with a wooden spoon until the sugar forms a crust round each nut.

Return to the heat. Stirring constantly, cook until the sugar has melted and caramelised. Pour on to an oiled place and cool for 30 minutes. When completely cold, break the praline into pieces and grind to a powder in a blender, grinder or food processor.

Meanwhile peel and core the pears, leaving them whole with the stalks on. Dissolve the sugar in the water, then add the lemon rind. Bring to the boil, then reduce to a simmer. Poach the pears in the syrup for 10 minutes, turning occasionally. Leave them in the syrup until cold.

Lift the pears out of the syrup and leave to drain. Place in four individual serving dishes. Whip the cream until it is stiff, then fold in half the praline. Cover the pears completely with the cream. Sprinkle with the remaining praline and serve.

## Cook's Tip

*To check that the sugar has reached the right temperature when making praline, spoon a little of it into a bowl of ice cold water. It should form a soft ball when pressed together with the fingers.*

# 23 | Kissel Cup

**Preparation time**
10 minutes, plus 30
minutes to cool and 1
hour to chill

**Cooking time**
20 minutes

**Serves 6**

**Calories**
255 per portion

**You will need**
225 g/8 oz mixed blackcurrants
　and redcurrants
50 g/2 oz caster sugar
4 tablespoons water
grated rind and juice of ½ orange
100 g/4 oz raspberries
100 g/4 oz strawberries, sliced
1 teaspoon arrowroot
4 tablespoons brandy
250 ml/8 fl oz whipping cream
1 tablespoon icing sugar, sifted
redcurrants to decorate

Place the currants in a pan with the caster sugar, water
and orange rind. Bring to the boil and simmer gently for
10 minutes, until softened. Strain, reserving the syrup.
Place the currants in a bowl with the raspberries and
strawberries.

Return the syrup to the pan and bring to the boil. Mix
the arrowroot with the orange juice and stir into the boiling syrup. Cook, stirring constantly, until thickened and
clear. Pour over the fruit with 2 tablespoons of the
brandy, mix well and leave to cool.

Spoon the fruit mixture into six serving dishes. Whip
the cream with the remaining brandy and the icing sugar
and spoon over the fruit mixture. Chill for an hour. Decorate with redcurrants to serve.

# 24 | Rhubarb and Ginger Compote

**Preparation time**
20 minutes

**Cooking time**
15-20 minutes

**Serves 6**

**Calories**
190 per portion

**You will need**
1 kg/2 lb rhubarb, washed
225 g/8 oz sugar
300 ml/½ pint water
75 g/3 oz preserved stem ginger,
　finely chopped

Top and tail the rhubarb. Remove the stringy skin. Cut
into 5 cm/2 in lengths.

Dissolve the sugar and water in a pan over a gentle
heat. Bring to the boil. Add the rhubarb and ginger to the
syrup, reserving two or three pieces of ginger for decoration. Simmer gently for 15 minutes.

Pour the compote into a serving dish and leave to cool.
Decorate with the reserved stem ginger. Serve with ice
cream or whipped cream.

## Cook's Tip

**To remove red or
blackcurrants quickly from
their stalks, run the stalk
through the prongs of a fork.**

## Cook's Tip

**The normal growing season
for rhubarb is from May to
July, but early, forced rhubarb
is available from January to
April.**

# 25 | Blackcurrants and Redcurrants in Cointreau

**Preparation time**
5 minutes, plus
overnight chilling

**Serves 4**

**Calories**
105 per portion

**You will need**
grated rind and juice of 1 orange
2 tablespoons clear honey
3 tablespoons Cointreau
225 g/8 oz redcurrants
225 g/8 oz blackcurrants

Mix together the orange rind and juice, honey and Cointreau. Place the redcurrants and blackcurrants in a serving bowl, pour over the orange-flavoured syrup and chill overnight. Serve with whipped cream.

# 26 | Mango Ice Cream

**Preparation time**
15 minutes, plus 3-4
hours to freeze

**Cooking time**
5-8 minutes

**Serves 4-6**

**Calories**
400 per portion

**You will need**
150 ml /¼ pint single cream
3 egg yolks
75 g/3 oz caster sugar
1 (425 g/15 oz) can sliced mango
   in syrup, drained
200 ml/⅓ pint double cream

Heat the single cream in a pan until just under boiling point. Put the egg yolks and sugar in a bowl and whisk well together. Pour the hot cream on to the egg mixture, stirring well, then whisk over a pan of gently simmering water for 5-6 minutes until the mixture thickens to coat the back of a spoon. Strain the mixture into a bowl and leave to cool.

Meanwhile purée the mango in a blender or food processor until smooth, then add to the custard mixture. Whip the double cream and fold into the custard.

Pour the mixture into a freezerproof container, cover and freeze for about an hour until partially frozen around the edges. Using a fork, stir the frozen parts into the unfrozen parts until thoroughly combined, then cover and freeze until firm.

Transfer the ice cream to the refrigerator 20 minutes before serving to soften. Serve with crisp wafers.

## Cook's Tip

*Macerating (or soaking) the fruit in a Cointreau-flavoured syrup softens its texture and improves the flavour – so prepare this fruit salad the day before you intend to serve it.*

## Cook's Tip

*For special occasions, frost the tops of serving glasses by dipping the rims lightly in beaten egg and then in sugar.*

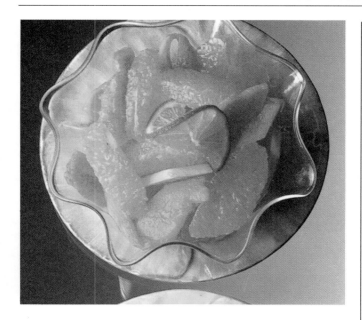

# 27 | Polynesian Pawpaw Salad

**Preparation time**
5 minutes

**Serves 4**

**Calories**
52 per portion

**You will need**
1 pawpaw
juice of ½ lime
1 pink-fleshed grapefruit
lime slices to decorate

Cut the pawpaw into quarters and remove the seeds. Peel and slice into a glass bowl. Pour over the lime juice. Peel the grapefruit, removing all pith, and cut into segments. Add to the bowl and chill until required. Decorate with lime slices to serve.

# 28 | Pears with Chocolate Sauce

**Preparation time**
15 minutes, plus 30 minutes to cool

**Cooking time**
about 15 minutes

**Serves 4**

**Calories**
851 per portion

**You will need**
225 g/8 oz sugar
600 ml/1 pint water
few strips of lemon rind
4 evenly-sized Comice pears, peeled
600 ml/1 pint vanilla ice cream

For the sauce
85 ml/3 fl oz double cream
100 g/4 oz dark plain chocolate, broken into pieces

To make the syrup, dissolve the sugar in the water, then add the lemon rind. Bring to the boil, then reduce to a simmer. Poach the pears in the syrup until they are tender. Leave to cool in the syrup.

Place two scoops of ice cream in each of four sundae glasses and top with a drained, cold poached pear.

To make the sauce, put the cream in a small saucepan and heat it gently just to boiling point. Remove the pan from the heat and add the chocolate. Stir until it is melted. Pour the warm sauce over the pears and serve immediately.

## Cook's Tip

**Pawpaw is also known as papaya. They are ready to eat when they yield to gentle pressure applied in the palm of your hand.**

## Cook's Tip

**If you have to leave a cooked sauce to stand for any time, place the bowl or pan in a water bath (bain marie). It keeps it warm but doesn't allow it to burn.**

# 29 | *Apple Salad Cups*

**Preparation time**
20 minutes

**Serves 4**

**Calories**
173 per portion

**You will need**
4 large red dessert apples
1 tablespoon lemon juice
1 small banana, peeled, quartered
  and sliced
50 g/2 oz sultanas
25 g/1 oz flaked almonds, chopped
3 tablespoons diced melon
  (optional)
150 ml /5.2 oz carton black cherry
  yogurt

Cut a thin slice of each apple at the flower end. Using a serrated grapefruit knife or a small sharp knife, carefully scoop out the apple flesh, cutting to within 5 mm/¼ in of the edge of each apple. Cut the apple flesh into small pieces and place in a bowl.

Brush the insides of the apple shells with the lemon juice and sprinkle the remainder over the diced apple. Toss well to prevent discoloration. Add the banana, sultanas, almonds and melon, if using. Stir in the yogurt and lightly mix together. Spoon the fruit mixture into the apple shells and serve immediately.

# 30 | *Caribbean Salad*

**Preparation time**
10 minutes

**Serves 4-6**

**Calories**
51 per portion

**You will need**
1 Charentais or Galia melon,
  halved and seeded
1 mango, peeled
1 banana
3 tablespoons white rum
lemon balm sprigs to decorate
  (optional)

Cut the flesh out of the melon halves and cut into slices. Reserve the shells.

Cut the mango in half lengthways, as close to the stone as possible. Using a sharp knife, remove the stone. Cut the flesh into slices and place in a bowl with the melon. Slice the banana and add to the fruit with the rum. Stir well, then spoon into the reserved melon shells and decorate with lemon balm, if using.

## Cook's Tip

**The flesh of apples, oranges, melons, pineapples and watermelons can be scooped out leaving the shells to provide impressive serving cups for ice cream, sorbet, fruit salads and fools.**

## Cook's Tip

**If you have to store cut melon in the refrigerator, cover it carefully with cling film as it quickly absorbs the smell and flavour of other foods.**

# 31 | *Fraises Plougastel*

**Preparation time**
5 minutes, plus 30
minutes to chill

**Serves 4**

**Calories**
76 per portion

**You will need**
500 g/1 lb strawberries
2 tablespoons caster sugar
grated rind and juice of ½ orange
2 tablespoons Grand Marnier

Divide half the strawberries between 4 individual serving dishes. Place the remaining strawberries in a bowl with the sugar and orange rind, then mash to a pulp using a fork. Add the orange juice and Grand Marnier and mix thoroughly. Pour this pulped mixture over the whole strawberries. Chill for at least 30 minutes. Serve with whipped cream.

# 32 | *Port and Cherry Compote*

**Preparation time**
5 minutes

**Cooking time**
8-10 minutes

**Serves 4**

**Calories**
143 per portion

**You will need**
750 g/1½ lb cherries, stoned
2 tablespoons redcurrant jelly
120 ml/4 fl oz port
thinly pared rind and juice of 1
orange
2 teaspoons arrowroot

Place the cherries in a pan with the redcurrant jelly, port and orange rind. Cover and bring slowly to the boil. Stir gently and simmer for 4-5 minutes. Transfer the cherries to individual glass bowls with a slotted spoon. Remove the orange rind.

Blend the orange juice with the arrowroot, then add to the syrup in the pan. Bring to the boil, stirring, and simmer for 1 minute. Cool, then pour over the cherries. Serve with whipped cream.

## Cook's Tip

*To make a strawberry purée, rub the fruit through a nylon sieve, pressing it with a wooden spoon, or blend in a liquidiser or food processor: 500 g/1 lb fruit yields 300 ml/½ pint of purée.*

## Cook's Tip

*As a delicious variation, replace the port with the same quantity of Amaretto, an almond-flavoured liqueur.*

# Cheese-cakes and Flans

*Rich and creamy, chilled and light or crisp and crumbly – there is a cheesecake or flan here to suit your taste. Many will suit your pocket too when made with storecupboard standbys or windfalls and gluts of home-grown fruit.*

## 33 | Blackcurrant Cheesecake

**Preparation time**
20 minutes plus 2-3 hours to chill

**Cooking time**
5 minutes

**Serves 8**

**Calories**
408 per portion

**You will need**
50 g/2 oz margarine, melted
100 g/4 oz digestive biscuits, crushed
25 g/1 oz demerara sugar
300 g/10 oz curd cheese
50 g/2 oz caster sugar
2 eggs, separated
grated rind and juice of ½ orange
15 g/½ oz gelatine
300 ml/½ pint whipping cream, whipped

**For the toppping**
1 (213 g/7½ oz) can blackcurrants
2 tablespoons arrowroot
finely grated rind and juice of 1 orange

Lightly grease a 20 cm/8 in loose-bottomed cake tin. Combine the margarine, biscuit crumbs and demerara sugar. Spread over the base of the prepared tin and chill.

Mix the cheese in a bowl with the sugar, egg yolks and orange rind. Dissolve the gelatine in the orange juice over a pan of simmering water. Stir into the cheese mixture with the cream. Whisk the egg whites until stiff, then fold into the mixture. Spread the filling evenly over the base and chill until set.

Drain the currants and heat the syrup. Blend the arrowroot with the orange rind and juice, then pour on the syrup, stirring. Bring to the boil, stirring. Add the currants and allow to cool. Pour the currants over the cheesecake.

## Cook's Tip

**Ring the changes. Replace the blackcurrants with a can of crushed pineapple and use the natural juices instead of the orange juice.**

## 34 | Rich Lemon Cheesecake

**Preparation time**
15 minutes, plus 2-3 hours to chill

**Serves 6**

**Calories**
569 per portion

**You will need**
50 g/2 oz margarine or butter, melted
25 g/1 oz soft dark brown sugar
100 g/4 oz chocolate digestive biscuits, crushed
crystallised lemon slices to decorate

**For the filling**
15 g/½ oz powdered gelatine
2 tablespoons hot water
350 g/12 oz full-fat soft cheese
75 g/3 oz caster sugar
grated rind of 1 lemon
4 tablespoons lemon juice
150 ml/¼ pint double cream

Grease an 18 cm/7 in flan ring. Mix the melted margarine or butter with the sugar and biscuit crumbs. Spoon into the prepared tin and press evenly over the base and sides. Chill.

Dissolve the gelatine in the hot water over a pan of simmering water. Beat the cheese, sugar, lemon rind and juice together until smooth, then add the gelatine. Whip the cream until it forms soft peaks, then fold it into the cheese mixture. Turn into the prepared tin and smooth the surface. Chill for several hours or until set. Remove from the tin and decorate with lemon slices. Serve chilled.

## Cook's Tip

**Add 1-2 teaspoons lemon juice when poaching eggs or boiling rice to prevent them from becoming grey-coloured when cooked.**

# 35 | Fresh Cranberry Cheesecake

**Preparation time**
45 minutes, plus 5-6 hours to chill

**Cooking time**
5 minutes

**Serves 8**

**Calories**
528 per portion

**You will need**
150 g/5 oz digestive biscuits, crushed
75 g/3 oz caster sugar
1 teaspoon mixed spice
75 g/3 oz butter
1½ tablespoons apricot jam
350 g/12 oz fresh cranberries
3 large strips orange peel
150 g/5 oz granulated sugar
1 tablespoon powdered gelatine
8 tablespoons orange juice
100 g/4 oz light brown sugar
2 tablespoons grated orange zest
200 g/7 oz full-fat soft cheese
200 g/7 oz curd cheese
120 ml/4 fl oz double or whipped cream, whipped

Grease and line a 20 cm/8 in springform tin. Mix the biscuit crumbs with the sugar and spice. Melt the butter and jam, stir in the crumb mixture and combine. Press into the tin. Place the cranberries in a pan and cover with water. Add the orange peel strips, bring to the boil and simmer. Stir in the granulated sugar and cool.

To make the filling, dissolve the gelatine in the orange juice over a pan of simmering water, mix with the brown sugar and orange zest. Add the cheeses and beat thoroughly. Reserve a little cream and fold the rest into the filling. Sieve the cranberries. Spread half the fruit over the base, cover with the filling and finish with the remaining fruit. Chill for 5-6 hours. Decorate as shown.

## Cook's Tip

*If you want to make this cheesecake when cranberries are out of season, substitute 330 ml/11 fl oz of cranberry jelly for the fresh fruit.*

# 36 | Summer Lime Cheesecake

**Preparation time**
15 minutes, plus 3 hours to chill

**Serves 8**

**Calories**
370 per portion

**You will need**
8 trifle sponges
4 tablespoons lime juice or sherry
175 g/6 oz full-fat soft cheese
175 g/6 oz caster sugar
2 eggs, separated
150 ml/¼ pint double cream
grated rind and juice of 2 limes
15 g/½ oz powdered gelatine
3 tablespoons hot water

**To decorate**
120 ml/4 fl oz whipping cream, whipped
1 tablespoon plain chocolate drops
1 lime, cut into 10 wedges

Cut the sponges in half horizontally and use to line the base of a 20 cm/8 in loose-bottomed cake tin. Sprinkle with the lime juice or sherry. Leave until beginning to set.

Beat together the cheese and sugar until well blended, then whisk in the egg yolks, cream, lime rind and juice. Dissolve the gelatine in the hot water over a pan of simmering water and stir into the mixture. Whisk the egg whites until stiff, carefully fold into the mixture and pour into the prepared tin. Chill until set. Remove from the tin and decorate with the piped cream, chocolate drops and lime wedges.

## Cook's Tip

*To cream fat and sugar, make sure they are at room temperature and soft. Use the flat side of a wooden spoon and beat in one direction, keeping the mixture down in the base of the bowl.*

# 37 | Baked Sultana Cheesecake

**Preparation time**
15 minutes

**Cooking time**
55 minutes

**Oven temperature**
190C, 375F, gas 5
then
180C, 350F, gas 4

**Serves 8**

**Calories**
486 per portion

**You will need**
500 g/1 lb full-fat soft cheese
150 ml/¼ pint double cream
75 g/3 oz caster sugar
grated rind of 1 lemon
1 tablespoon lemon juice
2 eggs
40 g/1½ oz cornflour
50 g/2 oz sultanas
100 g/4 oz shortcrust pastry
   (recipe 58)
icing sugar to decorate

Beat together the cheese, cream, sugar, lemon rind and juice and eggs until smooth. Toss the sultanas in the cornflour and add them to the mixture. Beat until the ingredients are thoroughly combined.

Roll out the pastry and use to line the base of a 20 cm/8 in springform tin. Prick with a fork and bake for 20 minutes. Reduce the temperature.

Pour the cheese mixture over the pastry and return to the oven for 35 minutes. Turn off the heat and leave the cheesecake in the oven until cold. Chill until required.

Remove from the tin. Dust the surface with icing sugar and mark with a lattice pattern using the back of a long-bladed knife.

## Cook's Tip

**Try peach or apricot cheesecake instead. Sprinkle 100 g/4 oz well-drained and chopped canned peaches or apricots over the baked pastry base. Omit the sultanas from the mixture and continue as instructed in the recipe above.**

# 38 | American Cheesecake

**Preparation time**
15 minutes, plus 2-3 hours to cool

**Cooking time**
45 minutes

**Oven temperature**
180C, 350F, gas 4

**Serves 10-12**

**Calories**
650 calories per portion

**You will need**
75 g/3 oz margarine or butter
   melted
175 g/6 oz digestive biscuits,
   crushed
fresh or drained canned cherries
   to decorate

**For the filling**
1 kg/2 lb full-fat soft cheese
250 g/9 oz caster sugar
4 eggs, lightly beaten
40 g/1½ oz plain flour, sifted
300 ml/½ pint soured cream
grated rind of 1 lemon

Grease a loose-bottomed or springform 23 cm/9 in cake tin. Mix the melted margarine with the biscuit crumbs. Spoon into the prepared tin and press evenly over the base. Place on a baking tray and bake for 10 minutes, then set aside to cool.

Beat together all the ingredients for the filling and pour into the tin. Bake in the oven for 35 minutes, or until set. Leave for 3-4 hours, until cold. Run a round-bladed knife around the sides of the cheesecake, then remove from the tin. Transfer to a serving plate and decorate with cherries.

## Cook's Tip

**Use a pastry brush to make it easier to remove lemon rind from a grater.**

# 39 | Kiwi and Gooseberry Cheesecake

**Preparation time**
25 minutes, plus 2-3 hours to chill

**Cooking time**
15-20 minutes

**Serves 6-8**

**Calories**
293 per portion

**You will need**
40 g/1½ oz butter
100 g/4 oz ginger snaps, crushed
500 g /1 lb gooseberries
100 g/4 oz caster sugar
2 heads of elderflower, tied in muslin (optional)
15 g/½ oz gelatine
3 tablespoons hot water
225 g/8 oz curd cheese
few drops green food colouring
150 ml/¼ pint double cream, whipped
3 kiwi fruit, peeled and thinly sliced

Lightly grease an 18 cm/7 in loose-bottomed cake tin. Melt the butter in a pan, stir in the biscuit crumbs and press on to the base of the prepared tin. Chill until firm.

Place the gooseberries in a pan with the sugar and elderflower, if using. Cover and simmer for 10-15 minutes, until soft. Leave to cool, then remove the elderflower. Sieve or blend in a liquidiser or food processor until smooth. Dissolve the gelatine in the hot water over a pan of simmering water, then stir into the gooseberry purée. Beat the cheese in a bowl to soften, then mix in the colouring, purée and cream. Turn the mixture into the tin and chill until set. Remove from the tin and decorate with the kiwi fruit.

## Cook's Tip

*Kiwi fruit came originally from China and are now largely grown in New Zealand. They are rich in vitamin C.*

# 40 | Plum Cheesecakes

**Preparation time**
1 hour

**Cooking time**
1 hour

**Oven temperature**
160C, 325F, gas 3

**Makes four
7.5 cm/3 in cakes**

**Calories**
673 per portion

**You will need**
10 large plums
250 ml/8 fl oz water
150 g/5 oz sugar
2 teaspoons cornflour

For the base
120 g/4½ oz digestive biscuits
40 g/1½ oz unsalted butter, melted
40 g/1½ oz caster sugar

For the filling
120 g/4½ oz curd cheese
2 eggs, separated
50 g/2 oz caster sugar

Slit the plums. Put the water and sugar in a pan and bring to the boil, stirring until the sugar has dissolved. Add the plums and poach for 15 minutes. Remove the stones and cut the plums in half. Four of these will be mixed into the filling, sixteen left whole for use on the top of the cheesecakes. Dissolve the cornflour in a little water. Measure 150 ml/¼ pint of the syrup into a small pan. Whisk in the cornflour and boil until thickened.
Crush the biscuits, mix with the butter and sugar. Divide the mixture between four 7.5 cm/3 in tins.

To make the filling, beat the cheese with the egg yolks, four plum halves and the sugar until light and creamy. Whisk the egg whites until stiff and fold into the cheese mixture. Pour the filling into the tartlet tins. Bake for 1 hour. Leave to cool. Arrange four of the reserved plum halves on each tartlet and spoon the syrup on top.

## Cook's Tip

*Baked cheesecakes crack if they cool too quickly, so when they are cooked, turn off the heat but allow them to cool in the oven before handling them.*

# 41 | *Orange Cheesecake*

**Preparation time**
30 minutes, plus 2-3 hours to chill

**Serves 6-8**

**Calories**
467 per portion

**You will need**
50 g/2 oz butter
50 g/2 oz soft dark brown sugar
175 g/6 oz digestive biscuits, crushed
225 g/8 oz full-fat soft cheese
225 g/8 oz curd cheese
2 eggs, separated
150 ml/¼ pint soured cream
25 g/1 oz caster sugar
grated rind and juice of 1 orange
2-3 tablespoons orange Curaçao
15 g/½ oz gelatine
2 tablespoons hot water

**To decorate**
150 ml/¼ pint double cream
½ orange, sliced

Melt the butter and stir in the brown sugar and biscuit crumbs. Press on to the base of a 23 cm/9 in loose-bottomed cake tin. Chill until firm.

Mix together the cheeses, then beat in the egg yolks, soured cream and caster sugar. Stir in the orange rind and juice and Curaçao. Dissolve the gelatine in the hot water over a pan of simmering water then stir into the mixture. Leave until almost set, then fold in the stiffly whisked egg whites. Pour on to the biscuit base and chill until firm. Decorate with piped whipped cream and orange slices.

# 42 | *Bistro Cheesecake*

**Preparation time**
20 minutes, plus 30 minutes to chill

**Cooking time**
1 hour 35 minutes

**Oven temperature**
180C, 350F, gas 4 then
150C, 300F, gas 2

**Serves 10**

**Calories**
463 per portion

**You will need**
200 g/7 oz plain flour
150 g/5 oz butter
50 g/2 oz caster sugar
1 egg yolk
1-2 tablespoons cold water

**For the filling**
750 g/1½ lb low-fat soft cheese
100 g/4 oz caster sugar
150 ml/¼ pint soured cream
3 eggs, beaten
1 teaspoon vanilla essence

**To decorate**
1 peach, sliced, or several canned peach slices
100 g/4 oz strawberries, sliced

Make the pastry as instructed in recipe 55. Use half to line the base of a 23 cm/9 in loose-bottomed cake tin and prick all over. Roll the remaining pastry into a 10 cm/4 in long roll and wrap in cling film. Chill both for 30 minutes.

Slice the pastry roll thinly and arrange in overlapping slices around the side of the tin. Bake blind for 20 minutes, then lower the temperature.

Beat the filling ingredients until smooth. Remove the paper and beans from the pastry case, pour in the filling and cook for 1¼ hours. Turn off the heat and leave the cheesecake in the oven until quite cool. Remove and decorate with the fruit.

## Cook's Tip

To dissolve gelatine, sprinkle it on the hot (but never boiling) water or specified liquid in a small bowl and stand it over a pan of gently simmering water. Stir until completely clear; if it is cloudy it has not dissolved completely. Never boil gelatine or it will be useless for setting.

## Cook's Tip

Baked cheesecakes freeze very well. When cold, freeze on a plate until solid, then remove from the plate and pack, label and freeze. To defrost, place on a wire rack for about 3 hours, then transfer to a serving plate.

# 43 | Tangy Cheesecake

**Preparation time**
10 minutes, plus 2-3
hours to chill

**Serves 6-8**

**Calories**
352 per portion

**You will need**
50 g/2 oz butter, melted
200 g/7 oz ginger biscuits, finely
 crushed
1 (397 g/14 oz) can condensed
 milk
225 g/8 oz full-fat soft cheese
grated rind and juice of 1 lime
grated rind and juice of 1 lemon
150 ml/¼ pint double cream,
 whipped
lemon and lime rind, cut into
 shapes, to decorate

Grease a 20 cm/8 in loose-bottomed cake tin. Combine
the butter, ginger biscuit crumbs and 2 tablespoons of
the condensed milk. Press the mixture into the base of
the prepared tin.

Beat the cheese in a bowl until softened, then gradually beat in the remaining condensed milk, lime and
lemon rind and juice. Leave until the mixture thickens,
then fold in the cream. Pour the mixture into the tin and
chill until set.

Remove from the tin and decorate with piped cream
and lime and lemon rind.

## Cook's Tip

**Condensed milk thickens
when mixed with citrus juice
and rind. With the addition of
cream cheese or cream, this
makes a quick and easy filling
for flans and cheesecakes.**

# 44 | Berry Bagatelle

**Preparation time**
1 hour, plus overnight
chilling

**Cooking time**
5 minutes

**Serves 10**

**Calories**
458 per portion

**You will need**
24 cm/9½ in sponge cake
75 g/3 oz granulated sugar
2 tablespoons water
6 tablespoons framboise liqueur
500 g/1 lb curd cheese
120 g/4½ oz caster sugar
4 eggs, separated
100 ml/3½ fl oz double cream
2 tablespoons powdered gelatine
5 tablespoons hot water
500 g/1 lb raspberries

**To decorate**
icing sugar
scented geranium leaves

Line the base and sides of a 23 cm/9 in springform tin.
Cut the sponge in half horizontally and drop one half into
the prepared tin. Heat the granulated sugar and water
until dissolved, then boil for 10 seconds. Cool slightly
then stir in 3 tablespoons of the liqueur. Brush the
sponge cake base with the syrup.

Cream the cheese and caster sugar. Beat in the egg
yolks, then the cream and remaining liqueur. Whip the
egg whites until stiff. Dissolve the gelatine in the hot
water over a pan of simmering water. Stir into the filling
mixture and immediately fold in the beaten egg white.
Spread a little filling over the sponge cake base.

Reserve a few raspberries and arrange the rest around
the base and centre. Pour the rest of the filling over the
fruit. Lay the second sponge layer on top and brush with
the remaining syrup. Chill. Decorate as shown.

## Cook's Tip

**To wash raspberries and other
soft fruit, place in a colander
or sieve and hold under a
slow-running cold tap. Do not
attempt to dry them or they
will become soggy and
squashed.**

# 45 | Peach Cheesecake

**Preparation time**
15 minutes, plus 2-3 hours to chill

**Serves 8**

**Calories**
394 per portion

**You will need**
18-20 cm/7-8 inch sponge cake layer, 1 cm/½ inch thick

For the filling
1½ (15 g/½ oz) sachets gelatine
6 tablespoons hot water
1 (410 g/14½ oz) can peach slices, drained
grated rind of ½ orange
2 tablespoons orange juice
225 g/8 oz full-fat soft cheese
2 eggs, separated
100 g/4 oz caster sugar
150 ml/¼ pint soured cream

To decorate
150 ml/¼ pint double cream
1 (410 g/14½ oz) can peach slices
whole strawberries

Grease an 18-20 cm/7-8 in loose-bottomed cake tin. Place the sponge cake in the tin, trimming it to fit exactly.

To make the filling, dissolve the gelatine in the hot water over a pan of simmering water. Set aside to cool slightly. Blend the peach slices and orange rind and juice to a purée in a liquidiser or food processor. Beat the cheese in a bowl, then add the egg yolks, half the sugar, the soured cream and peach purée. Stir in the gelatine and allow to cool until almost set.

Whisk the egg whites until stiff, then whisk in the remaining sugar. Fold into the cheese mixture. Turn the mixture into the tin. Chill for several hours. Remove from the tin and decorate with the cream and fruit.

## Cook's Tip

*If a loose-bottomed tin is not available, line a 20 cm/8 in cake tin and place double thickness foil or greaseproof paper strips inside it in a cross to lift out cheesecakes when set.*

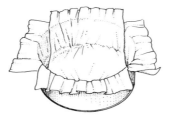

# 46 | Chocolate Orange Cheesecake

**Preparation time**
20 minutes, plus 2-3 hours to chill

**Serves 8**

**Calories**
437 per portion

**You will need**
50 g/2 oz butter
100 g/4 oz digestive biscuits, crushed
25 g/1 oz demerara sugar
500 g/1 lb curd cheese
50 g/2 oz caster sugar
grated rind and juice of 2 oranges
250 ml/8 fl oz single cream
15 g/½ oz gelatine
3 tablespoons hot water
50 g/2 oz plain chocolate, melted
120ml/4 fl oz double cream, whipped, to decorate

Grease a 20 cm/8 in loose-bottomed cake tin. Melt the butter in a pan and stir in the biscuit crumbs and sugar. Press into the base of the prepared tin. Chill until firm.

Place the cheese in a bowl with the sugar and orange rind and beat until smooth. Strain the orange juice and add to the mixture, then gradually stir in the cream. Dissolve the gelatine in the hot water over a pan of simmering water, then stir into the cheese mixture.

Spread the filling evenly over the crumb base. Pour the cooled, melted chocolate over the top, swirling with a fork to give a marbled effect. Chill until set. Remove from the tin and decorate with piped cream.

## Cook's Tip

*Agar-agar, which derives from seaweed, may be preferred to gelatine, particularly by vegetarians. It is used in the proportion of 2 teaspoons of powder dissolved in 600 ml/1 pint of liquid.*

# 47 | *Heavenly Cheesecake*

**Preparation time**
20 minutes, plus 4
hours to chill

**Cooking time**
1½-1¾ hours

**Oven temperature**
160C, 325F, gas 3

**Serves 8**

**Calories**
512 per portion

**You will need**
50 g/2 oz self-raising flour
½ teaspoon baking powder
50 g/2 oz butter, softened
50 g/2 oz caster sugar
1 egg
few drops cochineal

For the filling
275 g/10 oz full-fat soft cheese
40 g/1½ oz plain flour, sifted
150 ml/¼ pint whipping cream
few drops vanilla essence
5 egg whites
100 g/4 oz caster sugar
225 g/8 oz icing sugar, sifted
1 egg white, lightly whisked
crystallised rose petals

Grease a loose-bottomed 18-20 cm/7-8 inch cake tin. Sift the flour with the baking powder. Add the butter, sugar, egg and cochineal and blend thoroughly. Spread the mixture evenly over the base of the prepared tin.

To make the filling, beat the cheese until softened. Beat in the flour, cream, vanilla essence, 1 egg white and half the sugar. Whisk four egg whites until stiff, then whisk in the remaining caster sugar. Fold into the cheese mixture. Turn into the prepared tin. Bake for 1½-1¾ hours, or until set. Cool for 1 hour.

Beat the remaining egg white into the icing sugar. Swirl over the cheesecake and leave until almost set, then scatter over the rose petals. Chill for 2-3 hours.

## Cook's Tip

*If you are interrupted while mixing the filling after the egg whites have been added, cover with a large bowl inverted over the mixing bowl. It will save the day for some 20 minutes.*

# 48 | *Baked Cinnamon Cheesecake*

**Preparation time**
30 minutes

**Cooking time**
1 hour

**Oven temperature**
160C, 325F, gas 3

**Serves 8**

**Calories**
445 per portion

**You will need**
150 g/5 oz plain flour, sifted
75 g/3 oz butter
40 g/1½ oz caster sugar
225 g/8 oz full-fat soft cheese
225 g/8 oz curd cheese
50 g/2 oz soft light brown sugar
150 ml/¼ pint soured cream
2 teaspoons ground cinnamon
4 eggs

To decorate
whipped cream
ground cinnamon

Grease and line a 20 cm/8 in loose-bottomed cake tin. Rub the butter into the flour until the mixture resembles breadcrumbs. Stir in the caster sugar. Press into a stiff dough and knead until smooth.

Soften the cream cheese in a bowl. Beat in the curd cheese and brown sugar, then stir in the cream and cinnamon. Whisk in the eggs, one at a time.

Press the shortbread into the base and sides of the prepared tin and pour in the mixture. Bake for 1 hour, until set. Leave in the tin until cold. Remove from the tin, decorate with cream and sprinkle lightly with cinnamon.

## Cook's Tip

*When rubbing fat into flour use only the fingertips. Keep fingers spaced apart and lift the ingredients, rubbing quickly to make a light mixture which is not sticky.*

## 49 | Honey and Spice Cheesecake

**Preparation time**
30 minutes

**Cooking time**
1½-1¾ hours

**Oven temperature**
160C, 325F, gas 3

**Makes one 20 cm/8 in cake**

**Calories**
427 per portion

**You will need**
175 g/6 oz digestive biscuits
3 oz unsalted butter, melted
icing sugar

For the filling
225 g/8 oz curd cheese
120 g/4½ oz clear honey
1 teaspoon ground ginger
1 teaspoon mixed spice
40 g/1½ oz flour
3 eggs separated
10 g/¼ oz caster sugar
150 ml/¼ pint double cream

Grease a 20 cm/8 in springform tin. Crush the biscuits or blend them in a food processor. Combine the biscuit crumbs with the butter and press evenly into the base of the prepared tin.

To make the filling, beat the cheese, honey, ginger, spice, flour and egg yolks in a bowl for at least 5 minutes or blend in a food processor. Whisk the cream until it thickens. Combine with the filling mixture. Whisk the egg whites with the sugar until they are very stiff, then fold into the filling mixture.

Pour the filling into the tin and spread evenly. Bake for 1½-1¾ hours. Leave to cool in the oven.

Remove from the tin. Cut eight strips of paper 1 cm/½ in wide and arrange them in a criss-cross pattern on top of the cake. Dust with icing sugar and then carefully lift off the paper strips.

### Cook's Tip

*A springform tin is particularly useful for making cheesecakes. When the slide clip is unfastened, the sides expand by about 1 cm/½ in to free the base for the easy removal of fragile items such as cheesecakes.*

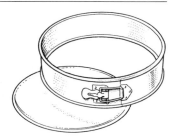

## 50 | Dreamy Cheesecake

**Preparation time**
20 minutes, plus 4-5 hours to chill

**Serves 8**

**Calories**
454 per portion

**You will need**
50 g/2 oz butter, melted
50 g/2 oz caster sugar
100 g/4 oz ratafias, crushed

For the filling
15 g/½ oz powdered gelatine
3 tablespoons hot water
225 g/8 oz full-fat soft cheese
2 eggs, separated
100 g/4 oz caster sugar
grated rind of 1 orange
few drops almond essence
150 ml/¼ pint double cream
225-350 g/8-12 oz mixed soft fruit
3 tablespoons redcurrant jelly
1 tablespoon strained orange juice

Grease a loose-bottomed 18-20 cm/7-8 inch cake tin. Mix the melted butter with the sugar and ratafia crumbs. Press evenly into the base of the prepared tin. Chill.

Meanwhile, dissolve the gelatine in the hot water over a pan of simmering water. Beat the cheese in a bowl, add the egg yolks, half the sugar, the orange rind, almond essence and cream. Stir in the gelatine. Leave the mixture until almost set. Whisk the egg whites until stiff, then whisk in the remaining sugar. Fold into the cheese mixture. Turn into the tin. Chill for 3-4 hours, or until set.

Remove the cheesecake from the tin and arrange the fruit over the top. Melt the jelly with the orange juice, cool slightly, then brush over the fruit. Chill and serve.

### Cook's Tip

*When adding any flavouring to double cream, reduce the likelihood of overbeating by adding the flavouring before whisking.*

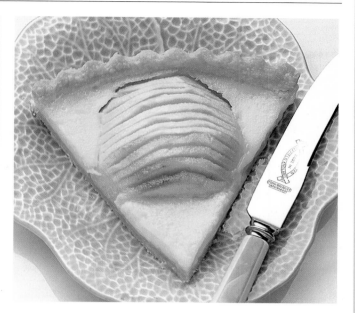

# 51 | *Blackberry Torte*

**Preparation time**
30 minutes, plus 30
minutes to chill

**Cooking time**
1¼ hours

**Oven temperature**
200C, 400F, gas 6 then
180C, 350F, gas 4
(pastry case) then
190C, 375F, gas 5
(torte)

**Serves 8**

**Calories**
279 per portion

**You will need**
120 g/4½ oz plain flour
pinch of salt
90 g/3½ oz butter, chilled
3 tablespoons caster sugar
½ teaspoon grated lemon zest
1 egg yolk
whipped cream to decorate

For the filling
1 egg white, for brushing
400 g/14 oz blackberries
65 g/2½ oz caster sugar
65 g/2½ oz macaroons, crushed
225 g/8 oz fromage frais, drained
2 tablespoons Kirsch
3 tablespoons double cream
2 egg yolks
1 egg white

Make the rich shortcrust pastry as instructed in recipe
55. Use it to line a 20 cm/8 in springform tin, extending
about 2.5 cm/1 in up the sides. Bake blind for 10 minutes
as instructed in recipe 52, brushing the base with beaten
egg white before baking for the final 5 minutes.

   Reserve 50 g/2 oz blackberries and sprinkle 50 g/2 oz
of the sugar over the rest. Scatter half the macaroons
over the pastry case and cover with blackberries. Beat together the cheese, Kirsch, cream, egg yolks and remaining sugar. Beat the egg white until stiff and fold in. Pour
the mixture into the tin and scatter the remaining macaroons on top. Bake for 45 minutes. Serve cold, decorated
with whipped cream and the reserved blackberries.

## Cook's Tip

*Fresh blackberries vary
enormously in colour,
depending on whether they
are cultivated or wild.
However, they should be
black all over; any red parts
are unripe and will taste sour.*

# 52 | *Normandy Apple Flan*

**Preparation time**
30 minutes, plus 15
minutes to chill

**Cooking time**
40-45 minutes

**Oven temperature**
200C, 400F, gas 6
then
180C, 350F, gas 4

**Serves 8**

**Calories**
327 per portion

**You will need**
175 g/6 oz plain flour
pinch of salt
100 g/4 oz unsalted butter
25 g/1 oz sugar
1 tablespoon cold water

For the filling
4 large firm dessert apples
4 tablespoons caster sugar
3 egg yolks
1 tablespoon cornflour
250 ml/8 fl oz mixed double cream
   and milk
few drops vanilla essence
large knob of butter

Make the shortcrust pastry as instructed in recipe 58
adding the sugar after the fat has been rubbed into the
flour. Use to line a 25 cm/10 in French fluted flan tin. Chill.

   Peel, core and halve the apples, then slice almost
through to give a fan effect. Arrange in the pastry case
and sprinkle with 1 tablespoon sugar. Bake for 20
minutes. Lower the temperature.

   Mix together the remaining sugar, egg yolks and cornflour. Heat the cream and milk together and pour over the
egg mixture, stirring all the time. Strain, and add the
vanilla essence, then pour carefully into the pastry case.
Return the tart to the oven for about 20 minutes until the
custard is set. Halfway through cooking, dot the apples
with the butter. Serve warm or cold.

## Cook's Tip

*Never leave peeled apples in a
bowl of water: they will lose
their flavour and absorb the
water. It is best to leave
peeling until just before they
are needed.*

# 53 | Mincemeat and Apple Flan

**Preparation time**
20 minutes, plus 30 minutes to chill

**Cooking time**
35-40 minutes

**Oven temperature**
190C, 375F, gas 5

**Makes one
23 cm/9 in flan**

**Calories**
969 per portion

**You will need**
225 g/8 oz plain flour
150 g/5 oz butter or margarine
1 tablespoon caster sugar
1 egg yolk
1-2 tablespoons iced water

For the filling
350 g/12 oz cooking apples
500 g /1 lb mincemeat
1 tablespoon sherry
2-3 dessert apples

To glaze
4 tablespoons apricot jam
2 teaspoons lemon juice

Make the rich shortcrust pastry as instructed in recipe 55. Use to line a 23 cm/9 in fluted flan rung placed on a baking tray. Chill for 30 minutes.

Peel, core and chop the cooking apples and mix with the mincemeat and sherry. Turn into the flan ring and spread evenly to the edges. Quarter, core and thinly slice the dessert apples and arrange them overlapping in a circle on top of the mincemeat mixture. Bake for 35-40 minutes. Remove the flan carefully from the flan ring and leave to cool on a wire rack.

Heat the jam with the lemon juice, stirring until the jam has melted. Sieve, reheat and brush over the apples to glaze. Serve warm or cold.

## Cook's Tip

*For a more traditional flavour, replace the sherry with 1 tablespoon of brandy.*

# 54 | Walnut Apricot Flan

**Preparation time**
15 minutes

**Cooking time**
40-45 minutes

**Oven temperature**
190C, 375F, gas 5

**Serves 6-8**

**Calories**
298 per portion

**You will need**
175 g/6 oz plain flour
100 g/4 oz margarine
50 g/2 oz walnuts, finely chopped
75 g/3 oz caster sugar
2 egg yolks
1 tablespoon cold water
500 g /1 lb apricots, halved and stoned
1 egg white, lightly beaten
1 tablespoon caster sugar

Sift the flour into a bowl and rub in the margarine until the mixture resembles breadcrumbs. Stir in the walnuts, sugar, egg yolks and water and mix to a soft dough. Roll out two-thirds of the pastry and use to line a 20 cm/8 in flan tin. Prick the base.

Arrange the apricots in the pastry case. Roll out the remaining pastry for a lid and use to cover the flan, brushing the edges with egg white to seal. Make a hole in the centre. Brush the flan with egg white and sprinkle with the caster sugar. Cook for 40-45 minutes, until golden. Cool in the tin, then turn out on to a serving plate.

## Cook's Tip

*To remove the stones from fruit such as apricots, make a cut right around the fruit and twist the two halves in opposite directions. The fruit will break cleanly and expose the stone for removal.*

# 55 | Franzipan Flan

**Preparation time**
30 minutes, plus 15
minutes to chill

**Cooking time**
40-50 minutes

**Oven temperature**
200C, 400F, gas 6
then
180C, 350F, gas 4

**Calories**
600 per portion

**You will need**
225 g/8 oz plain flour
150 g/5 oz butter
1 tablespoon caster sugar
1 egg yolk
1-2 tablespoons cold water

For the filling
50 g/2 oz cake crumbs
1 (411 g/14½ oz) can red cherries,
    drained and stoned
50 g/2 oz butter
50 g/2 oz caster sugar
1 egg
25 g/1 oz plain flour
75 g/3 oz ground almonds
1 teaspoon rosewater (optional)
1 tablespoon icing sugar, sifted

To make the rich shortcrust pastry, sift the flour into a bowl and rub in the butter until the mixture resembles breadcrumbs. Stir in the sugar. Add the egg yolk and enough water to mix to a firm dough. Knead the dough lightly and chill for 15 minutes. Roll out the pastry on a floured surface and use to line a 20 cm/8 in flan ring or tin. Bake blind for 10 minutes, then lower the temperature.

Sprinkle the cake crumbs over the base and arrange the cherries on top. Beat the butter and sugar together until light and fluffy. Beat in the egg, flour, ground almonds and rosewater, if using. Spread over the cherries and cook at the lower temperature for 30-40 minutes, until firm to the touch. Sprinkle with the icing sugar and serve warm or cold.

## Cook's Tip

**Add rosewater or orange flower water to creamy puddings, fillings, icings, jams and jellies to impart an unusual and delicate flavour to the food.**

# 56 | Chocolate Tipsy Flan

**Preparation time**
10 minutes, plus 2-3
hours to chill

**Cooking time**
20 minutes

**Oven temperature**
200C, 400F, gas 6
then
180C, 350F, gas 4

**Serves 6**

**Calories**
503 per portion

**You will need**
100 g/4 oz plain flour
75 g/3 oz butter
25 g/1 oz caster sugar
1 egg yolk
1-2 tablespoons cold water

For the filling
3 eggs, separated
2 tablespoons dark rum
175 g/6 oz plain chocolate, melted

To decorate
150 ml/¼ pint double cream,
    whipped
chocolate rose leaves

Make the pastry as instructed in recipe 55. Use to line a 20 cm/8 in flan tin. Prick the base and chill. Bake blind for 10 minutes, then lower the temperature and bake for another 10 minutes. Remove the beans and paper and cook for a further 5 minutes. Leave to cool.

Stir the egg yolks and rum into the melted chocolate. Whisk the egg whites until stiff, carefully fold into the chocolate mixture, then pour into the pastry case. Chill until set. Decorate with swirls of piped cream and chocolate rose leaves.

## Cook's Tip

**To make the chocolate rose leaves, paint the undersides of clean dry rose leaves with melted chocolate. Leave to set, chocolate side up, then carefully lift off the top of the leaf and peel away from the chocolate.**

# 57 | *French Apple Flan*

**Preparation time**
15 minutes, plus 1 hour
to chill

**Cooking time**
35-40 minutes

**Oven temperature**
190C, 375F, gas 5

**Serves 8**

**Calories**
459 per portion

**You will need**
175 g/6 oz plain flour
75 g/3 oz butter
75 g/3 oz caster sugar
3 egg yolks
few drops vanilla essence

For the filling
1.5 kg/3 lb cooking apples, peeled,
  cored and thinly sliced
50 g/2 oz caster sugar

To glaze
4 tablespoons apricot jam
juice of ½ lemon

To make the pâte sucrée, sift the flour on to a cool work surface. Make a well in the centre and add the butter, sugar, egg yolks and vanilla essence. Using the fingertips of one hand, work these ingredients together, then draw in the flour. Knead lightly until smooth and chill for 1 hour. Roll out the pastry very thinly and use to line a 25 cm/10 in fluted flan ring.

Fill the case generously with the apples, then arrange an overlapping layer of apples on top. Sprinkle with the sugar. Bake for 35-40 minutes.

Meanwhile, heat the jam with the lemon juice, then strain and brush over the apples. Serve hot or cold.

# 58 | *Royal Curd Tart*

**Preparation time**
30 minutes

**Cooking time**
50-55 minutes

**Oven temperature**
200C, 400F, gas 6
then
180C, 350F, gas 4

**Serves 6**

**Calories**
623 per portion

**You will need**
225 g/8 oz plain flour
100 g/4 oz butter or margarine
2-3 tablespoons iced water
icing sugar to decorate

For the filling
225 g/8 oz curd cheese
50 g/2 oz ground almonds
50 g/2 oz caster sugar
2 eggs, separated
grated rind and juice of 1 lemon
50 g/2 oz sultanas
150 ml/¼ pint double cream

To make the shortcrust pastry, sift the flour into a bowl. Rub in the butter or margarine until the mixture resembles fine breadcrumbs. Add the water gradually and mix to a firm dough. Turn out on to a floured surface and use to line a 23 cm/9 in flan ring placed on a baking tray. Prick the base.

Place the cheese in a bowl and blend in the ground almonds, caster sugar and egg yolks. Add the lemon rind and juice, sultanas and cream and mix well. Whisk the egg whites until stiff and fold into the mixture.

Pour the mixture into the flan case and bake for 20 minutes then lower the temperature and continue to cook for 30-35 minutes until firm and golden. Serve warm or chilled, dusted with icing sugar.

## *Cook's Tip*

**There is no need to grease trays and tins when cooking with this type of pastry because of the high fat content of the dough. In some other recipes the tins may need to be greased.**

## *Cook's Tip*

**A quick way to make the shortcrust pastry is to chill the fat in the freezer, dip in the flour, then grate coarsely. Mix into the flour with enough water to bind.**

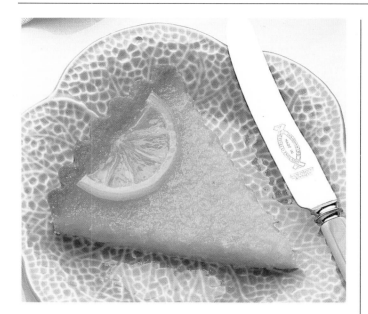

# 59 | Glazed Lemon Flan

**Preparation time**
30 minutes

**Cooking time**
45 minutes

**Oven temperature**
190C, 375F, gas 5

**Serves 8**

**Calories**
409 per serving

**You will need**
175 g/6 oz plain flour
pinch of salt
75 g/3 oz caster sugar
75 g/3 oz butter, softened
3 egg yolks

For the filling
3 eggs
175 g/6 oz caster sugar
grated rind and juice of 3 thin-
 skinned lemons
50 g/2 oz butter, melted

To decorate
50 g/2 oz sugar
300 ml/½ pint water
1 thin-skinned lemon, sliced

Make the rich shortcrust pastry as instructed in recipe 55. Use to line a 23 cm/9 in French fluted flan tin. Chill.

Meanwhile, beat together the ingredients for the filling. To make the decoration, dissolve the sugar in the water. Bring to the boil and boil for 2 minutes. Add the lemon slices and continue to boil gently until the syrup has almost disappeared, taking care that the lemon slices stay whole. Leave on a plate to cool.

Bake the pastry case blind for 15 minutes. Pour in the filling and return to the oven for a further 20-25 minutes until the filling is just set. Allow to cool slightly, then decorate with halved lemon slices. Leave until cold.

# 60 | Mincemeat Flan

**Preparation time**
30 minutes, plus 15 minutes to chill

**Cooking time**
35-40 minutes

**Oven temperature**
200C, 400F, gas 6

**Serves 6-8**

**Calories**
499 per portion

**You will need**
1 quantity rich shortcrust pastry
 (recipe 55)
water and caster sugar to glaze

For the filling
500 g /1 lb mincemeat
2 dessert apples, peeled, cored
 and chopped
100 g/4 oz grapes, halved and
 seeded
grated rind of 1 orange
2 tablespoons brandy

To serve
1 tablespoon brandy
150 ml/¼ pint double cream,
 whipped

Make the rich shortcrust pastry as instructed in recipe 55. Roll out two-thirds of the pastry thinly on a floured surface and use to line a 23 cm/9 in fluted flan ring. Chill the flan and remaining pastry for 15 minutes.

Mix the filling ingredients together and use to fill the flan case. Roll out the remaining pastry thinly and cut out about twelve 7.5 cm/3 in rounds, with a fluted cutter. Dampen the edges of the pastry in the flan ring and arrange the rounds overlapping around the edge. Brush with water, sprinkle with caster sugar and bake for 35-40 minutes, until golden.

Fold the brandy into the cream. Serve the flan hot or cold, topped with the brandy cream.

## Cook's Tip

*To make a different citrus decoration, use a potato peeler or canelle knife to pare off lemon, lime or orange peel, free of white pith, in long spirals.*

## Cook's Tip

*If you make your own mincemeat for Christmas puddings and recipes such as this one, you may prefer to use the vegetarian suet available from health shops and supermarkets to replace the traditional animal suet.*

# 61 | St. Clement's Whip Flan

**Preparation time**
15 minutes

**Cooking time**
15-20 minutes

**Oven temperature**
160C, 325F, gas 3

**Serves 6**

**Calories**
210 per portion

**You will need**
50 g/2 oz self-raising flour
¼ teaspoon baking powder
2 teaspoons cocoa powder
50 g/2 oz caster sugar
50 g/2 oz soft margarine
1 egg

For the filling
2 eggs, separated
50 g/2 oz caster sugar
grated rind and juice of 2 small
 lemons
grated rind of 1 small orange
2 teaspoons powdered gelatine
1 tablespoon hot water

To decorate
orange segments
120 ml/4 fl oz whipped cream

Grease and line a 20 cm/8 in flan tin. Sift the flour, baking powder and cocoa into a bowl. Add the sugar, margarine and egg and beat well. Spoon into the tin and bake for 15-20 minutes, until firm to touch. Cool on a wire rack.

Whisk the egg yolks and sugar in a bowl over a pan of simmering water. Remove from the heat and stir in the lemon juice and orange and lemon rinds. Dissolve the gelatine in the hot water over a pan of simmering water. Stir in and leave until just set. Whisk the egg whites until stiff, then fold into the mixture. Pour into the flan case and decorate with orange segments and piped cream.

## Cook's Tip

**To make a baking powder use three parts cream of tartar to one part bicarbonate of soda and add them to the mixture separately.**

# 62 | Walnut Treacle Tart

**Preparation time**
25 minutes, plus 1 hour
to rest

**Cooking time**
35 minutes

**Oven temperature**
190C, 375F, gas 5

**Makes one
20 cm/8 in tart**

**Calories**
303 per portion

**You will need**
175 g/6 oz plain flour
pinch of salt
40 g/1½ oz hard margarine
40 g/1½ oz lard
4 tablespoons milk

For the filling
175 g/6 oz maple syrup
50 g/2 oz treacle
150 g/5 oz walnuts, ground
25 g/1 oz brown breadcrumbs

To make the shortcrust pastry sift the flour and salt into a bowl. Rub in the butter and lard until the mixture resembles breadcrumbs. Gradually stir in the milk, and mix the pastry to a smooth dough with the fingers. Leave to rest for 30 minutes. Roll out on a lightly floured surface and use to line a 20 cm/8 in flan ring. Trim off the excess pastry and roll it out again. Cut into four 25 cm/10 in strips. Leave the flan case and strips to rest for 30 minutes.

Warm the syrup and treacle in a saucepan over a low heat. Add the walnuts and breadcrumbs. Mix well and pour into the flan case. Decorate with the strips of pastry and bake for 35 minutes, or until the pastry is golden.

## Cook's Tip

**Ensure that any pastry lattice work that you use to decorate open tarts or flans is not too thick or it will be indigestible and undercooked by the time the tart is ready.**

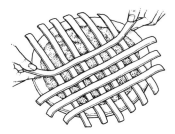

# 63 | Fluted Layer Flan

**Preparation time**
20 minutes, plus 2-3 hours to chill

**Cooking time**
30 minutes

**Oven temperature**
200C, 400F, gas 6
then
180C, 350F, gas 4

**Serves 8**

**Calories**
359 per portion

**You will need**
175 g/6 oz plain flour
100 g/4 oz butter
75 g/3 oz caster sugar
1 egg yolk
2 tablespoons water

For the filling
1 egg yolk
25 g/1 oz caster sugar
15 g/½ oz plain flour
¼ teaspoon vanilla essence
150 ml/¼ pint boiling milk
3 kiwi fruit, thinly sliced
150 ml/¼ pint whipping cream, whipped
225 g/8 oz strawberries, sliced
1 teaspoon powdered gelatine
150 ml/¼ pint tropical fruit juice

Make the rich shortcrust pastry as instructed in recipe 55. Use to line a 20 cm/8 in loose-bottomed cake tin. Bake blind (see Cook's Tip below) for 10 minutes, then lower the temperature and bake for 15 minutes. Remove the beans and paper and cook for a further 5 minutes.

Blend together the egg yolk, sugar, flour and vanilla essence. Add the milk, whisking well, then cook for 1 minute. Pour into the pastry case and leave to cool.

Arrange two-thirds of the kiwi fruit over the custard, spread with half the cream and top with the strawberries. Dissolve the gelatine in the fruit juice over a pan of simmering water, pour over the flan and chill until set. Decorate with the remaining cream and kiwi fruit.

# 64 | 18th-Century Tart

**Preparation time**
15-20 minutes

**Cooking time**
30 minutes

**Oven temperature**
180C, 350F, gas 4

**Serves 4**

**Calories**
509 per portion

**You will need**
½ quantity rich shortcrust pastry (recipe 55)
75 g/3 oz butter
75 g/3 oz caster sugar
4 egg yolks
25 g/1 oz candied peel
grated rind of 1 orange
1 dessert apple

Make the rich shortcrust pastry as instructed in recipe 55. Roll out the pastry on a floured surface and use to line an 18 cm/7 in flan ring or tin.

Beat the butter, sugar and egg yolks until light and fluffy. Stir in the candied peel and orange rind. Pour the mixture over the pastry. Quarter, core and grate the apple (do not peel) and spoon over the flan.

Bake for 30 minutes. Serve warm or cold.

## Cook's Tip

*Pastry cases for cheesecakes and flans are baked blind to prevent them becoming soggy. Use kitchen foil or greaseproof paper to cover the pastry base and sides, weighed down with dried beans, rice or pastry pebbles to prevent the pastry rising as it cooks. Remove the paper and weights for the last 5 minutes of the cooking time.*

## Cook's Tip

*When rubbing in fat in a pastry recipe, shake the bowl occasionally to bring any larger lumps to the surface so they can be rubbed in evenly.*

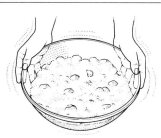

# Soufflés and Light Desserts

*Nothing is more beguiling than a feather-light, freshly-whipped soufflé, mouse, fool, syllabub, parfait, brûlée or fool to crown a meal. Here is a simply wicked selection to tempt the tastebuds.*

## 65 | Brandy Fruit Soufflé

**Preparation time**
15 minutes, plus 30 minutes to cool

**Cooking time**
25-30 minutes

**Oven temperature**
150C, 300F, gas 2

**Serves 6**

**Calories**
219 per portion

**You will need**
3 tablespoons redcurrant jelly
2 tablespoons brandy
75 g/3 oz mixed dried fruit
25 g/1 oz mixed peel
4 egg whites
175 g/6 oz caster sugar

Grease and lightly sugar a 15 cm/6 in soufflé dish. Place the redcurrant jelly, brandy, dried fruit and mixed peel in a small pan, and allow the jelly to melt slowly over a low heat, stirring occasionally. Set aside to cool.

Whisk the egg whites until very stiff then, using a metal spoon, fold in the sugar and the fruit mixture. Turn into the prepared soufflé dish and make peaks on the top with the back of a spoon. Bake in a preheated oven for 25-30 minutes until well risen and lightly browned. Serve hot with single cream handed separately.

## 66 | Soufflé Rothschild

**Preparation time**
40 minutes, plus 1 hour to soak

**Cooking time**
20 minutes

**Oven temperature**
180C, 350F, gas 4

**Serves 4-6**

**Calories**
148 per portion

**You will need**
1 peach or mango, diced
1 kiwi fruit, sliced
8 strawberries, sliced
2 slices fresh or canned pineapple, diced
1 miniature bottle Curaçao
4 eggs, separated
50 g/2 oz caster sugar
25 g/1 oz icing sugar, sifted, to serve

Place all the fruits in a shallow dish and pour over the Curaçao. Set aside for about 1 hour to absorb the flavour, turning the fruit occasionally.

Drain the excess juice from the fruit into a bowl and add the egg yolks and caster sugar. Place over a pan of simmering water and whisk until creamy and thick. Remove from the heat and whisk until cool. Whisk the egg whites until stiff and carefully fold into the mixture.

Place the fruit in a prepared 1.2 litre/2 pint soufflé dish on a baking tray. Spoon the soufflé mixture on top of the fruit. Bake immediately in a preheated oven for 20 minutes, until well risen, golden brown on top and creamy in the centre. Dredge with icing sugar and serve immediately.

## Cook's Tip

**Wash excess sugar from mixed dried fruit and peel by placing it in a sieve under a running hot water tap for a few minutes. Drain thoroughly before use.**

## Cook's Tip

**Other liqueurs such as Calvados, maraschino, framboise, fraise, Amaretto and Cointreau enhance the flavour of fruit desserts such as this.**

# 67 | Strawberry Soufflé

**Preparation time**
*30 minutes, plus 1 hour
to chill*

**Serves 6-8**

**Calories**
*386 per portion*

**You will need**
*500 g /1 lb strawberries, hulled
4 eggs, separated
100 g/4 oz caster sugar
15 g/½ oz powdered gelatine
juice of 1 orange
300 ml/½ pint whipping cream*

**To serve**
*15 g/½ oz ratafias, crushed
4 tablespoons double cream,
    whipped
few strawberry slices (optional)*

Prepare a 1 litre/1¾ pint soufflé dish (see Cook's Tip 75). Purée the strawberries in a blender or food processor, then sieve to remove the pips.

Put the egg yolks and sugar in a bowl and whisk until thick and mousse-like. Soak the gelatine in the orange juice, then dissolve over a pan of simmering water. Stir into the egg mixture. Whip the cream until it stands in soft peaks, then lightly fold in the strawberry purée. Carefully fold in the egg mousse mixture. Leave in a cool place until almost set.

Whisk the egg whites until stiff, stir 1 tablespoon into the soufflé mixture, and then fold in the remainder. Spoon the soufflé mixture into the prepared dish and chill for 1 hour or until set.

To serve, remove the paper and press the crushed ratafias around the sides. Decorate with the cream and strawberry halves, if used.

# 68 | Lemon Soufflé

**Preparation time**
*30 minutes, plus 2
hours to chill*

**Serves 6-8**

**Calories**
*366 per portion*

**You will need**
*3 large eggs, separated
175 g/6 oz caster sugar
grated rind and juice of 2 lemons
450 ml/¾ pint whipping cream,
    whipped
15 g/½ oz gelatine
3 tablespoons hot water
2 tablespoons chopped almonds,
    toasted, to decorate*

Place the egg yolks, sugar and lemon rind in a bowl. Heat the lemon juice in a small pan, then pour over the egg mixture. Whisk thoroughly until thick, then fold in two-thirds of the cream.

Dissolve the gelatine in the hot water over a pan of simmering water and gently stir into the soufflé until beginning to set. Whisk the egg whites until stiff, then fold into the mixture. Pour into a prepared 15 cm/6 in soufflé dish (see Cook's Tip 75) and chill for 2 hours or until set.

Remove the paper band from the soufflé and press the nuts around the sides. Decorate with the remaining cream. Chill before serving.

## Cook's Tip

**If ratafias are difficult to
obtain, use macaroons or any
other almond-flavoured
biscuits instead.**

## Cook's Tip

**Almonds that are dry and
brittle are much easier to chop
or cut into slivers if covered
with boiling water for 30
seconds, then drained.**

# 69 | *Chocolate Cinnamon Soufflé*

**Preparation time**
30 minutes, plus 2
hours to chill

**Serves 4-6**

**Calories**
397 per portion

**You will need**
1 tablespoon cocoa powder
2 tablespoons boiling water
4 eggs, separated
100 g/4 oz caster sugar
1½ teaspoons ground cinnamon
15 g/½ oz gelatine
2 tablespoons hot water
150 ml/¼ pint whipping cream,
   half whipped
150 g/6 oz plain chocolate to
   decorate

Blend the cocoa with the boiling water to a smooth paste; cool. Put the egg yolks, sugar, cinnamon and cocoa paste in a bowl over a pan of simmering water and whisk until creamy and thick. Remove from the heat and whisk until cool. Whisk the egg whites until stiff.

Dissolve the gelatine in the hot water over a pan of simmering water, and gently stir into the chocolate mixture. Carefully fold in the cream and the egg whites. Turn the mixture into a prepared 900 ml/1½ pint cold soufflé dish (see Cook's Tip 75) and chill for 2 hours or until set. Shave half the chocolate into curls using a potato peeler; finely grate the remainder. Remove the paper band from the soufflé and press the grated chocolate around the sides. Arrange the chocolate curls on top.

# 70 | *Soufflé Surprise*

**Preparation time**
20 minutes

**Cooking time**
8-10 minutes

**Oven temperature**
200C, 400F, gas 6

**Serves 4-6**

**Calories**
203 per portion

**You will need**
3 eggs, separated
50 g/2 oz caster sugar
1 tablespoon sweet sherry
2 (225 g/8 oz) packets frozen
   blackberries, half defrosted
⅓ litre/12 fl oz block vanilla ice
   cream
15 g/½ oz icing sugar, sifted

Lightly butter a 1.5 litre/2½ pint soufflé dish and place in a shallow dish or pan surrounded by ice cubes. Chill in the refrigerator while preparing the soufflé mixture.

Put the egg yolks, sugar and sherry in a bowl over a pan of simmering water and whisk until creamy and thick. Remove from the heat and whisk again until cool. Whisk the egg whites until stiff and, using a metal spoon, carefully fold in the yolk mixture.

Remove the prepared dish from the refrigerator and immediately put the blackberries in the bottom. Place the ice cream on top and quickly cover with the soufflé mixture. Sprinkle with the icing sugar and bake immediately on the top shelf of a preheated oven for 8-10 minutes, until well risen and golden brown. Serve immediately.

## Cook's Tip

**Keep a cinnamon stick in a jar of caster sugar. This sugar is good for flavouring fresh melon and if sprinkled on top of hot buttered toast gives delicious cinnamon toast.**

## Cook's Tip

**The cooler the air you whisk into egg whites, the more the mixture will rise when cooked to give an impressive look to the finished soufflé.**

# 71 | Lime Soufflé

**Preparation time**
30 minutes, plus 2
hours to chill

**Serves 4-6**

**Calories**
258 per portion

**You will need**
3 eggs, separated
75 g/3 oz caster sugar
grated rind and juice of 3 limes
15 g/½ oz gelatine
2 tablespoons hot water
150 ml/¼ pint whipping cream,
  half whipped

To decorate
50-75 g/2-3 oz chopped nuts
crystallised lemon slices (optional)

Place the egg yolks, sugar, lime rind and juice in a bowl over a pan of simmering water and whisk until cool. Whisk the egg whites until stiff.

Dissolve the gelatine in the hot water over a pan of simmering water, and gently stir into the lemon mixture. Carefully fold in the cream, reserving 2 tablespoonfuls for decoration, and the egg whites. Turn into a prepared 900 ml/1½ pint cold soufflé dish and chill for 2 hours.

Remove the paper band from the soufflé and press the nuts around the sides. Decorate with the reserved cream and lemon slices, if using.

# 72 | Tangerine Soufflé

**Preparation time**
25 minutes

**Cooking time**
10 minutes

**Oven temperature**
230C, 450F, gas 8

**Serves 4**

**Calories**
198 per portion

**You will need**
10 g/¼ oz unsalted butter, melted
65 g/2½ oz caster sugar, plus 2
  tablespoons
grated rind of 2 tangerines
250 ml/8 fl oz tangerine juice
  (about 12 tangerines)
25 g/1 oz arrowroot
25 ml/1 fl oz water
3 eggs, separated

Brush four 150 ml/¼ pint freezerproof soufflé dishes with the melted butter. Dust with 1 tablespoon of the sugar and place in the freezer.

Heat the rind, tangerine juice and 65 g/2½ oz of the sugar to simmering point. Blend the arrowroot and water together and whisk into the hot juice, stirring until it thickens. Cool slightly, then beat in the egg yolks. Whisk the egg whites with the remaining 1 tablespoon of sugar until stiff and fold into the tangerine mixture.

Pour the mixture into the prepared soufflé dishes and smooth the tops with a palette knife. Bake in a preheated oven for 10 minutes. Serve immediately.

## Cook's Tip

To remove the paper band
from a soufflé, hold a palette
knife against the side of the
soufflé and carefully peel off
the paper while sliding the
knife around the soufflé.

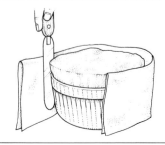

## Cook's Tip

Arrowroot is excellent for
thickening fruit juice for a
clear glaze for fruit flans. Use
in the proportion of 1
teaspoon to 150 ml/¼ pint
liquid.

# 73 | Soufflé Omelette

**Preparation time**
10 minutes

**Cooking time**
3-5 minutes

**Serves 1**

**Calories**
458 per portion

**You will need**
2 eggs, separated
2 teaspoons cold water
2 teaspoons caster sugar
¼ teaspoon vanilla essence
15 g/½ oz butter
2 tablespoons strawberry
    conserve
icing sugar to dredge

Whisk together the egg yolks, water, sugar and vanilla essence until pale and creamy. Whisk the egg whites until just stiff enough to stand in peaks, then gently fold into the mixture with a metal spoon.

Melt the butter until just beginning to sizzle. Add the egg mixture and spread evenly. Cook gently for about 2 minutes until set around the edge, then place under a preheated grill for 1-2 minutes until the surface feels firm to the touch and looks puffy.

Heat the jam in a small pan. Put two skewers in a flame until red hot. Remove the omelet from the grilll and quickly spread with jam. Fold over and dredge with icing sugar. Mark a lattice pattern across the top with the red hot skewers. Serve immediately.

# 74 | Banana and Rum Soufflé

**Preparation time**
30 minutes

**Cooking time**
30 minutes

**Oven temperature**
190C, 375F, gas 5

**Serves 8**

**Calories**
171 per portion

**You will need**
25 g/1 oz unsalted butter
60 g/2¼ oz caster sugar, plus 1
    tablespoon
4 eggs, separated
20 g/¾ oz flour
150 ml/¼ pint milk, warmed
2 bananas
50 ml/2 fl oz rum
icing sugar to dredge

For the sauce
3 egg yolks
50 g/2 oz caster sugar
40 ml/1½ fl oz rum
1 tablespoon orange juice

Use a little butter to grease inside a 1.25 litre/2¼ pint soufflé dish. Coat with 1 tablespoon of sugar. Chill.

Whisk the egg yolks, 40 g/1½ oz of the sugar and the flour, add the milk and blend thoroughly. Gently heat the mixture in a clean pan, stirring constantly until it thickens, then beat in the remaining butter.

Slice 1 banana and macerate in the rum. Purée the second banana and add to the custard. Whisk the egg whites and remaining sugar until stiff. Fold the rum, banana slices, and egg whites into the custard. Pour into the dish and bake in a preheated oven for 30 minutes. To make the sauce, whisk all the ingredients in a bowl over a pan of simmering water until light and fluffy. Dredge the soufflé with icing sugar and serve at once.

## Cook's Tip

*Other suitable fillings for soufflé omelette include: preserved ginger in syrup; 2 tablespoons of raisins soaked in either brandy or rum for 30 minutes; or marmalade with a little liqueur added.*

## Cook's Tip

*To coat the inside of cake tins or soufflé dishes, first grease the tin, add the flour or sugar, then tilt from side to side, tapping the edge to coat the base and sides evenly.*

# 75 | *Crystallised Ginger Soufflé*

**Preparation time**
30 minutes, plus 2 hours to chill

**Serves 4-6**

**Calories**
194 per portion

**You will need**
50-75 g/2-3 oz crystallised ginger, minced or finely chopped
2 tablespoons boiling water
4 eggs, separated
25 g/1 oz caster sugar
15 g/½ oz gelatine
2 tablespoons hot water
150 ml/¼ pint whipping cream, half whipped

**To decorate**
50-75 g/2-3 oz chopped nuts
few pieces crystallised ginger, chopped

Put the ginger in a bowl and sprinkle with the boiling water. Add the egg yolks and sugar. Place the bowl over a pan of simmering water and whisk until creamy and thick. Remove from the heat and whisk until cool. Whisk the egg whites until stiff.

Dissolve the gelatine in the hot water over a pan of simmering water, and gently stir into the ginger mixture. Carefully fold in the cream, reserving 2 tablespoons for decoration, and the egg whites. Turn into a prepared 900 ml/1½ pint cold soufflé dish and chill for 2 hours or until set.

Remove the paper band from the soufflé and press the nuts around the sides. Decorate with the reserved cream and ginger.

# 76 | *Mango Fool*

**Preparation time**
15 minutes, plus 1 hour to chill

**Cooking time**
10 minutes

**Serves 4**

**Calories**
315 per portion

**You will need**
1 large ripe mango
50 g/2 oz caster sugar
1 teaspoon lime or lemon juice
1 egg white
150 ml/¼ pint double or whipping cream, whipped

Peel and slice the mango and purée the flesh. Stir in 25 g/1 oz of the sugar and the lime or lemon juice. Chill for at least an hour.

Whisk the egg white until stiff, then whisk in the remaining sugar. Fold in the whipped cream. Fold the mango purée into the cream mixture and spoon into four individual dishes. Chill until required.

If preferred, place chopped mango in the dishes before spooning in the fool.

## Cook's Tip

**To prepare a soufflé dish, cut a band of double greaseproof paper long enough to fit around the outside of the dish and wide enough to stand 5 cm/2 in above the rim. Secure with string or an elastic band.**

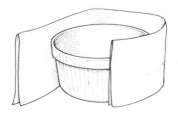

## Cook's Tip

**Use this recipe as the basis for almost any fruit fool. Cook currants and blackberries before puréeing; soft fruits like raspberries and strawberries just need puréeing, as in the mango version above.**

# 77 | Marbled Gooseberry Fool

**Preparation time**
12 minutes, plus 1 hour
to chill

**Cooking time**
about 30 minutes

**Serves 5-6**

**Calories**
360 per portion

**You will need**
750 g/1½ lb fresh or frozen and
    defrosted gooseberries, topped
    and tailed
175 g/6 oz caster sugar
1 teaspoon powdered gelatine
2 tablespoons hot water
150 ml/¼ pint whipping cream
1 (425 g/15 oz) can custard
few drops green food colouring
    (optional)

Put the gooseberries and sugar in a pan and heat gently until the sugar has dissolved. Simmer, uncovered, until the fruit forms a thick pulp. Stir the mixture occasionally to prevent it sticking. Purée the mixture in a liquidiser or food processor, then sieve to remove the seeds. Leave the mixture to cool for about 30 minutes.

Meanwhile, dissolve the gelatine in the hot water over a pan of gently simmering water. Whip the cream until it forms soft peaks and stir in the cooled but still liquid gelatine. Lightly whisk in the custard.

Tint the cooled gooseberry purée with a few drops of green colouring, if liked. Put alternate spoonfuls of the gooseberry purée and custard mixture in individual glasses, finishing with the custard. Pull the handle of a teaspoon from the top to the base at 2.5 cm/1 in intervals around the inside of each glass to create a marbled effect. Chill for at least an hour before serving.

# 78 | Strawberry Mousse

**Preparation time**
30 minutes, plus 2
hours to chill

**Serves 8**

**Calories**
245 per portion

**You will need**
350 g/12 oz strawberries
2 eggs
1 egg yolk
75 g/3 oz caster sugar
3 tablespoons orange juice
15 g/½ oz gelatine
300 ml/½ pint double cream,
    lightly whipped

Reserve a few of the best strawberries for decoration. Sieve the remainder or purée in a liquidiser or food processor, then sieve to remove the seeds. There should be about 250 ml/8 fl oz purée.

Place the eggs, egg yolk and sugar in a bowl over a pan of gently simmering water and whisk until thick. Place the orange juice in a small pan, sprinkle over the gelatine and leave for 5 minutes. Heat gently to dissolve the gelatine, then fold into the egg mousse with the strawberry purée and half the cream. Remove from the heat and stir over a bowl of iced water until beginning to set, then turn into a 900 ml/1½ pint ring mould. Chill for 2 hours or until set.

Turn out on to a serving plate. Whip the remaining cream until stiff and decorate the mousse with piped cream and the reserved strawberries.

## Cook's Tip

*The versatile gooseberry is good puréed and served cold in custard, yogurt or cream to make a fool, or hot in crumbles and pies. Puréed stewed gooseberries also go well with deep-fried cheeses such as Brie.*

## Cook's Tip

*When turning out a mousse on to a serving plate, wet the plate slightly so that the mousse can be moved a little if you turn it out slightly off-centre.*

# 79 | Liqueur Mousse

**Preparation time**
*25 minutes, plus 2
hours to chill*

**Serves 6**

**Calories**
*281 per portion*

**You will need**
*3 eggs, separated
100 g/4 oz caster sugar
grated rind and juice of 1 lemon
1 tablespoon Grand Marnier
2 tablespoons Kirsch
1 tablespoon rum
2 teaspoons powdered gelatine
50 ml/2 fl oz hot water
150 ml/¼ pint double cream*

**To decorate**
*double cream, whipped
6 small liqueur chocolates*

Prepare a 15 cm/6 in soufflé dish to form a collar 7.5 cm/ 3 in above the rim of the dish (see Cook's Tip 75). Put the egg yolks and sugar in a bowl placed over a pan of gently simmering water. Whisk until creamy and thick. Add the lemon rind, juice, liqueurs and rum.

Dissolve the gelatine in the hot water over a pan of simmering water. Stir well, cool slightly, then whisk the gelatine into the yolk and sugar mixture and allow to cool.

Whisk the cream until it holds its shape on the whisk. Using a clean whisk, whisk the egg whites until stiff. Fold the cream into the yolk and sugar mixture, then carefully fold in the egg whites. Pour the mixture into the prepared dish and chill for 2 hours or until set. Remove the paper band from the soufflé, pipe rosettes of cream on top and decorate with small liqueur chocolates.

# 80 | Honeycomb Fool

**Preparation time**
*10 minutes, plus 1 hour
to chill*

**Serves 4**

**Calories**
*242 per portion*

**You will need**
*4 milk chocolate honeycomb bars
1 egg white
250 ml/8 fl oz double or whipping
cream
twists of orange rind to decorate*

Place the honeycomb bars in a strong plastic bag. Hold the open end of the bag securely and crush into rough pieces with a rolling pin.

Whisk the egg white until stiff, then whip the cream until stiff. Fold the egg white into the cream. Stir in the crushed honeycomb bars. Spoon the mixture into four individual dishes. Chill until required. Decorate with twists of orange rind.

## Cook's Tip

**Choose any combination of
your favourite liqueurs. Why
not try Tia Maria or Drambuie
in this recipe instead of the
Grand Marnier.**

## Cook's Tip

**Bought confectionery can be
used to make a number of
short cuts in recipes. Bite-
sized miniature chocolate bars
decorate cakes and trifles and
melted chocolate bars make
quick sauces.**

# 81 | *Chocolate Marquise*

**Preparation time**
*25 minutes, plus 1½ hours to chill*

**Serves 4**

**Calories**
*685 per portion*

**You will need**
*165 g/5½ oz plain chocolate*
*1 tablespoon water*
*2 tablespoons whisky, armagnac or rum (optional)*
*90 g/3½ oz unsalted butter, softened*
*50 g/2 oz icing sugar*
*2 eggs separated*
*15 g/½ oz caster sugar*

Break the chocolate in pieces into a bowl. Add the water and alcohol, if using, and place in a bowl over a pan of simmering water until the chocolate melts. Remove from the heat, stir well and allow 5 minutes to cool.

Cream the softened butter and icing sugar together. Beat in the egg yolks, then fold in the melted chocolate. Whisk the egg whites and caster sugar until very stiff and fold into the chocolate mixture. Pour into a 600 ml/1 pint mould or four individual moulds lined with foil, and chill for 1½ hours or until set.

To serve, dip the mould or individual moulds in hot water for a few seconds to loosen the marquise from the sides, then turn out on to a dish. Peel off the foil and serve with orange segments.

# 82 | *Cheese and Yogurt Creams*

**Preparation time**
*15 minutes, plus 3-4 hours to drain*

**Serves 6**

**Calories**
*215 per portion*

**You will need**
*225 g/8 oz cream cheese*
*150 g/5.2 oz carton natural yogurt*
*2 tablespoons clear honey*
*1 egg white*
*225 g/8 oz soft fruit, e.g. strawberries, raspberries, blackcurrants or redcurrants*

Place the cheese, yogurt and honey in a bowl and mix well. Whisk the egg white until fairly stiff then fold into the cheese mixture.

Line six heart-shaped moulds with muslin, spoon in the cheese mixture and smooth the tops. Place on a plate and leave to drain in the refrigerator for 3-4 hours. Turn out on to individual dishes and surround with the fruit.

Alternatively, spoon the cheese mixture into six rame-kin dishes, arrange the fruit on top and chill for at least an hour.

## Cook's Tip

**To soften butter, place in a bowl standing in a larger bowl of hot, but not boiling, water. Alternatively, to chill butter, fill the larger bowl with ice cubes.**

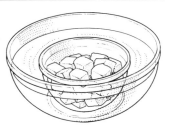

## Cook's Tip

**Whether homemade or bought, yogurt should be kept well covered. Keep in a cool place and eat no later than three days after the 'sell by' date or within three or four days of making.**

# 83 | *Redcurrant Tansy*

**Preparation time**
30 minutes, plus 2
hours to cool and chill

**Cooking time**
15 minutes

**Serves 6**

**Calories**
361 per portion

**You will need**
500 g /1 lb redcurrants, stalks
    removed
100 g/4 oz granulated sugar
3 egg yolks
1 tablespoon caster sugar
2 teaspoons cornflour
300 ml/½ pint milk
150 ml/¼ pint double cream,
    whipped

Put the redcurrants in a pan with the sugar and simmer gently for 8-10 minutes until softened. Leave to cool. Purée in a liquidiser or food processor until smooth, or work through a sieve.

   Put the egg yolks, caster sugar and cornflour in a bowl and beat until thoroughly blended. Bring the milk to the boil in a pan, then stir into the egg mixture. Strain into the top of a double boiler or a heatproof bowl over a pan of simmering water and cook gently, stirring constantly, until the custard is thick enough to coat the back of a spoon. Remove from the heat and fold in the redcurrant purée. Leave to cool, stirring occasionally to prevent a skin forming.

   Whisk the redcurrant mixture, then fold in the whipped cream to create a marbled effect. Spoon into individual glasses and chill until required. Serve with crisp biscuits.

# 84 | *Chestnut Creams*

**Preparation time**
10 minutes, plus 1 hour
to chill

**Serves 4**

**Calories**
301 per portion

**You will need**
150 ml/¼ pint double or whipping
    cream
2 tablespoons rum or brandy
1 (225 g/8 oz) can sweetened
    chestnut spread
chocolate curls to decorate

Whip the cream and rum or brandy together until just 'floppy'. Gradually fold in the chestnut spread. Spoon the mixture into a piping bag fitted with a large star nozzle. Pipe into four individual dishes. Chill until required or for at least 1 hour. Decorate with chocolate curls. Serve with single cream.

## *Cook's Tip*

*To freeze, pour the tansy into a rigid freezerproof container, seal and label, then freeze for up to three months. To defrost, leave at room temperature for 4-5 hours.*

## *Cook's Tip*

*To peel fresh chestnuts, place flat side down on a board and make a cut in the pointed end. Boil or bake the chestnuts in a hot oven for 10-20 minutes until the cuts open, then strip off the skins, using a sharp, pointed knife.*

# 85 | Lemon Wine Syllabub

**Preparation time**
10 minutes, plus 1 hour to infuse

**Serves 4-6**

**Calories**
280 per portion

**You will need**
150 ml/¼ pint white wine or sherry
75 g/3 oz caster sugar
2 tablespoons lemon juice
2 teaspoons grated lemon rind
300 ml/½ pint double or whipping cream
julienne strips of lemon rind to decorate

Place the wine, sugar, lemon juice and rind in a bowl. Leave to infuse for 1 hour.

Add the cream and whisk the mixture until it is stiff enough to stand in soft peaks. Spoon into individual glasses and decorate with the lemon rind. Chill until required. Use on the day it is made.

# 86 | Crème Brûlée

**Preparation time**
5 minutes, plus overnight chilling

**Cooking time**
35-45 minutes

**Oven temperature**
140C ,275F, gas 1

**Serves 6**

**Calories**
509 per portion

**You will need**
4 egg yolks
1 tablespoon sugar
600 ml/1 pint double cream
few drops vanilla essence
50 g/2 oz caster sugar to finish

Beat the egg yolks and sugar together. Warm the cream in a double saucepan. Carefully stir in the egg mixture. Continue cooking gently, stirring constantly, until thick enough to coat the back of a spoon. Add the vanilla essence. Strain into six ramekin dishes and place in a roasting tin containing 2.5 cm/1 in water. Bake for 30-40 minutes. Remove dishes from the tin, cool then chill overnight.

To finish, sprinkle evenly with the sugar. Place under a preheated hot grill until the sugar has caramelised. Cool, then chill for 2 hours before serving.

## Cook's Tip

**Do not make syllabub too far in advance of serving it as the alcohol it contains may cause it to separate.**

## Cook's Tip

**Ensure the sugar is spread evenly before placing under the grill: if thick in patches the caramelised coating will be hard to break through; too thin and the exposed custard may actually boil under the heat of the grill.**

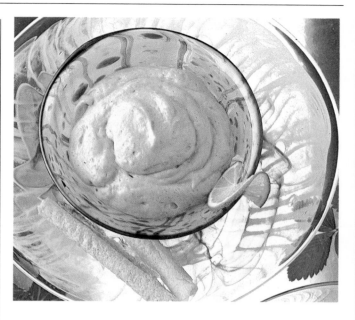

# 87 | Whim-Whams

**Preparation time**
20 minutes

**Serves 4**

**Calories**
553 per portion

**You will need**
450 ml/¾ pint double cream
65 g/2½ oz caster sugar
90 ml/3½ fl oz sweet white wine
20 ratafias
150 ml/¼ pint made-up blackberry
  jelly, set

Whip the cream and sugar together until it holds its shape on the whisk. Whisk in the wine: take care not to overbeat or the cream will separate.

Divide a third of the cream between four 150 ml/¼ pint stemmed wine glasses. Arrange 2 ratafias on top. Spread with half the jelly. Cover with half the remaining cream. Arrange 3 ratafias on top. Spread the remaining jelly on them. Top with the rest of the cream. Serve chilled.

# 88 | Avocado and Lime Whip

**Preparation time**
30 minutes

**Serves 4**

**Calories**
356 per portion

**You will need**
2 ripe avocados, peeled and
  stoned
2 limes
6 tablespoons single cream
2 egg whites
50 g/2 oz icing sugar, sifted

Chop the avocados into small cubes and place in a blender or food processor. Strain the juice of 1 lime and add to the blender or processor with the cream. Work to a purée.

Whisk the egg whites until stiff, then whisk in the icing sugar, 1 tablespoon at a time. Carefully fold in the avocado mixture and spoon into individual glasses. Slice half the remaining lime thinly, place a slice on each glass and spoon a little juice from the other half over each one. Serve immediately.

## Cook's Tip

*To make a jelly quickly, use just enough hot water to melt the jelly cubes, then make up the specified quantity with cold water.*

## Cook's Tip

*If you have to cut an avocado some time before serving, leave the stone in one of the halves, cover with cling film and chill in the refrigerator to prevent discoloration.*

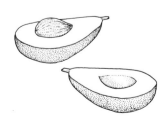

# 89 | *Coffee and Walnut Cream*

**Preparation time**
*10 minutes, plus 30 minutes to chill*

**Serves 4**

**Calories**
*457 per portion*

**You will need**
*12 marshmallows*
*120 ml/4 fl oz strong black coffee*
*300 ml/½ pint double cream*
*50 g/2 oz walnut pieces, chopped*

Place the marshmallows and coffee in a pan and heat gently, stirring until dissolved. Allow to cool. Whip the cream until it stands in soft peaks, then carefully fold into the coffee mixture with all but 2 teaspoons of the walnuts. Spoon into individual dishes and sprinkle the tops with the remaining walnuts. Chill for at least 30 minutes before serving.

# 90 | *Blackcurrant Parfait*

**Preparation time**
*30-40 minutes, plus 2-3 hours to chill*

**Cooking time**
*10 minutes*

**Serves 4-6**

**Calories**
*337 per portion*

**You will need**
*500 g /1 lb blackcurrants, stalks removed*
*4 tablespoons water*
*2 teaspoons lemon juice*
*50 g/2 oz granulated sugar*
*2 egg whites*
*75 g/3 oz caster sugar*
*300 ml/½ pint double cream*

Put the blackcurrants in a pan with the water, lemon juice and sugar. Simmer gently for 8-10 minutes until the blackcurrants are softened. Leave to cool. Purée in a liquidiser or food processor until smooth, then sieve to remove the pips.

Pour the purée into a rigid freezerproof container, cover and freeze for 2-3 hours until half-frozen. Transfer to a bowl and whisk thoroughly to break up the ice crystals. Whisk the egg whites until stiff, then whisk in the sugar, 1 tablespoon at a time. Continue whisking until the meringue is very stiff and holds its shape. Whip the cream until it stands in soft peaks, then fold into the meringue with the half-frozen blackcurrant mixture. Spoon into chilled glasses and serve immediately with thin, crisp biscuits.

## Cook's Tip

**Toasted marshmallows are delicious on an open-topped apple flan. Simply cover the apple filling with marshmallows and cook under the grill for a few minutes until they are golden brown.**

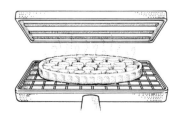

## Cook's Tip

**As a pretty decoration for this dessert, frost a few sprigs of blackcurrant. Dip each sprig in lightly beaten egg white, drain or brush off excess, then dredge in caster sugar and place on greaseproof paper to dry.**

# 91 | *Spiced Muscovado Swirl*

**Preparation time**
8 minutes, plus 2 hours
to chill

**Serves 8**

**Calories**
240 per portion

**You will need**
300 ml/½ pint double or whipping
  cream
500 g/1 lb plain unsweetened
  yogurt
grated rind of 1 lemon
100 g/4 oz Muscovado (raw cane)
  sugar
2 teaspoons mixed spice

Whip the cream, then stir in the yogurt and lemon rind. Spoon into a serving dish or eight individual dishes. Mix the sugar and spice and sprinkle in a thick layer over the mixture. Chill for at least 2 hours until the sugar is completely moist. Just before serving, carefully swirl the sugar through the mixture. Serve with thin crisp biscuits.

# 92 | *Pashka*

**Preparation time**
15 minutes, plus
overnight chilling

**Serves 6-8**

**Calories**
455 per portion

**You will need**
2 (225 g/8 oz) packets full-fat soft
  cheese
1 egg yolk
75 g/3 oz caster sugar
grated rind and juice of 1 lemon
120 ml/4 fl oz double cream,
  whipped
50 g/2 oz blanched almonds,
  chopped and browned
50 g/2 oz glacé cherries, quartered
50 g/2 oz raisins
25 g/1 oz flaked almonds, toasted,
  to decorate

Place the cheese in a bowl with the egg yolk, sugar and lemon rind. Beat thoroughly until smooth, then stir in the lemon juice. Fold in the cream with the chopped almonds and fruit.

Line a 1 litre/1¾ pint clean clay flower pot or pudding basin with a piece of muslin large enough to overlap the top. Spoon in the cheese mixture and fold the cloth over. Cover with a saucer and place a 500 g/1 lb weight on top. Place in a bowl and chill overnight.

To serve, unfold the cloth, invert on to a serving plate and carefully remove the muslin. Decorate with the flaked almonds.

## Cook's Tip

*For a tangy change, use the grated rind of an orange or a lime instead of the lemon.*

## Cook's Tip

*Clay flower pots can also be used for baking bread. Before use, brush the inside thoroughly with oil. Place the empty pot in a moderate oven (200C, 400F, gas 6) for 15 minutes. Allow to cool completely before use.*

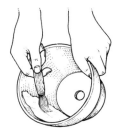

# Meringues, Jellies and Trifles

Here is a mouth-watering selection of those delicious nursery and party-time favourite desserts — meringues, jellies and trifles. However, flavoured with sherry, chocolate, ginger, caramel, coconut, coffee, fruit and given added crunch with nuts these tasty offerings have gained grown-up status.

## 93 | Meringue Croquembouches

**Preparation time**
15 minutes, plus 30 minutes to cool

**Cooking time**
50 minutes

**Oven temperature**
150C, 300F, gas 2

**Serves 4**

**Calories**
493 per portion

**You will need**
2 large egg whites
150 g/5 oz caster sugar
150 ml/¼ pint double cream
40 g/1½ oz sugar
225 g/8 oz fresh fruit in season, chopped

Line a baking tray with non-stick silicone paper. To make the Swiss meringue, whisk the egg whites until stiff. Gradually whisk in half the caster sugar until the mixture is thick and glossy. Carefully fold in the remaining caster sugar. Spoon into a piping bag fitted with a 1 cm/½ in nozzle and pipe twelve 7.5 cm/3 in rings on the paper. Bake for 50 minutes. Leave to cool.

   Whip the cream with the sugar until it holds its shape on the whisk. Spread eight of the twelve meringue rings with whipped cream and fruit and sandwich together with cream. Spread the four remaining meringue rings with cream and put them cream side down, on top. Decorate with fruit and serve.

## 94 | Pineapple Meringue Pie

**Preparation time**
30 minutes

**Cooking time**
50-55 minutes

**Oven temperature**
200C, 400F, gas 6
then
180C, 350F, gas 4
(pastry)
160C, 325F, gas 3
(pie)

**Serves 6**

**Calories**
431 per portion

**You will need**
175 g/6 oz plain flour
pinch of salt
75 g/3 oz butter or margarine
1-2 tablespoons iced water

For the filling
50 g/2 oz cornflour
450 ml/¾ pint pineapple juice
3 eggs, separated
25 g/1 oz butter
175 g/6 oz caster sugar
caster sugar for sprinkling

Make the pastry and bake blind in a 20 cm/8 in flan tin.
   Blend the cornflour with a little of the pineapple juice in a pan. Add the remaining juice and heat slowly, stirring, until thickened. Remove from the heat and beat in the egg yolks and butter. Pour into the pastry case and cool.
   Whisk the egg whites until very stiff and dry. Add the sugar a little at a time, whisking thoroughly between each addition until the meringue is glossy and forms soft peaks. Spoon into a large piping bag fitted with a 1 cm/½ in star nozzle and pipe over the pineapple filling. Sprinkle lightly with a little caster sugar. Bake for 15-20 minutes, until golden brown. Serve warm or cold.

## Cook's Tip

**To give a delicate flavour to the whipped cream, fold in a few drops of almond essence or a teaspoon of rosewater or orange flower water.**

## Cook's Tip

**When making meringues, ensure all utensils are completely free of grease and moisture, or the egg whites will not stiffen. For this reason, separate the eggs carefully so that no yolk mixes with the white.**

# 95 | *Coffee Meringues*

**Preparation time**
30 minutes

**Cooking time**
1-1½ hours

**Oven temperature**
140C, 275F, gas 1

**Serves 4-6**

**Calories**
177 per portion

**You will need**
225 g/8 oz sugar
150 ml/¼ pint water
4 egg whites
1 teaspoon coffee essence

Line a baking try with non-stick silicone paper. To make the Italian meringue, dissolve the sugar and water over a low heat without boiling. Once dissolved, bring to the boil without stirring until it reaches hard ball stage, 121C/250F on a sugar thermometer.

Meanwhile, whisk the egg whites until stiff. When the syrup is ready, pour it in a slow steady stream on to the stiff egg whites, beating constantly until the meringue is cool. Beat in the coffee essence. Reserve a quarter of the mixture and put the remainder in a piping bag fitted with a star nozzle. Pipe eight or twelve swirls on to the baking tray. Bake for about 1-1½ hours or until crisp. Cool, then remove the paper.

Place the reserved mixture in the piping bag. When the meringues are cold, pipe the uncooked meringue on to one half and sandwich the pairs together.

# 96 | *Hazelnut Meringue*

**Preparation time**
20 minutes

**Cooking time**
40-45 minutes

**Oven temperature**
180C, 350F, gas 4

**Serves 6**

**Calories**
319 per portion

**You will need**
4 egg whites
250 g/9 oz caster sugar
few drops vanilla essence
1 teaspoon vinegar
100 g/4 oz hazelnuts, toasted and
  ground

**For the filling**
300 ml/½ pint double cream,
  whipped
1 tablespoon caster sugar
225 g/8 oz raspberries
sifted icing sugar to finish

To make the meringue, whisk the egg whites until stiff, then whisk in the sugar, 1 tablespoon at a time. Continue whisking until the meringue is very stiff and holds its shape. Fold in the vanilla essence, vinegar and hazelnuts. Divide the mixture equally between two greased and lined 20 cm/8 in sandwich tins and spread evenly. Bake for 40-45 minutes. Turn out on to a wire rack to cool.

To make the filling, mix two-thirds of the cream with the sugar and raspberries, reserving a few for decoration. Sandwich the meringue rounds together with the filling and dust with icing sugar. Decorate with piped cream and the reserved raspberries.

## *Cook's Tip*

*Italian meringue is extremely versatile. Not only can it be cooked to form a crisp shell, but it can also be used as a filling. It can also be mixed with equal parts of whipped cream and fruit purée to make a cake filling.*

## *Cook's Tip*

*Keep a small wire-mesh tea strainer in a packet of icing sugar for use when sifting or dredging icing sugar for desserts.*

# 97 | *Chocolate Hazelnut Meringue*

**Preparation time**
25 minutes

**Cooking time**
2 hours

**Oven temperature**
120C, 250F, gas ½

**Serves 8**

**Calories**
414 per portion

**You will need**
4 egg whites
225 g/8 oz caster sugar
100 g/4 oz hazelnuts, toasted and
   ground
50 g/2 oz chocolate, melted, to
   decorate

**For the filling**
100 g/4 oz plain chocolate, broken
   into pieces
4 tablespoons water
450 ml/¾ pint double cream

To make the meringue, whisk the egg whites until stiff then whisk in 2 tablespoons of the sugar. Fold in the remaining sugar a little at a time, with the ground hazelnuts. Put the meringue in a piping bag fitted with a 1 cm/½ in plain nozzle and pipe into two 23 cm/9 in rounds on baking trays lined with silicone paper. Bake for 2 hours. Transfer to a wire rack to cool.

Place the chocolate and water in a small pan and heat very gently until melted; cool. Whip the cream until it begins to thicken, then whip in the cooled chocolate and continue to whip until stiff. Use three-quarters of the chocolate cream to sandwich the meringue rounds together. Pipe the remaining cream around the top edge. Put the melted chocolate in a greaseproof piping bag, snip off the end and drizzle the chocolate across the top.

# 98 | *Lemon Meringues*

**Preparation time**
20 minutes

**Cooking time**
2 hours

**Oven temperature**
140C, 275F, gas 1

**Serves 6**

**Calories**
573 per portion

**You will need**
4 egg whites
250 g/9 oz caster sugar
100 g/4 oz cream cheese
grated rind and juice of 1 lemon
150 ml/¼ pint double cream,
   whipped

**To decorate**
6 lemon twists
frosted currant leaves (optional)

Whisk the egg whites until stiff, then whisk in half the sugar. Fold in all but 2 tablespoons of the remaining sugar. Spoon the meringue into 12 mounds on a baking sheet lined with silicone paper. Bake for 2 hours. Peel off the paper and cool.

Beat together the cheese, reserved sugar, lemon rind and juice. Fold in the cream and use to sandwich the meringues together. Decorate with lemon twists and frosted leaves, if desired.

## *Cook's Tip*

**To toast hazelnuts, place in a single layer under the grill until just beginning to colour. Cool slightly, then rub the nuts against each other in a plastic bag to loosen the skins.**

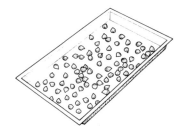

## *Cook's Tip*

**Use frosted petals and leaves for decoration. Wash the petals or leaves – e.g. rose, violet, currant – and shake dry. Dip in beaten egg white, then in caster sugar. Spread on lined baking sheets and bake in a very cool oven until dry and crisp. Cool on a wire rack, then store in an airtight tin.**

# 99 | *Hexenschaum*

**Preparation time**
25 minutes, plus 1 hour
to cool

**Cooking time**
about 15 minutes

**Serves 4**

**Calories**
206 per portion

**You will need**
500 g/1 lb Cox's Orange Pippin
  apples
100 g/4 oz canned apricots,
  drained
65 g/2½ oz sugar
2 egg whites
25 g/1 oz caster sugar

**To decorate**
4 canned apricot halves
a few flaked almonds

Peel, core and chop the apples and put them in a pan with 1 tablespoon of water. Simmer over a gentle heat until tender. Blend the apricots and the cooked apple in a liquidiser or food processor to make a smooth purée. Add the sugar to the mixture and cool.

Whisk the egg whites and caster sugar until very stiff and fold into the fruit purée. Spoon into four glasses or glass dishes and chill. To serve, place an apricot half on top of the mousse, rounded side uppermost, and arrange almonds around the apricot.

# 100 | *Strawberry Meringues*

**Preparation time**
30 minutes

**Cooking time**
2-2½ hours

**Oven temperature**
120C, 250F, gas ½

**Serves 6**

**Calories**
413 per portion

**You will need**
4 egg whites
250 g/9 oz caster sugar
few drops vanilla essence
few drops pink food colouring

**For the filling**
300 ml/½ pint double cream
175 g/6 oz fresh strawberries,
  hulled, sliced and sprinkled with
  caster sugar (optional)

Line two large baking trays with non-stick silicone paper. Whisk the egg whites until they form stiff peaks. Gradually whisk in half the sugar, beating well until thick and glossy. Fold in the remaining sugar, vanilla essence and colouring. Spoon the mixture into a piping bag fitted with a large rose nozzle and pipe six swirls on to each of the prepared baking trays. Bake for 2-2½ hours until crisp. Cool on a wire rack and then peel off the paper. Sandwich the meringues together with whipped cream and strawberries.

## Cook's Tip

**Hexenschaum is a popular Austrian dish which literally means 'witches foam'. To ring the changes, add 1 teaspoon of cinnamon to the stewed apples, or blend 1 tablespoon dark rum or brandy with the apples and apricots.**

## Cook's Tip

**The beauty of meringues is that you can make one large dessert with the mixture, or pipe individual rounds and nests as you need or prefer.**

# 101 | Floating Islands

**Preparation time**
30 minutes

**Cooking time**
25 minutes

**Serves 4-6**

**Calories**
186 per portion

**You will need**
2 egg whites
100 g/4 oz caster sugar
600 ml/1 pt milk
2 tablespoons caster sugar
3 eggs
1 tablespoon cornflour
few drops vanilla essence

**To decorate**
25 g/1 oz whole almonds
25 g/1 oz caster sugar

Whisk the egg whites until stiff. Whisk in the sugar, 1 tablespoon at a time, until thick and glossy. Heat the milk and sugar to simmering point. Slide 4 separate table-spoons of egg white mixture into the milk. Simmer for 3 minutes. Drain on a clean tea-towel. Repeat twice to make 12 meringue 'islands'.

Beat together the eggs and cornflour, stir in the hot milk and vanilla essence. Strain into a clean saucepan and cook gently, stirring constantly, until thick enough to coat the back of a wooden spoon. Cool and pour into a serving dish.

Place the whole almonds and sugar in a saucepan. Heat gently without stirring until the sugar turns caramel coloured. Pour on to a buttered baking tray and leave until cold. Chop fairly finely when set. Place the meringue 'islands' on the egg custard. Sprinkle with the almond caramel and serve at once.

# 102 | Meringue Baskets

**Preparation time**
25 minutes

**Cooking time**
1-1¼ hours

**Oven temperature**
150C, 300F, gas 2

**Serves 8**

**Calories**
240 per portion

**You will need**
4 egg whites
few drops vanilla essence
250 g/9 oz icing sugar, sifted

**For the filling**
150 ml/¼ pint double cream, whipped
100 g/4 oz strawberries
2 tablespoons redcurrant jelly, warmed

To make the meringue, whisk the egg whites until stiff, then whisk in the vanilla essence and icing sugar, 1 table-spoon at a time. Place the bowl over a pan of gently sim-mering water and continue whisking for about 5 minutes until the meringue is very stiff.

Line a baking tray with silicone paper and draw eight 7.5 cm/3 in circles on it. Spread half the meringue over the circles to form bases. Put the remaining meringue in a piping bag fitted with a large fluted nozzle, and pipe round the edge of each base. Bake for 1-1¼ hours. Cool on a wire rack. Remove the paper.

Spoon a little cream into each basket and arrange the strawberries on top. Brush with the redcurrant jelly.

## Cook's Tip

To shape the 'islands', take up a portion of the meringue mixture on 1 tablespoon. Using a second tablespoon, pass the mixture between the two until a smooth egg shape is formed.

## Cook's Tip

Whisk the egg whites evenly for meringues and ensure that none of the mixture sticks to the side of the bowl while whisking. Uneven whisking results in a rough mixture that does not hold its bulk.

# 103 | *Pudim Molokov*

**Preparation time**
20 minutes, plus 2-3
hours to chill

**Cooking time**
15 minutes

**Oven temperature**
180C, 350F, gas 4

**Serves 4-6**

**Calories**
226 per portion

**You will need**
100 g/4 oz sugar
2 large egg whites
50 g/2 oz flaked almonds, toasted
225 g/8 oz soft fruit (optional)
150 ml/¼ pint single cream to
    serve

Place the sugar in a heavy-based pan with 4 tablespoons of cold water. Heat gently, without boiling, stirring until all the sugar has dissolved. Increase the heat and boil briskly, without stirring, until the syrup turns a golden caramel colour. Remove from the heat and stir in 2 tablespoons of hot water, stand back – it can spit – then add another 2 tablespoons. If the mixture is lumpy, return to a low heat and stir until smooth.

Pour a little of the caramel into a warm, lightly greased 600 ml/1 pint ring mould. Reheat the remaining caramel to boiling point. Whisk the egg whites until stiff, then add the caramel, pouring in a steady stream and whisking continuously until the mixture is stiff and glossy. Fold in the almonds and spoon into the mould. Stand the mould in a hot water bath and bake for 15 minutes.

Cool slightly, then turn out on to a serving plate and chill. Just before serving, fill the centre with soft fruit, if using, and serve with the cream.

## Cook's Tip

**To clean a sticky toffee pan,
fill it with water and bring to
the boil. The toffee melts and
can then be poured away with
the water.**

# 104 | *Lemon Cheese Meringue*

**Preparation time**
15 minutes

**Cooking time**
20 minutes

**Oven temperature**
200C, 400F, gas 6

**Serves 4**

**Calories**
217 per portion

**You will need**
25 g/1 oz cornflour
300 ml/½ pint milk
25 g/1 oz granulated sugar
75 g/3 oz medium fat curd cheese
grated rind and juice of 1 lemon
2 eggs, separated
50 g/2 oz caster sugar

Blend the cornflour with a little of the milk, then add the granulated sugar. Heat the remaining milk until almost boiling, then pour on to the blended custard, stirring. Return to the heat, stirring, until the custard thickens. Cool slightly.

Blend in the cheese, lemon rind and juice, and egg yolks. Whisk until smooth, then spoon into a greased 600 ml/1 pint ovenproof dish. Whisk the egg whites until stiff. Whisk in 25 g/1 oz of the caster sugar, then fold in the remainder. Pile on top of the lemon custard and bake for 15 minutes. Serve with soured cream.

## Cook's Tip

**Soured cream is delicious
with both sweet and savoury
dishes: fruit pies and
pancakes, soups and sauces
as well as pasta and salad
dressings all benefit from its
slightly tart flavour.**

# 105 | *Chestnut Meringue Nests*

**Preparation time**
20 minutes

**Cooking time**
1½ hours

**Oven temperature**
140C, 275F, gas 1

**Serves 8**

**Calories**
500 per portion

**You will need**
3 egg whites
225 g/8 oz caster sugar
8 chocolate rose leaves to
decorate

For the filling
½ (439 g/15½ oz) can sweetened
chestnut purée
1 tablespoon caster sugar
2 tablespoons brandy
150 ml/¼ pint whipping cream,
whipped

To make the meringue, whisk the egg whites until stiff, then gradually whisk in the caster sugar. Line a baking tray with silicone paper and draw eight 7.5 cm/3 in circles on it. Put the meringue in a piping bag fitted with a large fluted nozzle. Pipe a round to fill each circle, then pipe round the edge of each base to form a nest. Bake for 1½ hours. Cool on a wire rack. Remove the paper.

Beat the chestnut purée with the sugar and brandy until blended, then fold in the cream. Put in a piping bag fitted with a large fluted nozzle and pipe into the nests. Decorate each nest with a chocolate rose leaf (see Cook's Tip 56).

# 106 | *Caramel Vacherin*

**Preparation time**
20 minutes

**Cooking time**
2 hours

**Oven temperature**
120C, 250F, gas ½

**Serves 6-8**

**Calories**
344 per portion

**You will need**
4 egg whites
225 g/8 oz soft brown sugar
50 g/2 oz hazelnuts, toasted and
chopped
300 ml/½ pint double cream
8 hazelnuts to decorate

Whisk the egg whites until stiff and dry. Gradually whisk in the sugar. Put the meringue in a piping bag, fitted with a 1 cm/½ in plain nozzle. Pipe two 23 cm/9 in rounds on baking trays lined with silicone paper. Sprinkle a few of the chopped nuts over one round. Bake for 2 hours until crisp. Peel off the paper and cool the rounds on a wire rack.

Whip the cream until it holds its shape. Combine three-quarters of the cream with the remaining chopped nuts and use to sandwich the meringues together, with the nutty round on top. Pipe the remaining cream around the edge and decorate with the hazelnuts.

## Cook's Tip

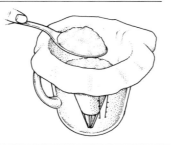

**To fill a large piping bag, put it in a large jug and fold the open end over the rim of the jug. Spoon in the meringue or other type of mixture.**

## Cook's Tip

**Prevent leftover egg yolks from drying out in the refrigerator by covering them in water.**

# 107 | Ginger Queen of Puddings

**Preparation time**
15 minutes

**Cooking time**
35-40 minutes

**Oven temperature**
180C, 350F, gas 4
then
150C, 300F, gas 2

**Serves 6**

**Calories**
313 per portion

**You will need**
600 ml/1 pint milk
pared rind of ½ lemon
50 g/2 oz butter
175 g/6 oz caster sugar
75 g/3 oz fine fresh white
  breadcrumbs
3 eggs, separated
3-4 tablespoons ginger marmalade

Put the milk and lemon rind in a pan over a very low heat and leave for 10 minutes. Discard the lemon rind. Add the butter and 50 g/2 oz of the sugar to the milk and stir until melted. Add the breadcrumbs and egg yolks and mix well. Transfer to a well-buttered shallow 1.2 litre/2 pint ovenproof dish. Leave to stand for 10 minutes then bake for 15-20 minutes or until set. Cool slightly, then spread with the marmalade. Lower the oven temperature.

Whisk the egg whites until stiff. Whisk in half the re-maining sugar, then fold in all but 2 teaspoons of the rest. Pipe or spoon the meringue over the baked pudding and sprinkle with the reserved sugar. Bake for 8-10 minutes, until golden brown. Serve warm.

# 108 | Baked Alaska

**Preparation time**
25 minutes

**Cooking time**
3-4 minutes

**Oven temperature**
200C, 400F, gas 6

**Serves 6**

**Calories**
337 per portion

**You will need**
1 15-18 cm/6-7 in sponge flan case
225 g/8 oz strawberries, sliced
  (optional)
⅓-½ litre/12 fl oz-1 pint strawberry
  ice cream

**For the meringue topping**
4 egg whites
225 g/8 oz caster sugar
½ teaspoon vanilla essence

**To decorate**
25-50 g/1-2 oz flaked almonds
  (optional)
caster sugar

Place the flan case on an ovenproof plate and arrange the strawberries on the base, if using. Spoon the ice cream over the top and place in the freezer.

To make the meringue topping, whisk the egg whites until very stiff and dry. Add the sugar 1 tablespoon at a time, whisking very thoroughly between each addition. Whisk in the vanilla essence. The meringue should be smooth, glossy and form soft peaks. Working quickly, pile the meringue on to the prepared base, completely enclosing the ice cream. Stick the almonds, if using, into the meringue and sprinkle with a little caster sugar. Bake for 3-4 minutes or until the meringue peaks are lightly browned. Serve immediately.

## Cook's Tip

**Make breadcrumbs by placing slices of bread in the bottom of the oven while you are cooking something else, then crush with a rolling pin. They can be frozen in a polythene bag and used straight from the freezer.**

## Cook's Tip

**For a dinner party, the baked alaska can be prepared in advance, covered with meringue. Freeze uncovered ready to put in a preheated oven at the last minute.**

# 109 | *Pineapple Meringue Cake*

**Preparation time**
1 hour

**Cooking time**
55 minutes

**Oven temperature**
190C, 375F, gas 5
(cake)
180C, 350F, gas 4
(meringue)

**Serves 8**

**Calories**
580 per portion

**You will need**
50 g/2 oz plain flour, sifted with a
    pinch of salt
2 eggs
50 g/2 oz caster sugar

For the meringue
3 egg whites
175 g/6 oz caster sugar
few drops vanilla essence
1 teaspoon lemon juice
75 g/3 oz hazelnuts, toasted and
    ground

To decorate
500 ml/18 fl oz whipped cream
1 pineapple, cored and sliced
75 g/3 oz hazelnuts, toasted and
    chopped

Grease four 18 cm/7 in sandwich tins. Whisk the eggs and sugar over a pan of simmering water until thick. Fold in the flour. Divide the mixture between two tins and bake for 15 minutes. Reduce the temperature.

For the meringue, whisk the egg whites until stiff, then add a little sugar, the vanilla essence and lemon juice. Fold in the remaining sugar and hazelnuts. Divide between the two remaining tins and bake for 40 minutes.

Reserve 1 pineapple slice. To assemble, spread each cake with alternate layers of cream, pineapple slices and meringe, then sandwich together with cream. Decorate as shown with the hazelnuts, cream and pineapple.

## Cook's Tip

To remove the centre core
from a slice of pineapple,
stamp it out with a small plain
pastry cutter.

# 110 | *Coconut Jelly*

**Preparation time**
25 minutes, plus 2-3
hours to set

**Serves 6**

**Calories**
321 per serving

**You will need**
1 fresh coconut
200 ml/⅓ pint milk
100 ml/3½ fl oz double cream
15 g/½ oz powdered gelatine
50 ml/2 fl oz hot water

Make two holes in the coconut shell and drain the milk into a measuring jug. Add sufficient water to make the milk up to 200 ml/⅓ pint. Split open the coconut and grate 225 g/8 oz of the flesh. Blend the coconut 'milk', milk and grated coconut in a liquidiser or food processor. Leave to stand for 5 minutes. Strain the milk through a muslin cloth to obtain about 400 ml/14 fl oz, then stir in the cream.

Dissolve the gelatine in the hot water over a pan of simmering water. Remove from the heat. Add to the milk and stir well. Pour into four individual moulds and chill until set, then turn out. Dip the mould in hot water for a few seconds to loosen the jelly from the sides. This jelly can be served with a fruit sauce, if desired.

## Cook's Tip

To unmould jellies and similar
cold desserts, dip the mould
in hot water for a few seconds
to loosen the contents from
the sides.

# 111 | Coffee Bavarois

**Preparation time**
1 hour, plus 5-6 hours
to set

**Serves 6**

**Calories**
183 per portion

**You will need**
200 ml/⅓ pint milk
3 egg yolks
75 g/3 oz sugar
15 g/½ oz powdered gelatine
50 ml/2 fl oz hot water
120 ml/4 fl oz strong black coffee
120 ml/4 fl oz double cream

Heat the milk to simmering point. Whisk the egg yolks and sugar until light, then pour the milk on to the yolks. Mix well. Return the custard to the rinsed pan and heat without boiling until it coats the back of a wooden spoon. Remove from the heat and pour into a deep baking tin.

Dissolve the gelatine in the hot water over a pan of simmering water. Remove from the heat and stir into the custard. Add the black coffee, then chill for several hours until on the point of setting.

Whip the cream and fold into the custard. Pour the bavarois into a 900 ml/1½ pint mould. Chill until completely set. Unmould on to a serving dish. Decorate with piped cream and confectionery coffee beans.

# 112 | Strawberry Cream Jelly

**Preparation time**
20 minutes, plus 2-3
hours to set

**Serves 6**

**Calories**
170 per portion

**You will need**
3 squares of strawberry jelly from
    a packet
150 ml/¼ pint boiling water
225 g/8 oz fresh or frozen
    strawberries, defrosted
50 g/2 oz caster sugar
150ml/¼ pint double cream,
    whipped
15 g/½ oz powdered gelatine
4 tablespoons hot water
2 egg whites, lightly whisked

Melt the jelly cubes in the boiling water and pour into a dampened 900 ml/1½ pint jelly mould. Leave to set in the refrigerator. Purée the strawberries in a liquidiser or food processor or press them through a sieve. Add the sugar. Fold in the cream.

Dissolve the gelatine in the hot water over a pan of simmering water. Stir into the strawberry cream. Fold in the egg whites, then pour the strawberry mixture over the set jelly. Chill until completely set. Unmould and serve.

## Cook's Tip

*When turning out any moulded dish, place a plate over the mould, making sure it is in the right position. Invert the mould and the plate and give them both a firm jerk.*

## Cook's Tip

*When making jellies, mousses and similar cold desserts in a mould, plunge the mould in water before filling to make turning out easier.*

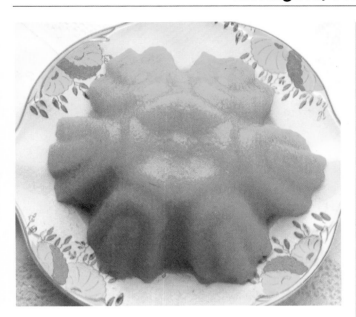

# 113 | *Apricot Jelly*

**Preparation time**
10 minutes, plus
overnight soaking and
3-4 hours to set

**Cooking time**
20-30 minutes

**Serves 4-6**

**Calories**
83 per portion

**You will need**
225 g/8 oz dried apricots, soaked
   overnight
juice of ½ lemon
1-2 tablespoons clear honey
15 g/½ oz gelatine
3 tablespoons hot water

Place the apricots in a pan with the liquid in which they were soaked, adding more water if necessary to cover. Simmer gently for 20-30 minutes until tender. Blend the apricots and their liquid, the lemon juice and honey in a liquidiser or food processor until smooth. Add water to make up to 750 ml/1¼ pints if necessary. Dissolve the gelatine in the hot water over a pan of simmering water and stir into the apricot mixture. Pour into a 900 ml/1½ pint ring mould and chill until set. Unmould on to a serving dish.

# 114 | *Orange Brûlée*

**Preparation time**
25 minutes, plus
cooling

**Cooking time**
40 minutes

**Oven temperature**
160C, 325F, gas 3

**Serves 6**

**Calories**
396 per portion

**You will need**
1 egg
4 egg yolks
50 g/2 oz vanilla sugar
400 ml/14 fl oz double cream
2 tablespoons Grand Marnier
50 g/2 oz sugar
rind of 1 orange, cut into julienne
   strips
65 g/2½ oz caster sugar

Beat the egg, yolks and vanilla sugar until light and creamy. Add the cream and liqueur and mix well. Pour into six 150 ml/¼ pint ramekin dishes. Stand the ramekins in a water bath and bake for 40 minutes. Remove from the oven and cool.

Place the sugar in a pan with a little water and boil until a mid-amber caramel. Stir in the orange rind and cook for 2 minutes, taking care that the caramel does not burn. Using a pair of tweezers, lift the rind on to a sheet of non-stick silicone paper. Sprinkle the caster sugar over the cooked crèmes, then place under a grill until glazed. Cool until the sugar hardens. Arrange caramelised orange strips on the top of each ramekin. Serve within 1 hour or the caramel will lose its brittleness.

## Cook's Tip

**Soaking the apricots in apple juice plumps them up and adds flavour. Pear juice may be used instead, if preferred.**

## Cook's Tip

**To make vanilla sugar, fill an airtight container with caster sugar and add a vanilla pod. Store in a cool place.**

# 115 | Exotic Fruit Terrine

**Preparation time**
1 hour, plus 5-6 hours
to set

**Serves 6**

**Calories**
315 per portion

**You will need**
500 ml/18 fl oz milk
6 egg yolks
150 g/5 oz vanilla sugar
25 g/1 oz powdered gelatine
120 ml/4 fl oz hot water
200 ml/⅓ pint double cream
300 g/11 oz chopped lychees
100 g/4 oz ripe mango, chopped

**To decorate**
½ mango
vanilla sugar, to taste

Heat the milk to simmering point. Whisk the egg yolks
and sugar until light and creamy. Pour over the milk and
mix. Return the custard to the rinsed pan and heat without boiling until it coats the back of a wooden spoon. Remove from the heat and pour into a deep baking tin.

Dissolve the gelatine in the hot water over a pan of
simmering water. Remove from the heat and stir into the
custard. Chill for several hours until almost set.

Whip the cream and fold into the custard. Fold in the
lychees and mango. Pour the mixture into a rectangular
loaf tin, cover with cling film and chill for 4 hours until set.
Unmould the terrine and, reserving a few slices of mango
for decoration, blend the remainder in a liquidiser or food
processor. Sweeten to taste with vanilla sugar. Coat six
chilled plates with the purée. Slice the terrine and
arrange some in the centre of each plate. Decorate with
the reserved mango.

## Cook's Tip

*This dessert is best eaten on
the day it is made. If preferred,
replace the exotic fruits with
soft fruits, such as
strawberries, raspberries, kiwi
fruit, peaches and nectarines.*

# 116 | Raspberry Wine Jelly

**Preparation time**
15 minutes, plus 3-4
hours to chill

**Cooking time**
5 minutes

**Serves 6**

**Calories**
192 per portion

**You will need**
225 g/8 oz raspberries
3 tablespoons brandy
300 ml/½ pint water
2 tablespoons gelatine
thinly pared rind and juice of
    1 orange
50 g/2 oz caster sugar
250 ml/8 fl oz port
4 tablespoons whipping cream,
    whipped, to decorate

Reserve six raspberries for decoration. Divide the remainder between six wine glasses. Pour a little brandy
into each glass and leave for 1 hour.

Pour a little of the water into a small bowl, sprinkle with
the gelatine and soak for 5 minutes. Place the remaining
water in a pan with the orange rind and sugar. Heat gently
to dissolve the sugar then bring to the boil. Remove from
the heat, add the soaked gelatine and stir until dissolved.
Add the orange juice and port and allow to cool.

Strain the wine mixture into the glasses and chill until
set. Decorate each with a rosette of cream and the reserved raspberries.

## Cook's Tip

*When dissolving gelatine,
don't pour the hot water or
specified liquid on to the
gelatine powder. Sprinkle the
gelatine over the water
instead to enable it to absorb
the liquid quickly and evenly.*

# 117 | *Italian-style Trifle*

**Preparation time**
25 minutes

**Cooking time**
3-4 minutes

**Oven temperature**
200C, 400F, gas 6

**Serves 6-8**

**Calories**
206 per portion

**You will need**
4 trifle sponges
2 tablespoons sherry (optional)
1 (439 g/15½ oz) can pineapple
  pieces
300 ml/½ pint cold custard

**For the meringue topping**
3 egg whites
175 g/6 oz caster sugar
½ teaspoon vanilla essence

Crumble the trifle sponges into an ovenproof dish. Sprinkle with the sherry, if using. Drain the pineapple and sprinkle half of the juice over the cake. Arrange the pineapple pieces on top and pour over the custard.

Prepare the meringue topping as instructed in recipe 108. Spoon it over the custard and bake for 3-4 minutes until just the tips of the meringue are golden brown. Serve warm or cold.

# 118 | *Raspberry Trifle*

**Preparation time**
40 minutes, plus 35
minutes to cool and
chill

**Cooking time**
15 minutes

**Serves 4**

**Calories**
494 per portion

**You will need**
1 quantity langues de chat (recipe
  13)
65 g/2½ oz sugar
50 ml/2 fl oz water
25 ml/1 fl oz raspberry liqueur
4 ratafias
4 heaped teaspoons raspberry jam
½ quantity hot crème anglaise
  (recipe 212)
12 raspberries to decorate

**For the crème chantilly**
150 ml/¼ pint double cream
25 ml/1 fl oz egg white
25 g/1 oz caster or vanilla sugar

Make the langues de chat as instructed in recipe 13. Boil the sugar and water until the sugar dissolves. Cool, then add the liqueur. Break the langues de chat in pieces and mix in a bowl with the ratafias. Pour over the syrup. Spoon half the biscuit mixture into four glass serving dishes. Cover with the raspberry jam and the remaining biscuit mixture.

Make the hot crème anglaise as instructed in recipe 212 and pour over the biscuit mixture. Stand for 15 minutes to cool, then chill for 15 minutes.

To make the crème chantilly, put the cream in a bowl, add the egg white and whisk until quite stiff. Add the sugar and whisk until the cream is smooth and holds its shape. Spoon into a piping bag fitted with a star nozzle and decorate the trifles. Place three raspberries in the centre of each and chill before serving.

## Cook's Tip

*This is good served with crème chantilly (see recipe 118). Alternatively substitute crème anglaise (see recipe 212) for the custard.*

## Cook's Tip

*To freeze biscuits, cool thoroughly then spread out on a tray to freeze until solid. Pack in a rigid freezerproof container. To defrost, spread on a wire rack and leave at room temperature for about an hour.*

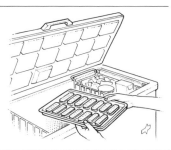

# 119 | *Zuppa Inglese*

**Preparation time**
*35 minutes*

**Cooking time**
*1-1½ hours*

**Oven temperature**
*140C, 275F, gas 1
(meringue)
then 240C,475F, gas 9*

**Serves 4**

**Calories**
*277 per portion*

**You will need**
*150 g/5 oz sponge cake, cubed
150 ml/¼ pint Marsala
65 g/2½ oz raspberry jam, melted
½ quantity Italian Meringue
   mixture (recipe 95)*

*For the chocolate sauce
15 g/½ oz unsalted butter
50 g/2 oz plain chocolate, broken
   into squares
1½ tablespoons double cream*

Arrange the sponge cake in an ovenproof dish and pour over the Marsala. Spoon the jam over the sponge cake. Press the sponge lightly with the back of a spoon.

To make the chocolate sauce, put the butter and chocolate in a flameproof bowl over a pan of simmering water until it melts, then beat in the cream. Trail the warm sauce over the sponge cake.

Make the Italian meringue as instructed in recipe 95 and spoon it into a piping bag fitted with a star tube. Pipe stars or scrolls over the top of the sponge cake. Bake at the higher temperature for 2 minutes or just long enough to colour the meringue.

# 120 | *Ginger Wine Trifle*

**Preparation time**
*40 minutes, plus 1½
hours to cool and chill*

**Serves 4**

**Calories**
*215 per portion*

**You will need**
*120 g/4½ oz sponge cake, cut into
   cubes
120 ml/4 fl oz ginger wine
65 g/2½ oz strawberry jam
150 ml/¼ pint milk
300 ml/½ pint double cream
4 egg yolks, beaten
50 g/2 oz caster sugar
1 teaspoon cornflour
grated rind of ½ lemon
1 pinch cinnamon*

*To decorate
12 ratafias
1 piece crystallised stem ginger,
   finely chopped*

Arrange the sponge cake evenly in the base of a trifle dish. Moisten with the ginger wine and spread with the strawberry jam.

In a small heavy pan, scald the milk and 65 ml/2½ fl oz of the cream. Mix the egg yolks with 25 g/1 oz of the sugar and the cornflour. Add the hot milk and cream to the egg yolk mixture, stirring constantly. Return the mixture to a clean pan. Heat gently, stirring until thickened. Pour the hot custard over the jam. Leave to cool, then chill.

Whip the remaining cream with the grated lemon rind, cinnamon and remaining sugar. Pile on top of the custard. Decorate with the ratafias and ginger.

## Cook's Tip

*When melting chocolate, don't overheat it or it will go grainy. Also take care not to get any drops of water in the chocolate – always dry the bottom of the bowl.*

## Cook's Tip

*For a stronger ginger flavour, sprinkle finely chopped stem ginger over the sponge.*

# Chocolate Desserts

*Here is a purely indulgent and certainly sinful selection of sumptuous desserts using chocolate in all its guises. Chocoholics can feast on delicious, velvety-smooth chocolate ices, beautifully-risen soufflés, sticky sponge puddings all the better for serving with custard, light-as-air, elegant roulades, liqueur-flavoured gâteau, creamy pies, crunchy nut biscuits, melt-in-the-mouth crêpes and nursery-style, chocolate semolina.*

## 121 | Chocolate Boxes

**Preparation time**
30 minutes

**Cooking time**
10 minutes

**Oven temperature**
220C, 425F, gas 7

**Serves 6**

**Calories**
401 per portion

**You will need**
225 g/8 oz plain dark chocolate
3 eggs
75 g/3 oz caster sugar
grated rind of 1 orange
75 g/3 oz plain flour, sifted with a
   pinch of salt
2 tablespoons Curaçao
4 tablespoons apricot jam,
   warmed and sieved
150 ml/¼ pint double cream,
   whipped
6 strawberries, halved
12 chocolate leaves

Grease and line a 28 × 18 × 4 cm/11 × 7 × 1½ in Swiss roll tin. Melt the chocolate in a bowl over a pan of hot water, then pour on to a piece of waxed paper to make a 30 × 23 cm/12 × 9 in rectangle. Leave to cool.
Whisk the eggs, sugar and orange rind in a bowl over a pan of simmering water until thick and light. Fold in the flour and turn the mixture into the prepared tin. Bake for 10 minutes until light golden brown and springy to the touch. Cool on a wire rack.

   Sprinkle the cake with the Curaçao and cut it into twelve equal cubes 5 × 6 cm/2 × 2½ in. Brush the sides of each with a little of the melted jam. Cut the chocolate into 48 squares to fit and press them on to the sides of the cakes. Spoon or pipe whipped cream into the boxes and top each with a halved strawberry and chocolate leaf (see Cook's Tip 56).

## 122 | Chocolate Mint Ice Cream

**Preparation time**
15 minutes, plus 4-5 hours to freeze

**Serves 4-6**

**Calories**
268 per portion

**You will need**
25 g/1 oz custard powder
300 ml/½ pint milk
1 (170 g/6 oz) can evaporated milk
2 eggs, separated
40 g/1½ oz icing sugar
25 g/1 oz butter
½ teaspoon peppermint flavouring
½ teaspoon green food colouring

**For the topping**
50 g/2 oz chocolate, melted
2 tablespoons single cream
3-4 tablespoons double cream,
   whipped, to decorate

Blend the custard powder with 2 tablespoons of the milk in a large bowl. Heat the remaining milk and evaporated milk until boiling and stir into the mixture. Return to the pan and heat, stirring, until very thick. Return to the bowl and beat in the egg yolks, one at a time. Beat in the icing sugar, butter, flavouring and colouring and set aside until cold, whisking occasionally.

   Whisk the egg whites until very stiff and fold into the cold custard. Transfer to a rigid freezerproof container, cover and freeze for about 1 hour. Whisk well, cover and partially freeze again. Repeat the process twice. Spoon into individual freezerproof dishes. Cover and freeze for several hours until firm. Combine the chocolate and single cream and spoon over the ice cream. Decorate with piped double cream.

## Cook's Tip

**To make jam easier to brush on to cakes, heat for a few seconds in a small bowl in a microwave, then pass through a sieve.**

## Cook's Tip

**When making ice cream it is important to measure out the quantity of sugar needed. Too much sugar prevents it from freezing firmly and too little means the ice cream will be rough in texture.**

# 123 | Chocolate and Orange Ice Cream

**Preparation time**
10 minutes, plus 4-5
hours to freeze

**Serves 6**

**Calories**
524 per portion

**You will need**
2 egg yolks
50 g/2 oz caster sugar
grated rind and juice of 1 orange
175 g/6 oz plain chocolate,
chopped
300 ml/½ pint single cream
300 ml/½ pint double cream,
whipped
finely shredded orange rind to
decorate

Beat the egg yolks, sugar and orange rind together. Put the chocolate and single cream in a bowl over a pan of simmering water until the chocolate has melted. Pour on to the egg mixture, stirring vigorously, then return to the bowl and heat gently until thickened. Add the orange juice and leave to cool.

Fold in three-quarters of the double cream and turn into a 900 ml/1½ pint loaf tin. Cover with foil, seal and freeze until firm. Turn out on to a plate 30 minutes before serving. Decorate with the remaining cream and orange rind and place in the refrigerator to soften.

# 124 | Crowning Glory

**Preparation time**
20 minutes, plus 4
hours to chill

**Serves 8-10**

**Calories**
377 per portion

**You will need**
225 g/8 oz plain chocolate, broken
into pieces
50 g/2 oz butter
2 eggs
175 g/6 oz bourbon biscuits,
crushed
50 g/2 oz hazelnuts, chopped and
toasted
50 g/2 oz glacé cherries, quartered
2 tablespoons rum

**To decorate**
150 ml/¼ pint double or whipping
cream, whipped
6 glacé cherries

Grease a 600 ml/1 pint ring mould. Melt the chocolate and butter in a heatproof bowl set over hot water. Stir vigorously until smooth. Beat the eggs in a large bowl, then add the chocolate mixture a little at a time and stir vigorously until blended. Stir the biscuits, nuts, glacé cherries and rum into the chocolate mixture, then spoon into the prepared ring mould. Chill for 4 hours until set.

Unmould the cake (see Cook's Tip 110); avoid any water running over the mixture. Invert a serving dish over the gâteau then turn both upside down. Lift off the mould. To decorate, pipe six large rosettes of cream on top of the gâteau and top each with a cherry.

## Cook's Tip

**Citrus fruit can be microwaved to extract more juice. Prick the orange and cook on full power for 5-10 seconds.**

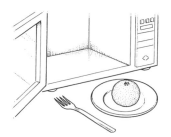

## Cook's Tip

**This gâteau can be frozen after removing it from the ring mould and before decorating with cream and the glacé cherries. Defrost for 4 hours in the refrigerator before decorating and serving.**

# 125 | Mocha Bombe

**Preparation time**
15 minutes, plus 4-5
hours to freeze

**Serves 6-8**

**Calories**
375 per portion

**You will need**
225 g/8 oz plain chocolate,
   chopped

For the coffee ice cream
2 tablespoons instant coffee
   powder
2 tablespoons boiling water
2 egg whites
100 g/4 oz caster sugar
300 ml/½ pint double cream

Put a 1.2 litre/2 pint freezerproof basin in the freezer to chill for 10 minutes. Melt the chocolate in a bowl over a pan of simmering water. Pour the chocolate into the basin and rotate to coat inside completely. Place the basin in a bowl of crushed ice and continue rotating until the chocolate has set in a layer.

To make the ice cream, mix the coffee with the water and leave to cool. Whisk the egg whites until stiff, then gradually whisk in the sugar. Whip the cream with the coffee mixture until it forms soft peaks and fold into the meringue mixture. Spoon into the chocolate mould, smooth the top evenly, cover with foil and freeze until firm. Unmould on to a serving plate.

## Cook's Tip

**To melt the chocolate in a microwave, break it into squares and place in a bowl. Microwave for 4-5 minutes until soft.**

# 126 | Chocolate Mousse Cake

**Preparation time**
20 minutes, plus 2
hours to chill

**Serves 6-8**

**Calories**
650 per portion

**You will need**
175 g/6 oz chocolate digestive
   biscuits, finely crushed
50 g/2 oz butter, melted
2 egg yolks
2 tablespoons caster sugar
rind and juice of 1 orange
225 g/8 oz full-fat soft cheese
100 g/4 oz plain dark chocolate,
   melted
10 g/¼ oz powdered gelatine
150 ml/¼ pint double cream,
   lightly whipped
3 egg whites, lightly whisked

To decorate
150 ml/¼ pint double cream,
   whipped
chocolate buttons
grated chocolate

Lightly grease a 20 cm/8 in loose-bottomed cake tin. Mix the biscuit crumbs with the melted butter. Spread them over the base of the tin and press down firmly. Chill.

Whisk the egg yolks, sugar and orange rind until they are thick and light. Beat in the cheese and melted chocolate, then add the cream. Dissolve the gelatine in the orange juice over a pan of simmering water. Stir and add to the mixture. Fold in the egg whites, then pour the mixture over the chilled biscuit base and chill until set. Unmould the cheesecake and decorate with rosettes of cream, chocolate buttons and grated chocolate.

## Cook's Tip

**The large slabs of chocolate sold as 'cooking chocolate' often have a fatty consistency and a rather synthetic taste. For a superior flavour use a good quality plain or dessert chocolate instead.**

# 127 | Apricot Cheesecake

**Preparation time**
25 minutes, plus 1 hour
to set

**Serves 6-8**

**Calories**
292 per portion

**You will need**
1 (200 g/7 oz) chocolate Swiss roll
2 (425 g/15 oz) cans apricot halves
450 g/1 lb curd cheese
3 tablespoons caster sugar
juice of half a lemon
2 eggs, separated
15 g/½ oz powdered gelatine
150 ml/¼ pint whipping cream

**To decorate**
15 g/½ oz plain cooking chocolate
10 g/¼ oz butter or margarine

Cut the Swiss roll into 1 cm/½ inch slices and use to line a 1.2 litre/2 pint glass dish. Drain the apricots and reserve 4 tablespoons of the juice. Reserve 4 apricot halves and purée the remainder. Blend the cheese, sugar and lemon juice together, then add the apricot purée. Beat in the egg yolks. Dissolve the gelatine in the reserved juice over a pan of simmering water. Blend into the cheesecake mixture and chill for 1 hour, until almost set.

Whip the cream until it holds its shape on the whisk, then fold into the cheesecake mixture. Beat the egg whites until stiff and fold into the mixture. Pour the filling over the Swiss roll, and level with a spatula. To decorate, melt the chocolate and butter over a pan of hot water, stirring constantly, and use to create a feathered effect (see Cook's Tip below). Decorate with cream. Halve each reserved apricot, cut in a small fan shape and place on the cheesecake.

## Cook's Tip

Fill a paper piping bag with the chocolate mixture and pipe parallel lines about 2.5 cm/1 inch apart. Turn the cheesecake 45° so the chocolate lines run horizontally and draw a sharp knife down the lines 2.5 cm/ 1 inch apart. Turn through 180° and draw the knife across the lines in the opposite direction to create a feathered effect.

# 128 | Crêpes au Chocolat

**Preparation time**
15 minutes, plus 30
minutes to stand

**Cooking time**
25 minutes

**Serves 6**

**Calories**
589 per portion

**You will need**
100 g/4 oz plain flour
pinch of salt
2 tablespoons caster sugar
1 tablespoon coffee powder
1 tablespoon cocoa powder
2 eggs, beaten
250 ml/8 fl oz milk
1 tablespoon oil

**For the sauce and filling**
175 g/6 oz plain chocolate,
  chopped
150 ml/¼ pint water
1 teaspoon instant coffee powder
100 g/4 oz sugar
300 ml/½ pint whipped cream
2 tablespoons rum

To make the batter, sift the dry ingredients into a bowl. Add the eggs, then gradually add half the milk, stirring constantly. Add the oil and beat thoroughly until smooth. Add the remaining milk. Leave to stand for 30 minutes. Cook the pancakes as instructed in recipe 152.

To make the sauce, heat the chocolate, 2 tablespoons of the water and the coffee in a pan. Add the remaining water and the sugar and heat, stirring, until dissolved. Simmer, uncovered, for 10 minutes. Cool.

To make the filling, fold the rum into the cream and spoon on to each pancake, then roll up and place on a serving dish. Pour over a little of the chocolate sauce and serve the rest separately.

## Cook's Tip

Stir the batter before making each crêpe to ensure a light, even texture for the finished crêpe.

# 129 | Chocolate Sponge Pudding

**Preparation time**
20 minutes

**Cooking time**
1½-2 hours

**Serves 4**

**Calories**
467 per portion

**You will need**
175 g/6 oz self-raising flour
2 tablespoons cocoa powder
100 g/4 oz butter or margarine
100 g/4 oz caster sugar
2 large eggs
2 tablespoons milk

For the chocolate sauce
75 g/3 oz plain chocolate, broken
    into pieces
3 tablespoons golden syrup
2 tablespoons water

Grease a 1.2 litre/2 pint pudding basin. Sift the flour and cocoa together. Cream the fat and sugar together until light and fluffy. Beat in the eggs, one at a time, adding a little of the flour and cocoa with the second egg. Fold in the remaining flour and cocoa, then mix in the milk. Spoon into the prepared basin. Cover with buttered foil, making a pleat across the centre to allow the pudding to rise. Steam for 1½-2 hours.

To make the sauce, melt the chocolate with the syrup and water in a small bowl over a pan of boiling water, then beat until smooth. Turn the pudding out on to a warmed serving dish and pour the hot sauce over before serving.

# 130 | Chocolate Pie

**Preparation time**
15 minutes, plus 3
hours to rest and set

**Cooking time**
15-20 minutes

**Oven temperature**
200C, 400F, gas 6

**Serves 4-6**

**Calories**
221 per portion

**You will need**
100 g/4 oz plain or white
    chocolate, broken into pieces
2 teaspoons powdered gelatine
50 ml/2 fl oz hot water
150 ml/¼ pint single cream

For the pastry
25 g/1 oz caster sugar
40 g/1½ oz butter
2 eggs, separated
65 g/2½ oz plain flour

To make the pastry, cream the sugar and butter until light and fluffy, then beat in 1 egg yolk. Gradually work in the flour to a soft, pliable dough. Knead lightly, then roll out the pastry to fit a 15 cm/6 inch fluted flan ring. Prick the base with a fork and rest for 30 mintues. Bake blind (see Cook's Tip 52) for 15-20 minutes, removing the beans and paper for the last 5 minutes. Turn out on to a wire rack. Cool.

Reserve 1 square of chocolate and melt the remainder in a heatproof bowl over a pan of hot water, stirring constantly. Remove from the heat and beat in the remaining egg yolk. Dissolve the gelatine in the hot water over a pan of simmering water. Stir into the chocolate mixture, then stir in the cream. Cool until almost set. Whisk the egg whites until soft peaks form, then gently fold into the chocolate mixture. Chill for about 2 hours, or until set. Just before serving, pile the chocolate mixture into the pastry case and grate over the reserved chocolate.

## Cook's Tip

**When tying the string around a steamed pudding basin, leave a loop on either side to form handles for making removal of the basin from the pan of water both safer and easier.**

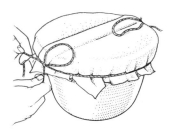

## Cook's Tip

**Chocolate decorations such as grated chocolate, leaves and curls can be frozen uncovered and then stored in rigid containers for 2-3 months.**

# 131 | *Hazelnut and Chocolate Fingers*

**Preparation time**
*5 minutes, plus 1½ hours to set*

**Cooking time**
*5-10 minutes*

**Makes 12**

**Calories**
*372 per portion*

**You will need**
*50 g/2 oz butter or margarine*
*175 g/6 oz plain chocolate*
*2 tablespoons clear honey*
*225 g/8 oz digestive biscuits, crushed*
*50 g/2 oz shelled hazelnuts, chopped and toasted*

Grease and line an 18 cm/7 in square cake tin. Put the butter or margarine, chocolate and honey in a pan and heat gently until melted. Stir in the biscuit crumbs and hazelnuts until thoroughly mixed, turn into the prepared tin and smooth the top. Leave until set, then cut into fingers before serving.

# 132 | *Chocolate Brandy Gâteau*

**Preparation time**
*20 minutes, plus overnight chilling*

**Serves 8**

**Calories**
*601 per portion*

**You will need**
*350 g/12 oz plain chocolate, broken into pieces*
*4 tablespoons strong black coffee*
*4 tablespoons brandy*
*225 g/8 oz digestive biscuits, broken into small pieces*
*175 g/6 oz glacé cherries, quartered*

**To decorate**
*250 ml/8 fl oz double cream, whipped*
*chocolate caraque, made with 50 g/2 oz chocolate*

Grease an 18 cm/7 in loose-bottomed cake tin. Place the chocolate and coffee in a pan and heat gently until melted; do not allow to become more than lukewarm. Remove form the heat and add the brandy, biscuits and cherries. Mix thoroughly, then turn into the prepared cake tin. Smooth the top and chill overnight in the refrigerator.

Remove from the tin and slide on to a plate. Pipe the cream over the top and decorate with chocolate caraque (see Cook's Tip below).

## Cook's Tip

**Add some raisins, sultanas or chopped glacé cherries to the mixture for a change. These quickly-made uncooked biscuits freeze well and can be kept in the freezer for up to six months.**

## Cook's Tip

**To make chocolate caraque, spread a thin layer of melted chocolate on to a cold surface. Leave until firm, but not hard. Draw a sharp, thin-bladed knife at a slight angle across the chocolate with a slight sawing movement, scraping** **off thin layers to form long scrolls.**

# 133 | *Iced Chocolate Soufflés*

**Preparation time**
20 minutes, plus 4
hours to freeze

**Serves 4-6**

**Calories**
387 per portion

**You will need**
4 eggs, separated
100 g/4 oz icing sugar, sifted
75 g/3 oz plain chocolate, chopped
1 tablespoon water
250 ml/8 fl oz double cream
2 tablespoons rum
grated chocolate to decorate

Tie a double thickness band of foil very tightly around six freezerproof ramekin dishes to stand 2.5 cm/1 in above the rim. Whisk the egg yolks and icing sugar until thick and creamy. Place the chocolate and water in a small pan and heat very gently until melted. Cool slightly, then whisk into the egg mixture. Whip the cream with the rum until it stands in soft peaks, then fold in the chocolate mixture. Whisk the egg whites until stiff and carefully fold into the mousse. Pour into the prepared ramekins and freeze for 4 hours until firm.

   Transfer to the refrigerator 10 minutes before serving to soften. Remove the foil carefully. Sprinkle the grated chocolate over the top to cover completely.

# 134 | *Sicilian Chocolate Cake*

**Preparation time**
30-40 minutes, plus 2
hours to cool and chill

**Cooking time**
25-30 minutes

**Oven temperature**
180C, 350F, gas 4

**Serves 6-8**

**Calories**
420 per portion

**You will need**
3 eggs
90 g/3½ oz caster sugar
50 g/2 oz plain flour, sifted
200 g/7 oz Ricotta cheese
75 g/3 oz mixed crystallised or
   glacé fruits, chopped
150 g/5 oz chocolate, cut into very
   small pieces or coarsely grated
grated rind of 1 orange
2 tablespoons Maraschino
50 g/2 oz unsalted butter
175 g/6 oz icing sugar, sifted
1 glacé cherry
piece angelica, cut into leaves.
2 glacé orange slices

Grease and line an 18 cm/7 in cake tin. Whisk 2 of the eggs with 65 g/2½ oz of the caster sugar over a pan of simmering water until light. Remove from the heat and beat until cold. Fold in the flour and pour into the tin. Bake for 25-30 minutes until golden. Cool on a wire rack.

   Cream the cheese with the remaining sugar, add the fruit, 25 g/1 oz of the chocolate and the orange rind. Cut the cake in three layers and sprinkle each with a little liqueur. Sandwich with the cheese mixture, then chill.

   Melt the remaining chocolate in a bowl over hot water, then add the butter. Beat the remaining egg and stir into the chocolate. Beat in the icing sugar, leave to cool. Spread some icing over the cake and pipe the rest. Decorate with the crystallised fruit. Chill before serving.

## *Cook's Tip*

**To grate chocolate quickly, make sure the block is not too cold. Using a potato peeler, scrape curls directly from the block.**

## *Cook's Tip*

**The easiest way to quarter and chop cherries – and any other sticky glacé or dried fruit – is to use clean kitchen scissors, frequently dipping the blades in a jug of hot water to remove the sugary build up.**

# 135 | *Chocolate Fudge Pudding*

**Preparation time**
*10 minutes*

**Cooking time**
*45-50 minutes*

**Oven temperature**
*160C, 325F, gas 3*

**Serves 6-8**

**Calories**
*359 per portion*

**You will need**

For the fudge topping
*40 g/1½ oz butter*
*40 g/1½ oz soft dark brown sugar*
*40 g/1½ oz golden syrup*
*15 g/½ oz cocoa powder*
*2 tablespoons single cream*
*50 g/2 oz walnuts or pecans,
  finely chopped*

For the cake mixture
*2 eggs*
*100 g/4 oz caster sugar*
*100 g/4 oz butter or margarine*
*100 g/4 oz self-raising flour*
*1 teaspoon baking powder*

Grease and line a 20 cm/8 in sandwich tin or 1.5 litre/2½ pint ring mould. To make the fudge topping, place all the fudge ingredients in a small heavy-based pan. Heat gently until boiling, stirring constantly, then boil for 30 seconds. Pour into the prepared tin and leave until cold.

Beat the cake mixture ingredients in a large bowl for 2 minutes. Turn on to the cooled fudge mixture and spread evenly. Bake for 40-45 minutes, until well risen, golden brown and firm to the touch. Cool in the tin for 5 minutes. Invert on to a serving plate and peel off the lining paper. Serve hot with cream.

# 136 | *Chocolate Chip Bombe*

**Preparation time**
*15 minutes, plus
overnight freezing*

**Serves 6-8**

**Calories**
*513 per portion*

**You will need**
*450 ml/¾ pint double cream*
*175 g/6 oz plain dark chocolate,
  melted and slightly cooled*
*120 ml/4 fl oz water*
*100 g/4 oz raisins*
*50 g/2 oz glacé cherries, quartered*
*75 g/3 oz chocolate drops or
  chocolate chips*
*75 g/3 oz plain dark chocolate,
  melted, to finish*

To make the ice cream, whip the cream very lightly. Add the cooled melted chocolate, the water, raisins, cherries and chocolate drops or chips, and stir together. Spoon the mixture into a 1 litre/1¾ pint pudding basin and freeze overnight.

To serve, unmould on to a plate. Pour the melted chocolate over the ice cream. It will freeze instantly. Serve immediately or return to the freezer. If the bombe has been kept in the freezer for 24 hours, transfer it to the refrigerator for about 30 minutes to soften slightly before serving.

## Cook's Tip

**To cut desserts or cakes into neat portions so the knife doesn't drag any cream or icing, dip the knife blade in hot water, shake off the excess liquid and cut the slice or portion quickly.**

## Cook's Tip

**This dessert is a wonderful children's alternative to Christmas pudding. If desired, decorate with a sprig of holly. To vary the ice cream filling, add pieces of crystallised fruits such as pineapple or apricot.**

# 137 | Baked Chocolate Soufflé

**Preparation time**
15 minutes

**Cooking time**
40-45 minutes

**Oven temperature**
180C, 350F, gas 4

**Serves 4**

**Calories**
202 per portion

**You will need**
25 g/1 oz cocoa powder
40 g/1½ oz cornflour
300 ml/½ pint milk
50 g/2 oz caster sugar
50 g/2 oz butter
4 eggs, separated
1 teaspoon vanilla essence
25 g/1 oz icing sugar, sifted,
    to serve

Blend the cocoa and cornflour with a little of the milk in a pan. Add the remaining milk, the sugar and butter and cook, stirring, until thickened. Cool slightly, then beat in the egg yolks, one at a time, and vanilla essence.

Whisk the egg whites until stiff. Stir about 2 table-spoons into the chocolate mixture, then carefully fold in the remainder. Turn into a greased 1.2 litre/2 pint soufflé dish and bake immediately in a preheated oven for 35-40 minutes, until risen and firm on top. Sprinkle with icing sugar and serve immediately.

# 138 | Layered Chocolate Crunch

**Preparation time**
15 minutes, plus 4
hours to chill

**Serves 6**

**Calories**
407 per portion

**You will need**
100 g/4 oz wholemeal
    breadcrumbs
100 g/4 oz demerara sugar
6 tablespoons drinking chocolate
2 teaspoons instant coffee
    powder
150 ml/¼ pint single cream
150 ml/¼ pint double cream or
    whipping cream
6 tablespoons black cherry or
    strawberry jam
chocolate lacework to decorate

Combine the breadcrumbs, sugar, cocoa and coffee powder. Whip the creams together until the whisk makes a trail but the cream is still 'floppy'.

Spoon 1 tablespoon of jam into each of six individual dishes, then cover with alternate layers of cream and breadcrumb mixture, finishing with a layer of bread-crumb mixture and a spoonful of cream. Chill for several hours. To make the chocolate lacework draw a lacework design on a template and cover with non-stick silicone paper. Fit a piping bag with a fine nozzle and fill with melted chocolate. Pipe following the stencil, moving it behind the silicone paper as each motif is completed. Chill until set. Use to decorate the pudding.

## Cook's Tip

**When folding whisked egg whites into a slightly heavier mixture, such as the one above, it is a good idea to stir in a small amount of egg white first to soften it.**

## Cook's Tip

**A paper doyley or a design on a birthday card or in a magazine could easily be used as the template for the chocolate lacework, provided it is flat and won't cause the silicone paper to slip as you pipe the chocolate.**

# 139 | *Chocolate Bombe Noël*

**Preparation time**
20 minutes, plus 1 hour
to soak and 4-5 hours
to freeze

**Serves 6-8**

**Calories**
437 per portion

**You will need**
100 g/4 oz glacé cherries, chopped
100 g/4 oz raisins
50 g/2 oz angelica, chopped
50 g/2 oz crystallised pineapple (optional)
50 g/2 oz sultanas
6 tablespoons rum
3 egg yolks
75 g/3 oz caster sugar
175 g/6 oz plain chocolate, chopped
300 ml/½ pint single cream
300 ml/½ pint double cream, whipped
100 g/4 oz blanched almonds, chopped and toasted

Place the fruit in a bowl, stir in the rum and leave to soak for 1 hour. Beat the egg yolks and sugar until thick and mousse-like. Gently melt the chocolate in a pan with the single cream, then heat to just below boiling point. Beat into the egg yolk mixture. Place over a pan of simmering water and stir until thickened. Strain and cool.

Fold the custard into half the double cream. Pour into a rigid freezerproof container, cover, seal and freeze for 2 hours. Stir well and mix in the fruit, rum and almonds. Turn into a 1.75 litre/3 pint pudding basin, cover with foil, seal and freeze until firm. Unmould on to a chilled plate. Smooth the surface and decorate with the remaining whipped cream.

## Cook's Tip

*Make a change by using pistachio nuts instead of the more traditional almonds or hazelnuts suggested in many recipes. Their bright green colour enlivens the blander ice cream or milk pudding.*

# 140 | *Caramel Crunch Biscuits*

**Preparation time**
30 minutes, plus 2
hours to chill

**Cooking time**
about 8 minutes

**Makes 24 squares**

**Calories**
174 per portion

**You will need**
100 g/4 oz butter or margarine
25 g/1 oz caster sugar
25 g/1 oz drinking chocolate powder
1 teaspoon vanilla essence
175 g/6 oz digestive biscuits, crushed
50 g/2 oz chopped nuts
100 g/4 oz plain or milk chocolate

**For the filling**
1 (400 g/14 oz) can condensed milk
25 g/1 oz butter
3 tablespoons golden syrup
1 teaspoon vanilla essence

Grease an 18 × 28 cm/7 × 11 inch Swiss roll tin. Melt the butter or margarine, sugar, chocolate powder and vanilla essence in a pan over low heat. Stir well. Stir the biscuits and nuts into the mixture until all the fat has been absorbed. Press the mixture into the prepared tin.

Place all the filling ingredients in a pan and heat until beginning to bubble. Boil gently for 3 minutes, stirring constantly. Do not allow the mixture to burn. Pour the mixture over the biscuit base and spread evenly.

Place the chocolate in a small bowl over a pan of hot water. Stir until melted. Pour over the caramel, and mark with a pattern. Chill for 2 hours or until set. Mark the chocolate into 24 equal squares and cut in the tin.

## Cook's Tip

*If using a non-stick Swiss roll tin, line the base with greased greaseproof paper to avoid scratching the coated surface of the tin.*

# 141 | Creole Cake

**Preparation time**
30 minutes, plus 4 hours to soak

**Cooking time**
25-30 minutes

**Oven temperature**
180C, 350F, gas 4

**Makes one 18 cm/7 in square cake**

**Calories**
1008 per portion

**You will need**
50 g/2 oz dried apricots, chopped
4 tablespoons dark rum
240 g/8½ oz butter
225 g/8 oz caster sugar
4 eggs
200 g/7 oz self-raising flour
50 g/2 oz cocoa powder
2 tablespoons warm water
75 g/3 oz unsweetened
 desiccated coconut
100 g/4 oz plain chocolate
1 tablespoon coffee powder
1 tablespoon soft brown sugar
4 tablespoons boiling water
4 tablespoons apricot jam
300 ml/½ pint double cream
chocolate curls to decorate

Soak the apricots in the rum for 4 hours. Grease and line two 18 cm/7 inch square tins. Prepare the cake mixture as instructed in recipe 129, using 225 g/8 oz of the butter. Stir in the water and 50 g/2 oz of the coconut. Divide the mixture between the tins and bake for 25-30 minutes. Cool. Cut one cake in half horizontally.

Melt the chocolate and the remaining butter in a double boiler and stir in the remaining coconut. Blend the coffee with the sugar and water. Crumble the uncut cake into a bowl. Add one-third of the cake crumbs each to the rum and apricot, chocolate and coffee mixtures. Spread the two cut surfaces of the remaining cake with the jam and spread one half with the three mixtures in turn. Sandwich together and decorate with whipped cream and chocolate curls.

## Cook's Tip

*When icing cakes or gâteaux ensure the top of the cake is complely flat. Turn it upside down and ice the underside if this is more level.*

# 142 | Chocolate Charlotte

**Preparation time**
30 minutes, plus 2 hours to set

**Cooking time**
10 minutes

**Serves 8**

**Calories**
909 per portion

**You will need**
100 g/4 oz plain chocolate,
 chopped
300 ml/½ pint milk
2 eggs, separated
50 g/2 oz soft light brown sugar
15 g/½ oz gelatine
3 tablespoons hot water
½ (439 g/15½ oz) can
 unsweetened chestnut purée
300 ml/½ pint whipped cream
, 30 langues de chat biscuits
 (recipe 13)
chocolate triangles to decorate

Grease a deep 18 cm/7 in cake tin. Gently heat the chocolate ina small pan with the milk until melted. Beat the egg yolks and sugar together until creamy, then stir in the chocolate mixture. Return to the pan and heat gently, stirring until thickened. Dissolve the gelatine in the hot water over a pan of simmering water, then stir into the egg yolks and chocolate.

Beat the chestnut purée with a little of the custard until smooth, then mix in the remainder. Cool, then fold in two-thirds of the cream. Whisk the egg whites until stiff and fold in. Turn into the prepared tin and chill until set.

Make the langues de chat as instructed in recipe 13. Turn the charlotte out on to a plate and cover with a thin layer of cream. Press the biscuits around the sides; trim to fit if necessary. Decorate with the remaining cream and chocolate triangles (See Cook's Tip below).

## Cook's Tip

*To make chocolate triangles, melt 40 g/1½ oz chocolate and spread thinly on a piece of greaseproof paper. When set, but not hard, cut into triangles, using a sharp knife and a ruler.*

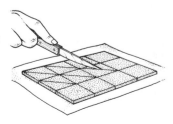

# 143 | *Chocolate Semolina*

**Preparation time**
10 minutes

**Cooking time**
25 minutes

**Oven temperature**
190C, 375F, gas 5

**Serves 4-6**

**Calories**
186 per portion

**You will need**
600 ml/1 pint milk
50 g/2 oz semolina
100 g/4 oz dark chocolate
1 tablespoon sugar
1 egg
caster sugar, for sprinkling

Bring the milk to the boil in a saucepan and stir in all the semolina. Cook over a gentle heat for 3-4 minutes, stirring constantly. Remove from the heat and add the chocolate and sugar. Stir until they are melted. Allow the mixture to cool a little, then beat in the egg. Pour into a 900 ml/1½ pint ovenproof dish and sprinkle with caster sugar. Bake for 20 minutes until the surface is set. Serve either hot or cold.

# 144 | *Mocha Roulade*

**Preparation time**
25 minutes, plus
overnight chilling

**Cooking time**
20-25 minutes

**Oven temperature**
180C, 350F, gas 4

**Serves 8**

**Calories**
423 per portion

**You will need**
175 g/6 oz plain chocolate
3 tablespoons water
1 tablespoon instant coffee
  powder
5 eggs, separated
225 g/8 oz caster sugar
icing sugar to dredge

**For the filling**
1 tablespoon instant coffee
  powder
1 tablespoon boiling water
300 ml/½ pint double cream,
  whipped
1 tablespoon icing sugar

Grease and line a 20 × 30 cm/8 × 12 in Swiss roll tin. Place the chocolate, water and coffee in a pan and heat gently until the chocolate has melted. Beat the egg yolks with the sugar until thick and creamy, then fold in the warm chocolate mixture. Whisk the egg whites until stiff and fold into the chocolate mixture. Turn into the prepared tin. Bake for 20-25 minutes until firm. Leave for 5 minutes, cover with a damp cloth and leave until cool. Chill overnight.
Carefully remove the cloth and turn the roulade out on to a sheet of greaseproof paper, sprinkled thickly with icing sugar. Peel off the lining paper. Dissolve the coffee in the water, cool, then fold into the cream with the sugar. Spread evenly over the roulade and roll up like a Swiss roll. Dust with icing sugar.

## Cook's Tip

*Semolina is a granular durum (hard) wheat flour rich in protein. It is often used with plain flour to increase the gluten content of a recipe and this is what enables pastries to hold their shape successfully.*

## Cook's Tip

*If you find it difficult to roll up a roulade or swiss roll without breaking it, try turning in a 2.5 cm/1 in 'hem' at one end and press it nearly flat before rolling.*

# Fritters, Pancakes and Waffles

Out of the frying pan and on to these pages come some tasty ideas for hot, melt-in-the-mouth pancakes, fritters, crêpes and waffles.

## 145 | Apricot Fritters in Brandy

**Preparation time**
30 minutes, plus 2 hours to macerate

**Cooking time**
25-30 minutes

**Serves 4**

**Calories**
455 per portion

**You will need**
225 g/8 oz sugar
450 ml/¾ pint water
12 ripe apricots, peeled and stoned
4 tablespoons brandy

For the fritter batter
100 g/4 oz plain flour
pinch of salt
25 g/1 oz butter, melted
1 egg, separated
150 ml/¼ pint milk
oil for deep frying
icing sugar to decorate

Put the sugar and water in a large pan and bring to the boil, stirring constantly, then simmer for 1 minute. Add the apricots to the syrup and poach for 10-15 minutes until completely tender. Strain the apricots and macerate them in 3 tablespoons of the brandy for 2 hours.

To make the fritter batter, sift the flour and salt into a bowl. Add the butter and egg yolk. Using a wooden spoon gradually incorporate into the flour mixture, adding the milk a little at a time to make a smooth batter. Whisk the egg white until it is stiff and fold it into the batter.

Heat the oil in a large heavy pan to 190C/375F or until a cube of bread browns in 30 seconds. Add the remaining brandy to the fritter batter. Dip the apricots in the batter and fry them, until crisp and golden. Drain on absorbent paper. Sprinkle with icing sugar and serve immediately.

### Cook's Tip

**If using canned fruit instead of fresh when making fritters, be sure to drain the syrup thoroughly from the fruit and dry each piece on absorbent kitchen paper, otherwise the batter won't stick properly.**

## 146 | Choux Fritters with Fruit Sauce

**Preparation time**
15 minutes

**Cooking time**
about 25 minutes

**Serves 6**

**Calories**
220 per portion

**You will need**
50 g/2 oz butter
150 ml/¼ pint water
65 g/2½ oz plain flour, sifted
25 g/1 oz caster sugar
2 eggs, beaten
oil for deep frying
icing sugar
50 g/2 oz granulated sugar
300 ml/½ pint water
2 teaspoons cornflour
2 tablespoons brandy
lemon juice
100 g/4 oz redcurrants
225 g/8 oz strawberries, chopped

Heat the butter and 150 ml/¼ pint water until the butter melts, then boil. Remove from the heat, add the flour and sugar and beat well. Allow to cool slightly, then beat in the eggs, a little at a time. Spoon into a piping bag fitted with a large star nozzle. Chill until required.

For the sauce, heat the sugar and remaining water until the sugar dissolves. Boil rapidly for 2 minutes. Mix the cornflour, brandy and lemon juice, add to the syrup and bring to the boil. Add the fruit and simmer for 5 minutes.

Heat the oil for deep frying to 182C/360F. Test the temperature by placing a cube of bread in the pan; the cube should rise instantly to the surface. Pipe 4 cm/1½ in lengths of choux paste into the oil. Fry in 3 or 4 batches, for 2-3 minutes until golden. Drain on absorbent paper. Sprinkle with icing sugar and serve with the sauce.

### Cook's Tip

**To make it easier to cut each length of piped choux paste free of the nozzle, use a wetted knife.**

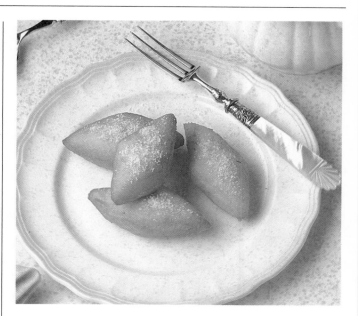

# 147 | Honey Fritters

**Preparation time**
10-15 minutes, plus 1
hour to froth and rise

**Cooking time**
3-4 minutes per batch

**Makes 20-24**

**Calories**
89 per fritter

**You will need**
15 g/½ oz fresh yeast or
  2 teaspoons dried yeast
200 ml/⅓ pint tepid water
225 g/8 oz strong plain flour,
  sifted with a good pinch of salt
4 tablespoons milk
1 egg
oil for deep frying
50 g/2 oz toasted flaked almonds
  to decorate

**For the syrup**
175 g/6 oz granulated sugar
100 g/4 oz clear honey
4 tablespoons water
2 tablespoons lemon juice

Mix the yeast in 3 tablespoons of tepid water and stir.
Cover and leave in a warm place until frothy. Mix the
flour, milk, half the remaining water, the egg and yeast
and beat well to make a smooth batter. Leave for an hour.
  To make the syrup, gently heat all the ingredients, stirring occasionally until the sugar dissolves. Boil the syrup
without stirring until it is thick enough to coat a spoon
lightly. Remove from the heat.
  When the batter has risen, heat a deep pan of oil to
180-190C/350-375F or until a cube of bread browns in 30
seconds. Carefully place 6-7 tablespoons of batter in the
oil, turning the fritters frequently until golden brown.
Drain on absorbent kitchen paper and keep hot while frying the remaining fritters. Decorate with the almonds and
serve the syrup separately.

## Cook's Tip

*Use a stainless steel knife
when cutting lemons. The high
acidity levels in lemons
discolour ordinary steel
knives.*

# 148 | Beignets Bourguignons

**Preparation time**
15 minutes, plus 2
hours to rest

**Cooking time**
about 5 minutes

**Makes 24**

**Calories**
68 per fritter

**You will need**
175 g/6 oz self-raising flour
50 g/2 oz caster sugar
2 eggs, lightly beaten
2 tablespoons dark rum
75 g/3 oz unsalted butter
oil for deep frying
caster sugar to decorate

Mix the flour and sugar together, then beat in the eggs
and rum. Cream the butter and combine it with the batter
to make a soft pastry. Cover and leave the pastry to rest
for about 2 hours.
  Roll out the pastry on a floured surface and cut into
24 diamond-shaped pieces. Heat the oil in a large heavy
saucepan to 190C/375F or until a cube of bread browns in
30 seconds. Fry the pieces a few at a time for 5 minutes,
until golden brown. Drain on absorbent kitchen paper.
Dust with caster sugar and serve immediately, with a
sweetened apple sauce if desired. Serve hot.

## Cook's Tip

*Dusting the beignets with the
sugar after cooking is best
done by putting the sugar in a
bag with the beignets and
gently shaking them.*

# 149 | Apple Fritters

**Preparation time**
10 minutes, plus 3
hours to rest

**Cooking time**
4-5 minutes per batch

**Makes about 12**

**Calories**
104 per fritter

**You will need**
100 g/4 oz plain flour, sifted
200 ml/⅓ pint light ale
3 medium cooking apples
100 g/4 oz caster sugar
1-1½ teaspoons ground cinnamon
oil for deep frying
2-3 tablespoons caster sugar
lemon twist to decorate

Place the flour in a bowl and add half the ale. Gently fold
in the flour, gradually adding the remaining ale until the
batter is smooth. Leave for 3 hours at room temperature.

About 15-20 minutes before the fritters are needed,
peel and core the apples and cut in 1 cm/½ in slices. Mix
the sugar and cinnamon. Place the apple slices on a
sheet of greaseproof paper or cling film and sprinkle with
the sugar mixture. Turn over and repeat.

Heat the oil in a deep pan to 180-190C/350-375F or until
a cube of bread browns in 30 seconds. Dip the apple
slices in the batter and fry a batch of three or four fritters
for 4-5 minutes, turning occasionally until they are golden
brown. Drain on absorbent kitchen paper. Keep hot while
frying the remaining fritters. Sprinkle with the caster
sugar, decorate with the lemon twist and serve
immediately.

# 150 | Churros

**Preparation time**
10 minutes

**Cooking time**
3-4 minutes

**Serves 4-6**

**Calories**
139 per portion

**You will need**
300 ml/½ pint water
175 g/6 oz plain flour
pinch of salt
2 eggs, beaten
groundnut or sunflower oil for
    deep frying
caster sugar mixed with ground
    cinnamon to coat

Boil the water in a heavy pan, then tip in the flour and salt,
and beat vigorously until the ball of dough leaves the side
of the pan. Beat in the eggs gradually, until the mixture is
smooth and glossy. Put the mixture in a large piping bag
fitted with a large rose nozzle. Heat the oil in a saucepan
to 190C/375F or until a cube of bread browns in 30
seconds. Pipe sections of dough about 10 cm/4 in long
and fry them until golden brown. Remove with a slotted
spoon and toss in cinnamon sugar. Serve immediately.

## Cook's Tip

**Don't use a frying basket
when making fritters as the
batter will stick to the mesh.
Instead, carefully lower the
fritters into the oil on the
prongs of a fork or on a
slotted spoon.**

## Cook's Tip

**If your bottle of cooking oil
has clouded because it has
become too cold, stand it in a
bowl of hot water until it
clears and thins again.**

# 151 | Almond Crêpes with Praline

**Preparation time**
35 minutes, plus 30 minutes to cool

**Cooking time**
35 minutes

**Oven temperature**
200C, 400F, gas 6

**Serves 6**

**Calories**
555 per portion

**You will need**
100 g/4 oz plain flour
pinch of salt
2 eggs
300 ml/½ pint milk
25 g/1 oz butter, melted
1 tablespoon caster sugar
100 g/4 oz ground almonds, toasted

**For the praline butter**
50 g/2 oz sugar
50 g/2 oz whole almonds
175 g/6 oz unsalted butter
3 tablespoons caster sugar
caster sugar for baking

Make and cook the crêpes as instructed in recipe 128. adding the butter, sugar and almonds to the batter.

To make the praline butter, moisten the sugar with water and boil for 3 minutes. Test the sugar temperature (see Cook's Tip 22). Add the almonds and remove from the heat. Stir until the sugar forms a crust around each nut. Return to the heat and cook, stirring constantly, until the sugar has melted and caramelised. Pour on to an oiled plate and cool for 30 minutes. Break the praline into pieces and grind to a powder in a blender, grinder or food processor. Cream the butter and caster sugar together, then add the praline.

Spread praline butter on each crêpe and roll it up. Place in a greased dish, with a dot of praline on top. Sprinkle with sugar and bake for 15 minutes. Serve immediately.

## Cook's Tip

*Make the job of pouring the batter for crêpes and pancakes into the pan less messy and easier to control by using a measuring jug, milk jug or soup ladle.*

# 152 | Lemon Soufflé Pancakes

**Preparation time**
20 minutes

**Cooking time**
40 minutes

**Oven temperature**
200C, 400F, gas 6

**Serves 4**

**Calories**
368 per portion

**You will need**

**For the pancakes**
50 g/2 oz plain flour, sifted
1 egg, beaten
200 ml/⅓ pint milk
oil for greasing

**For the lemon soufflé filling**
25 g/1 oz butter
25 g/1 oz plain flour
300 ml/½ pint milk
25 g/1 oz caster sugar
grated rind and juice of 1 lemon
2 eggs, separated
1 egg white
25 g/1 oz icing sugar

Combine the flour, egg and milk to make a thin batter. Grease a 15 cm/6 in frying pan and pour in just enough batter to cover the base thinly. Cook until golden, then turn over and cook the other side. Remove from the pan and keep warm while making the remaining pancakes.

To make the filling, melt the butter in a pan and fold in the flour. Stir in the milk, sugar, lemon rind and juice and bring to the boil, stirring. Cool slightly, then beat in the egg yolks. Whisk the egg whites and fold into the mixture. Spoon a little of the mixture on to each pancake, fold over and dust with icing sugar. Bake for 10-15 minutes. Serve hot with a raspberry coulis (see recipe 157).

## Cook's Tip

*For an alternative to the lemon soufflé filling, use a 410 g/14½ oz can of pears, drained then blended in a liquidiser or food processor. Make the purée up to 300 ml/½ pint, if necessary using some of the canned syrup,* *and proceed with the recipe as above.*

# 153 | Apricot Pancake Tower

**Preparation time**
20 minutes

**Cooking time**
1-1½ hours

**Oven temperature**
180C, 350F, gas 4

**Serves 8**

**Calories**
362 per portion

**You will need**
12 small pancakes (recipe 154)
100 g/4 oz dried apricots, soaked
  overnight
100 g/4 oz caster sugar
4 egg yolks
300 ml/½ pint double cream
grated rind of 1 lemon
1½ quantity ground praline (recipe
  22)
25 g/1 oz fresh, fine white
  breadcrumbs
50 g/2 oz flaked almonds, toasted

Make and cook the pancakes as in recipe 128. Simmer the apricots in their soaking liquid until tender. Blend in a liquidiser or purée through a sieve. Add 1 tablespoon of the caster sugar. Cream the egg yolks and remaining sugar until thick. Add the cream and lemon rind and whisk together. Transfer 8 tablespoons of the mixture to a clean bowl and stir in the ground praline. Transfer 4 tablespoons of the mixture to a clean bowl and add the purée. Reserve the remaining egg and cream mixture.

Grease a 900 ml/1½ pint soufflé dish and sprinkle with the breadcrumbs. Place a pancake in the dish. Spoon a layer of praline cream over it, then place another pancake on top and spoon a layer of apricot cream over it. Continue to layer, ending with a pancake. Pour the reserved egg and cream mixture over the pancakes. Cover with silicone paper and bake for 1-1½ hours until set. Cool. Turn out on to a serving dish. Sprinkle with almonds.

## Cook's Tip

*When making the pancakes use the same diameter frying pan as the soufflé dish if possible; otherwise you will have to trim the finished pancakes to fit the dish.*

# 154 | Apple Pancakes

**Preparation time**
30 minutes

**Cooking time**
35-45 minutes

**Oven temperature**
180C, 350F, gas 4

**Serves 6**

**Calories**
288 per portion

**You will need**
100 g/4 oz plain flour
pinch of salt
1 egg, beaten
300 ml/½ pint milk
1 tablespoon oil

**For the filling**
25 g/1 oz butter
750 g/1½ lb cooking apples,
  peeled, cored and sliced
50 g/2 oz brown sugar
½ teaspoon ground cinnamon
50 g/2 oz sultanas

**To finish**
3 tablespoons apricot jam,
  warmed
25 g/1 oz flaked almonds, toasted
whipped cream (optional)

Make and cook the pancakes as instructed in recipe 128. Melt the butter in a pan. Add the apples, sugar, cinnamon and sultanas. Cover and simmer gently for 10-15 minutes until the apples are tender.

Place a pancake on a greased ovenproof dish and cover with some of the apple mixture. Repeat until all the apple mixture and pancakes are used, finishing with a pancake. Spoon over the apricot jam to glaze.

Bake for 10-15 minutes until heated through. Cut into wedges and sprinkle with almonds. Serve with whipped cream if liked.

## Cook's Tip

*If making the pancakes in advance, it is a good idea to layer them with greaseproof paper to prevent them from sticking together.*

# 155 | *Scotch Pancakes*

**Preparation time**
*15 minutes*

**Cooking time**
*1-2 minutes per
pancake*

**Serves 6**

**Calories**
*205 per portion*

**You will need**
*100 g/4 oz plain flour
2 teaspoons baking powder
50 g/2 oz caster sugar
pinch of salt
1 egg, beaten
1 tablespoon lemon juice
65 ml/2½ fl oz milk
25 g/1 oz butter, melted*

**For the sauce**
*100 g/4 oz clear honey
grated rind and juice of 1 lemon*

Sift the flour, baking powder, sugar and salt into a bowl. Add the egg and lemon juice. Mix together to make a smooth batter, gradually adding the milk. Stir in the melted butter.

Heat a frying pan or griddle and grease lightly. Drop 3 or 4 tablespoons of batter on to the pan, keeping them well apart. Cook a few pancakes at a time. When golden brown on one side, turn them over and cook the other side. Keep them warm on a serving dish while cooking the others.

To prepare the sauce, gently heat the honey in a small pan with the lemon rind and juice. Serve the pancakes hot with the hot sauce poured over, and whipped cream, if liked.

# 156 | *Buckwheat Pancakes*

**Preparation time**
*15 minutes, plus 2
hours to rest*

**Cooking time**
*about 1 minute per
pancake*

**Makes 12-15
pancakes**

**Calories**
*64 per pancake*

**You will need**
*120 g/4½ oz buckwheat flour
small pinch of salt
300 ml/½ pint milk
3 eggs
2 tablespoons groundnut oil
    for frying*

Sift the flour and salt. Beat the milk with the eggs, then pour half the mixture into the flour. Stir in well, gradually adding the rest of the milk and eggs. Beat in the oil. Cover and leave the batter to rest for 2 hours.

Heat a 20 cm/8 in frying pan and brush with a little oil. Pour about 3 tablespoons of batter into the pan, tilting the pan to ensure that the pancakes are of even thickness. Cook the pancake for about half a minute, then turn it over and cook the other side. Keep it warm in a moderate oven while frying the remaining pancakes. To serve, fold each pancake in half and in half again so it looks like a wedge of cake.

## *Cook's Tip*

**Use a bristle pastry brush –
not a nylon one – for greasing
the griddle or frying pan when
making Scotch pancakes or
crêpes.**

## *Cook's Tip*

**Serve buckwheat pancakes
with lemon and sugar, fruit
purées, chocolate sauce, jams
or liqueurs.**

# 157 | Nut Waffles with Fruit Coulis

**Preparation time**
20 minutes

**Cooking time**
1-1½ minutes per waffle

**Serves 4-6**

**Calories**
216 per portion

**You will need**
75 g/3 oz plain flour
2 teaspoons baking powder
50 g/2 oz caster sugar
2 eggs, separated
300 ml/½ pint milk
25 g/1 oz butter, melted
50 g/2 oz nuts (walnuts, pecan nuts or hazelnuts), chopped

**For the fruit coulis**
juice of ½ lemon
275 g/10 oz fresh raspberries
75 g/3 oz caster sugar

Prepare and cook the waffles as instructed in recipe 158, folding the chopped nuts into the batter before cooking.

To make the fruit coulis, blend the lemon juice and raspberries in a liquidiser or food processor to make a purée. Strain the purée through a sieve into a bowl to remove the seeds. Add the sugar, stirring until completely dissolved. Sandwich the waffles together immediately with whipped cream or praline cream (see recipe 22) and serve with the coulis.

# 158 | Waffles with Maple Syrup

**Preparation time**
10 minutes

**Cooking time**
1-1½ minutes per waffle

**Serves 4-6**

**Calories**
386 per portion

**You will need**
75 g/3 oz plain flour
2 teaspoons baking powder
50 g/2 oz caster sugar
1 teaspoon ground cinnamon
2 eggs, separated
300 ml/½ pint milk
25 g/1 oz butter, melted

**To serve**
300 ml/½ pint double cream, whipped
maple syrup

Sift the flour, baking powder, sugar and cinnamon into a bowl. Make a well in the centre and drop in the egg yolks. Gradually stir in the yolks, adding the milk a little at a time, until a smooth batter is formed. Add the melted butter. Whisk the egg whites until they are stiff and fold them into the batter.

Heat a well-greased waffle iron until a drop of batter placed on it sizzles immediately. Pour some batter on to the iron and cook until golden brown on both sides. Sandwich the waffles immediately with whipped cream and serve with maple syrup poured over the top.

## Cook's Tip

*If your waffle iron does not have a thermostat, place a teaspoon of water in it as a temperature gauge; the iron is ready for use when it stops steaming.*

## Cook's Tip

*Any leftover waffles can be toasted briefly to crisp them up and heat them through.*

# 159 | Poor Knights of Windsor

**Preparation time**
10 minutes

**Cooking time**
15-20 minutes

**Serves 4-6**

**Calories**
344 per portion

**You will need**
8 medium thick slices white bread
300-450 ml/½-¾ pint milk
25 g/1 oz caster sugar
2 tablespoons sweet sherry
2 egg yolks
100-175 g/4-6 oz unsalted butter

**To serve**
2-3 tablespoons caster sugar
¼-½ teaspoon ground cinnamon
raspberry jam, heated

Remove the crusts from the bread, trim each slice to a square and cut into two triangles. Mix about half the milk with the sugar and sherry. Stir until the sugar has dissolved. Dip the bread into this mixture, then drain on a wire rack over a plate or tray.

Mix the egg yolks with the remaining milk, together with any remaining sherry-flavoured milk and any which drains from the bread. Heat two-thirds of the butter in a large frying pan. Dip both sides of each piece of bread in the egg mixture and fry on both sides until golden brown. Add more butter as necessary and reheat before adding any more bread to the pan. Combine the caster sugar and cinnamon. Pile the bread on to a hot dish, sprinkle with the sugar mixture and serve with hot jam.

# 160 | Swiss Waffles

**Preparation time**
10 minutes

**Cooking time**
1-1½ minutes per waffle

**Serves 4-6**

**Calories**
138 per portion

**You will need**
100 g/4 oz plain flour
1½ teaspoons baking powder
50 g/2 oz caster sugar
pinch of salt
1 egg, separated
50 ml/2 fl oz soured cream
25 ml/1 fl oz milk
1 tablespoon Kirsch
juice and grated rind of 1 lemon

Sift the flour, baking powder, sugar and salt into a bowl. Whisk the egg yolk, cream, milk and Kirsch together. Beat the mixture into the flour to form a smooth batter. Add the lemon juice and rind. Whisk the egg whites until they form stiff peaks and fold them into the batter. Cook the waffles as instructed in recipe 158. Serve with soured cream, jam or a fruit coulis (see recipe 157).

## Cook's Tip

**Add a pinch of cinnamon to the flour for extra flavour when making scone dough or apple pie pastry.**

## Cook's Tip

**This batter makes very light waffles. To keep them hot, lay them on a baking tray lined with absorbent kitchen paper and place them in the oven heated to 150C, 300F, gas 2 for up to 15 minutes.**

# Ice Creams and Cold Desserts

Here are some deliciously cool ideas for cold desserts and ice creams. You'll find many of the old favourites, few with a new flavour, twist or decoration and some fantastic new creations. These are desserts to push the boat out with so serve scooped into chilled glasses or fruit cases; or slice on to fine china or glass.

## 161 | Redcurrant Sorbet

**Preparation time**
10 minutes, plus 5-6 hours to freeze

**Serves 4**

**Calories**
153 per portion

**You will need**
500 g/1 lb redcurrants
100 g/4 oz icing sugar, sifted
juice of 1 orange
1 egg white

**To decorate**
frosted currant leaves
few sprigs redcurrants

Blend the redcurrants, icing sugar and orange juice in a liquidiser or food processor until smooth. Sieve to remove the pips. Place in a rigid freezerproof container, cover, seal and freeze for 2-3 hours. Whisk to break up the crystals. Whisk the egg white until stiff, then whisk into the half-frozen purée. Return to the freezer until firm.

Transfer to the refrigerator 15 minutes before serving to soften. Scoop into chilled glasses and decorate with frosted currant leaves (see Cook's Tip below) and redcurrant sprigs.

## 162 | Ginger Snap Ice Cream

**Preparation time**
20 minutes, plus 5-6 hours to freeze

**Serves 6-8**

**Calories**
328 per portion

**You will need**
3 eggs, separated
50 g/2 oz soft dark brown sugar
4 tablespoons green ginger wine
50 g/2 oz butter, melted
150 g/5 oz ginger biscuits, finely crushed
300 ml/½ pint double cream

Place the egg yolks in a bowl over a pan of hot water. Add the sugar and half the ginger wine and whisk until pale and creamy. Remove from the heat and whisk until cool. Stir in 1 tablespoon of the remaining ginger wine, the melted butter and all but 25 g/1 oz of the biscuit crumbs.

Whisk the cream and egg whites together until stiff enough to form soft peaks. Whisk in the remaining ginger wine. Fold both mixtures together and transfer to a rigid freezerproof container. Cover with cling film and freeze for about an hour, until just beginning to freeze around the edge. Whisk well, cover and partially freeze again. Repeat the process at least twice more. Cover, seal and freeze until firm.

Transfer to the refrigerator 30 minutes before serving to soften. Scoop into chilled glasses and sprinkle with the remaining biscuit crumbs.

## Cook's Tip

To make the frosted leaves, paint egg white all over the leaves with a fine paintbrush. Brush off any excess and dip in caster sugar until coated. Dry on greaseproof paper for 1-2 hours.

## Cook's Tip

The time required to freeze ice cream, sorbets, water ices and parfaits will depend on the efficiency of your freezing equipment, the size of container you are using and the depth of the mixture, but an indication has been included throughout to enable you to plan menus and estimate the time you will need to make a cold dessert.

## 163 | Thyme and Honey Sorbet

**Preparation time**
15 minutes, plus 4-5
hours to freeze

**Serves 4**

**Calories**
139 per portion

**You will need**
4 large lemons
600 ml/1 pint water
75 g/3 oz caster sugar
large bunch of thyme
3 tablespoons clear honey
1 egg white
4 thyme sprigs to decorate

Cut a thin slice from the base of each lemon so that they will stand. Cut the tops off the lemons and carefully scrape out the flesh. Sieve to extract the juice. Reserve the shells.

Place the water, sugar and thyme in a pan and heat gently until the sugar has dissolved. Bring to the boil, then simmer for 3 minutes. Add the honey and lemon juice and leave to cool.

Strain into a rigid freezerproof container, cover, seal and freeze for 2-3 hours, until half frozen. Whisk the egg white until stiff, then whisk into the ice. Spoon the sorbet into the lemon shells, piling it up well. Freeze any remaining sorbet in a rigid container, for another occasion.

Transfer to the refrigerator 10 minutes before serving to soften. Decorate with thyme sprigs.

## 164 | Ginger Parfait

**Preparation time**
20 minutes, plus 4-5
hours to freeze

**Serves 4**

**Calories**
328 per portion

**You will need**
3 egg yolks
75 g/3 oz caster sugar
300 ml/½ pint double cream
75 g/3 oz stem ginger, finely diced
2 tablespoons stem ginger syrup

Whisk the egg yolks until light and creamy, then whisk in the sugar. In a separate bowl, whisk the cream until it holds its shape on the whisk. Fold the yolk mixture into the cream, then fold in the ginger. Turn the mixture into a rigid freezerproof container and freeze for about 2-3 hours, or until almost set. Beat well, then freeze for a further 1-2 hours, or until firm.

If the parfait has been in the freezer for 24 hours or longer, transfer it to the refrigerator 15 minutes before serving to soften. To serve, scoop a ball of the parfait into a coupe. Pour over a teaspoon of the stem ginger syrup and serve with langues de chat biscuits (see recipe 13), if desired.

## Cook's Tip

**Keep the freezerproof container steady while you beat the ice crystals by placing it on a clean damp dish-cloth spread out on the work surface.**

## Cook's Tip

**Do not chop highly flavoured foods such as ginger, garlic or onions on the same board as you use for making pastry or preparing blander foods as the stronger flavours may blend.**

## 165 | Orange Givré

**Preparation time**
25 minutes, plus 4-5
hours to freeze

**Serves 4**

**Calories**
382 per portion

**You will need**
4 oranges
200 g/7 oz sugar
200 ml/⅓ pint water
1 egg white
1 teaspoon caster sugar

Cut the tops off the oranges, about two-thirds of the way up. Trim the bottoms so that the oranges stand upright. Squeeze the juice from the oranges without damaging the outer peel. Scrape away the flesh and any membranes sticking to the peel with a grapefruit knife, then blend and sieve the juice. Stand the hollowed shells and caps in the freezer.

Place the sugar and water in a pan and heat to boiling point, stirring constantly until the sugar has dissolved. Leave to cool, then mix with the orange juice in a rigid freezerproof container. Freeze for 2-3 hours, or until almost firm. Whisk the egg white and caster sugar until stiff, and fold into the sorbet. Whisk well. Return to the freezer for 1-2 hours, or until set. If the givré has been in the freezer for 24 hours or longer, transfer to the refrigerator 15 minutes before serving to soften slightly. To serve, spoon the sorbet into the frozen orange shells and place the orange lids on top.

## 166 | Raspberry Yogurt Sorbet

**Preparation time**
15 minutes, plus 4-5
hours to freeze

**Serves 6**

**Calories**
105 per portion

**You will need**
225 g/8 oz raspberries
2 150 g/5.2 oz cartons natural
  yogurt
15 g/½ oz gelatine
3 tablespoons hot water
2 egg whites
75 g/3 oz caster sugar

Blend the raspberries in a liquidiser or food processor until smooth. Sieve to remove the seeds. Stir in the yogurt. Dissolve the gelatine in the hot water over a pan of simmering water, then add to the purée. Whisk the egg whites until stiff, then gradually whisk in the sugar. Carefully fold the purée into the meringue, turn into a rigid freezerproof container, cover, seal and freeze until very firm.

Transfer to the refrigerator 30 minutes before serving to soften. Scoop into chilled glasses to serve.

## Cook's Tip

**To make orange-flavoured cream, run a sugar cube over the outside of an orange then crumble the sugar cube into the cream.**

## Cook's Tip

**Ensure that the sieve you use to remove the raspberry seeds in this recipe and others is a nylon one. A metal one not only discolours the fruit but also gives it an unpleasant flavour.**

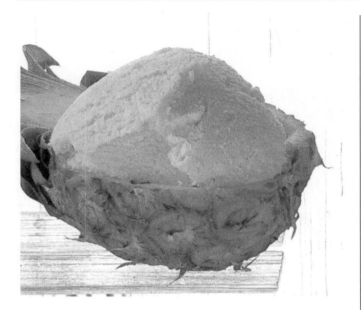

# 167 | Pina Colada Ice

**Preparation time**
30 minutes, plus 5-6 hours to freeze

**Serves 8-10**

**Calories**
568 per portion

**You will need**
1 large pineapple
25 g/1 oz creamed coconut, chopped
2 tablespoons boiling water
2 egg whites
100 g/4 oz caster sugar
6 tablespoons white rum
300 ml/½ pint whipping cream, whipped

Cut the pineapple in half lengthways. Scrape out the flesh and juice into a bowl, discarding the hard core. Chill the shells. Blend the flesh and juice in a liquidiser or food processor to make a purée.

Blend the coconut cream with the boiling water and leave to cool. Whisk the egg whites until stiff, then gradually whisk in the sugar. Mix the pineapple purée with the coconut and rum. Fold this into the cream with the meringue mixture. Turn into a rigid freezerproof container, cover, seal and freeze for 1½ hours. Remove from the freezer and stir well, then re-freeze until firm.

Transfer to the refrigerator 30 minutes before serving to soften. Scoop into the chilled pineapple shells and arrange on a dish.

# 168 | Coffee Granita with Vanilla Ice Cream

**Preparation time**
10 minutes, plus 2-3 hours to freeze

**Serves 4**

**Calories**
213 per portion

**You will need**
50 g/2 oz sugar
450 ml/¾ pint hot strong black coffee
4 scoops vanilla ice cream
4 teaspoons liqueur (Tia Maria, Sambuca, Amaretto di Saronno) (optional)

Stir the sugar into the coffee until it has dissolved. Pour the sweetened coffee into a shallow-sided tray and leave to cool. Transfer the tray to the freezer for about 30 minutes, until beginning to freeze. Scrape the ice crystals from the side of the tray to the centre. Return the tray to the freezer and repeat the scraping at regular intervals until all the mixture has a grainy texture.

Divide the granita between four glass coupes or sundae dishes and spoon or arrange scoops of vanilla ice cream on top. Spoon a little liqueur, if using, over the ice cream and serve immediately.

## Cook's Tip

*To make attractive ice cubes to serve with cocktails such as pina colada, use mineral water (which freezes clear, not opaque as tap water) with garnishes such as shreds of lemon or orange rind added when freezing.*

## Cook's Tip

*Granita is a type of Italian sorbet. It is half frozen with a granular texture, and is popular as a light, refreshing dessert or can be eaten between courses.*

## 169 | Grapefruit Sorbet

**Preparation time**
15 minutes, plus 5-6
hours to freeze

**Serves 8**

**Calories**
51 per portion

**You will need**
2 grapefruit (preferably pink)
15 g/½ oz gelatine
2 tablespoons hot water
600 ml/1 pint grapefruit juice
25 g/1 oz caster sugar
1 150 g/5.2 oz carton natural
   yogurt
2 egg whites, stiffly beaten
8 mint sprigs to decorate

Finely grate the rind from both grapefruit. Place in a large bowl and add just enough boiling water to cover. Leave to soak for 5 minutes, then drain. Dissolve the gelatine in the hot water over a pan of simmering water.

Cut the grapefruit in half and squeeze thoroughly so that the flesh comes out with the juice. Add to the soaked rind, together with the dissolved gelatine, grapefruit juice, sugar and yogurt. Stir well, then turn the mixture into a rigid freezerproof container, cover with cling film and freeze for about an hour, until just beginning to freeze around the edge. Whisk, then fold in the egg whites. Partly freeze and whisk twice more. Cover, seal and freeze until firm.

Transfer to the refrigerator 10 minutes before serving to soften. Scoop into chilled glasses and decorate with mint sprigs.

## 170 | Coupe Glacé à la Mangue

**Preparation time**
15 minutes

**Serves 4**

**Calories**
355 per portion

**You will need**
4 scoops vanilla ice cream
1 mango, peeled, stoned and
   quartered
50 g/2 oz caster sugar
juice of 1 orange
1 quantity crème chantilly (recipe
   118)

Place a scoop of ice cream in four coupes and chill. Cut half of the mango into fine slices for decoration. Pass the remaining mango through a sieve or blend in a liquidiser or food processor. Whisk in the sugar and orange juice. Arrange the mango slices around the ice cream. Pour the mango purée on top. To decorate, pipe rosettes of crème chantilly on top.

## Cook's Tip

**Because all liquids expand on freezing, it is important to leave a space of about 2.5 cm/1 inch at the top of the container to prevent the lid being forced off.**

## Cook's Tip

**Save the containers for bought ice cream for use when you make your own. These are also useful for storing other foods such as flour, teabags, coffee, sugar and packets of herbs which need to be kept dry.**

# 171 | Vanilla Ice Cream

**Preparation time**
20 minutes, plus 3-5
hours to freeze

**Cooking time**
10-15 minutes

**Serves 6-8**

**Calories**
249 per portion

**You will need**
3 egg yolks
100 g/4 oz vanilla sugar
250 ml/8 fl oz mlk
300 ml/½ pint double cream

Whisk the egg yolks and sugar until thick and creamy. Heat the milk to simmering point and pour over the yolks. Mix well. Return the custard to the rinsed pan and heat gently until it coats the back of a spoon. Pour into a bowl and cool.

Whisk the cream until it thickens, then fold into the custard. Pour the custard into a rigid freezerproof container and freeze for about 2-3 hours, or until it begins to set at the edges. Whisk thoroughly to break down the ice crystals. Return to the freezer for 1-2 hours, or until firm.

# 172 | Elderflower Sorbet

**Preparation time**
15 minutes, plus 4-5
hours to freeze

**Serves 6**

**Calories**
81 per portion

**You will need**
450 ml/¾ pint water
100 g/4 oz caster sugar
thinly pared rind and juice of 2
lemons
25 g/1 oz elderflower heads
1 egg white
elderflower or mint leaves to
decorate

Place the water, sugar and lemon rind in a pan and heat gently, stirring until the sugar has dissolved. Bring to the boil, then simmer for 5 minutes. Add the elderflower and lemon juice, cover and leave to cool.

Strain into a rigid freezerproof container. Cover, seal and freeze for 2-3 hours, until half frozen. Whisk the egg white until stiff, then whisk into the ice. Cover, seal and freeze until firm.

Transfer to the refrigerator 10 minutes before serving to soften. Scoop into chilled glasses and top with elderflower or mint leaves.

## Cook's Tip

**If the ice cream has been in the freezer for 24 hours or longer, transfer to the refrigerator 15 minutes before serving to soften.**

## Cook's Tip

**Dipping the ice cream scoop in water before use makes scooping easier and ensures that the shape of the ice cream or sorbet is smooth and unragged.**

# 173 | Truffle and Coffee Ripple

**Preparation time**
15 minutes, plus 5-6
hours to freeze

**Serves 8**

**Calories**
313 per portion

**You will need**

For the truffle mixture
100 g/4 oz plain chocolate,
    chopped
2 tablespoons single cream
2 tablespoons rum

For the coffee ice cream
2 tablespoons instant coffee
    powder
2 tablespoons boiling water
2 egg whites
100 g/4 oz caster sugar
300 ml/½ pint double cream

Place the chocolate, cream and rum in a heatproof bowl over a pan of simmering water until the chocolate has melted. Mix well, then leave to cool.

To make the ice cream, dissolve the coffee in the water and leave to cool. Whisk the egg whites until stiff, then whisk in the sugar. Whip the cream with the coffee until it forms soft peaks. Fold into the meringue.

When the truffle mixture begins to thicken, stir until smooth and soft. Fold into the ice cream mixture very lightly to create a marbled effect. Turn into a rigid freezerproof container, cover, seal and freeze until firm.

Transfer to the refrigerator 15 minutes before serving to soften. Scoop into chilled glasses and serve with chocolate sauce if desired.

# 174 | Cherry Brandy Sorbet

**Preparation time**
15 minutes, plus 5-6
hours to freeze

**Serves 4**

**Calories**
335 per serving

**You will need**
250 g/9 oz sugar
450 ml/¾ pint water
juice of 1 lemon
1 egg white
100 ml/3½ fl oz cherry brandy
4 teaspoons cherry brandy to
    serve

Place the sugar and 300 ml/½ pint of the water in a pan and heat to boiling point, stirring constantly until the sugar has dissolved. Leave to cool, then mix with the lemon juice and remaining water in a rigid freezerproof container. Freeze for 3-4 hours, or until almost solid. Whisk the egg white until stiff and fold into the sorbet. Whisk well and add the cherry brandy. Return to the freezer for 1-2 hours, or until completely firm.

If the sorbet has been in the freezer for 24 hours or longer, transfer to the refrigerator 15 minutes before serving to soften. To serve, scoop the sorbet into portions and pour a teaspoon of cherry brandy over each.

## Cook's Tip

**Eggs separate more easily
when cold, but their whites
froth up better when at room
temperature.**

## Cook's Tip

**Remove frozen ice cubes from
their trays by briskly rubbing a
cloth wrung out in hot water
over the base and sides of the
trays.**

# 175 | Vanilla and Blackcurrant Ripple Ice

**Preparation time**
15 minutes, plus 5-6 hours to freeze

**Serves 4-5**

**Calories**
365 per serving

**You will need**
150 ml/¼ pint single cream
3 egg yolks
50 g/2 oz caster sugar
1 teaspoon vanilla essence
300 ml/½ pint whipping cream
2 tablespoons blackcurrant jelly preserve

Heat the single cream until hot but not boiling. Place the egg yolks in a heatproof bowl and mix with a fork. Pour the hot cream on to the egg yolks, stirring constantly. Stir in the sugar and vanilla essence. Place over a pan of gently simmering water and stir for about 8-10 minutes until the mixture is thick enough to coat the back of a spoon. Strain into a bowl and leave to cool.

Whip the whipping cream until it forms soft peaks and lightly fold it into the custard. Turn the mixture into a 1 kg/2 lb loaf tin, cover and freeze for 1½ hours, or until partly frozen.

Melt the blackcurrant jelly in a pan and leave to cool but do not allow to set. Whisk the ice cream until smooth, make three holes along the centre of the ice cream and pour in the melted blackcurrant jelly. Run a sharp knife through the jelly and ice cream to give a marbled effect. Return to the freezer for another 4 hours, or until completely frozen.

Transfer to the refrigerator 30 minutes before serving to soften.

## Cook's Tip

*Break off a piece of vanilla pod, split it and add to heating milk to impart a lovely flavour to rice puddings, sauces and so on. It should be washed and dried after use and, if stored in a jar of sugar, will provide vanilla sugar.*

# 176 | Strawberry Water Ice

**Preparation time**
10 minutes, plus 4-5 hours to freeze

**Cooking time**
5 minutes

**Serves 4-6**

**Calories**
87 per portion

**You will need**
75 g/3 oz sugar
250 ml/8 fl oz water
1½ teaspoons lemon juice
275 g/10 oz strawberries, puréed
1 egg white
1½ tablespoons icing sugar, sieved

Dissolve the sugar in the water over a gentle heat. Bring to the boil and boil rapidly for 3 minutes. Leave to cool.

Stir in the lemon juice and strawberry purée. Turn into a freezerproof container and freeze for 2-3 hours, until half frozen. Whisk the egg whites until stiff, then whisk in the icing sugar. Whisk this mixture into the strawberry ice until evenly combined. Return to the freezer and freeze until solid. To serve, make small scoops of water ice with a melon baller.

## Cook's Tip

*Water ices are good with a little liqueur spooned over them before serving. Suitable combinations include blackcurrant water ice with creme de cassis and orange water ice with Cointreau.*

## 177 | Minty Chocolate Chip Ice

**Preparation time**
20 minutes, plus 5-6 hours to freeze

**Serves 8**

**Calories**
204 per portion

**You will need**
2 egg whites
100 g/4 oz caster sugar
1 (410 g/14.5 oz) can evaporated milk, chilled
4 drops green food colouring
½ teaspoon peppermint essence
75 g/3 oz plain chocolate, finely chopped

Whisk the egg whites until stiff, then gradually whisk in the sugar. Place the evaporated milk in a bowl with the colouring and peppermint essence and whisk until thick, then fold into the meringue mixture with the chocolate. Turn into a rigid freezerproof container, cover, seal and freeze for 2 hours. Remove from the freezer and stir vigorously. Re-freeze until firm.

Transfer to the refrigerator 1 hour before serving to soften. Scoop into chilled glass dishes.

## 178 | Coppa Cleopatra

**Preparation time**
15 minutes, plus 30 minutes to cool

**Serves 4**

**Calories**
373 per portion

**You will need**
100 g/4 oz sugar
1 tablespoon water
small pinch of cream of tartar
50 ml/2 fl oz double cream
50 ml/2 fl oz cognac
4 scoops vanilla ice cream
4 pieces crystallised stem ginger, finely diced

Place the sugar, water and cream of tartar in a pan and heat until the sugar has completely dissolved. Bring to the boil, stirring constantly until the sugar turns a mid-amber caramel. Remove from the heat and whisk in the cream. Beat in the cognac and leave to cool.

Put a scoop of ice cream in four glass coupes. Pour over the sauce and sprinkle the diced ginger on top.

### Cook's Tip

**A mouli grater grates chocolate much more quickly and easily than an ordinary upright grater.**

### Cook's Tip

**Cream of tartar is a humble but essential ingredient of this dessert, for it prevents the sugar crystallising even though it is heated at a temperature hot enough to turn it to caramel.**

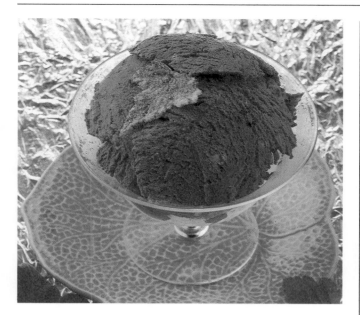

## 179 | Apple and Blackcurrant Ice Cream

**Preparation time**
20 minutes, plus 5-6 hours to freeze

**Serves 8-10**

**Calories**
238 per portion

**You will need**
225 g/8 oz cooking apples, peeled, cored and sliced
225 g/8 oz blackcurrants
2 tablespoons granulated sugar
4 tablespoons water
4 eggs, separated
100 g/4 oz caster sugar
300 ml/½ pint double cream, whipped
frosted currant leaves to decorate

Place the apples in a large pan with the blackcurrants, granulated sugar and water. Cover and cook over a gentle heat until soft. Cool slightly, then blend in a liquidiser or food processor until smooth. Sieve to remove the pips. Leave to cool completely.

Whisk the egg whites until stiff, then gradually whisk in the caster sugar and egg yolks. Fold the fruit purée into the cream, then fold into the egg mixture. Turn into a rigid freezerproof container, cover, seal and freeze until firm.

Transfer to the refrigerator 30 minutes before serving to soften. Scoop into chilled glasses and decorate with frosted currant leaves (see Cook's Tip 161).

## 180 | Punch à la Romaine

**Preparation time**
15 minutes, plus 4-6 hours to freeze

**Makes 6-8 portions**

**Calories**
219 per portion

**You will need**
400 g/14 oz sugar
400 ml/14 fl oz water
50 ml/2 fl oz orange juice
50 ml/2 fl oz lemon juice
120 ml/4 fl oz dry white wine
1 egg white
1 teaspoon caster sugar
6-8 teaspoons white rum

Place the sugar and water in a pan and heat to boiling point, stirring constantly until the sugar has dissolved. Leave to cool, then mix with the fruit juices and wine in a rigid freezerproof container. Freeze for 3-4 hours, or until almost solid. Whisk the egg white and sugar until stiff, then fold into the sorbet. Whisk well. Return to the freezer for 1-2 hours, or until completely firm.

If the punch has been in the freezer for 24 hours or longer, transfer to the refrigerator 15 minutes before serving to soften. To serve, scoop the mixture into individual bowls, and pour a teaspoon of rum over each portion.

## Cook's Tip

*If you don't have an ice cream scoop but want to serve the ice cream decoratively in neat shapes, use a soup spoon to remove the ice cream from its container.*

## Cook's Tip

*Use an ice cube tray to freeze items you may need to defrost only in small quantities, such as lemon juice, stocks, or cream.*

# 181 | Orange and Rosemary Ice Cream

**Preparation time**
20 minutes, plus 5-6 hours to freeze

**Serves 4**

**Calories**
185 per portion

**You will need**
200 ml/⅓ pint water
150 g/5 oz sugar
grated rind of 2 oranges
2 (15 cm/6 in) sprigs of rosemary
juice of 2 oranges
120 ml/4 fl oz double cream

Place the water and sugar in a pan and bring to the boil, stirring constantly until the sugar has dissolved. Add the orange rind and rosemary and leave to stand for 15 minutes.

Remove the rosemary and discard. Stir in the orange juice, then turn into a rigid freezerproof container and freeze for 2-3 hours, until almost set. Whip the double cream until it holds its shape on the whisk, then beat into the orange mixture. Freeze for 2-3 hours or until firm. If the ice cream has been in the freezer for 24 hours or longer, transfer to the refrigerator 15 minutes before serving to soften.

# 182 | Melon and Grape Sorbet

**Preparation time**
25 minutes, plus 4-5 hours to freeze

**Serves 4**

**Calories**
131 per portion

**You will need**
120 g/4½ oz black or white grapes, seeded
120 g/4½ oz ripe melon flesh, chopped
2 fresh mint leaves, finely chopped
40 g/1½ oz sugar
3 tablespoons water
2 ogen melons, halved and seeded, to serve

**To decorate**
2-4 sprigs of mint
black grapes, halved and seeded

Blend the grapes, chopped melon and mint leaves in a liquidiser or food processor, and pass them through a sieve to remove the grape skins. Place the sugar and water in a small pan over a gentle heat and bring to the boil, stirring constantly until the sugar has completely dissolved. Add the sugar syrup to the fruit purée. Pour the mixture into an ice cube tray and freeze until almost set. Beat well to break down the ice crystals and return to the freezer to set completely.

Fill the ogen melons with the sorbet and decorate with halved grapes and sprigs of mint. Serve immediately.

## Cook's Tip

Rosemary, with its lovely blue flowers, is among the many herbs you can grow yourself. Keep a pot of chives, mint, parsley and thyme on your kitchen windowsill and snip off as much as you need when in season.

## Cook's Tip

To test a melon for ripeness, gently press the stem end – a ripe melon will yield slightly.

# 183 | Gooseberry Sorbet

**Preparation time**
20 minutes, plus 4-5
hours to freeze

**Serves 4**

**Calories**
162 per portion

**You will need**
500 g/1 lb gooseberries
2 heads elderflower, tied in muslin
   (optional)
100 g/4 oz sugar
150 ml/¼ pint water
1 egg white
mint leaves to decorate

Place the gooseberries in a pan with the elderflower, if using, sugar and water. Cover and simmer for 15 minutes until tender. Remove the elderflower, cool slightly, then blend in a liquidiser or food processor until smooth. Sieve, then leave to cool. Turn into a rigid freezerproof container, cover, seal and freeze for 2-3 hours, until slushy. Whisk the egg white until stiff, then fold into the purée. Freeze until firm.

Transfer to the refrigerator 10 minutes before serving to soften. Scoop into glasses and decorate with mint leaves.

# 184 | Iced Zabaglione

**Preparation time**
10 minutes, plus 1-2
hours to freeze

**Cooking time**
10 minutes

**Serves 6-8**

**Calories**
162 per portion

**You will need**
6 egg yolks
6 tablespoons caster sugar
6 tablespoons Marsala
200 ml/⅓ pint double or
   whipping cream

**To decorate**
whipped cream
cystallised violets and/or angelica
leaves

Combine the egg yolks, sugar and Marsala in a large heat-proof basin. Place over a pan of simmering water and whisk for about 10 minutes, until thick and pale. Remove from the heat and continue whisking for 5 minutes until cool. Whip the cream until it stands in soft peaks. Fold into the cool egg mixture. Spoon into ramekin dishes and freeze until required. Decorate with whipped cream, violets and/or angelica leaves.

## Cook's Tip

**To speed up the preparation
of gooseberries, use a pair of
kitchen scissors when topping
and tailing them.**

## Cook's Tip

**For special occasions, scoop
the flesh out of lemons to
make baskets and fill these
with zabaglione. Freeze as
instructed above.**

# 185 | Marshmallow Pie

**Preparation time**
45 minutes, plus 4-5
hours to chill

**Cooking time**
15 minutes

**Serves 6-8**

**Calories**
453 per portion

**You will need**
175 g/6 oz digestive biscuits,
 crushed
75 g/3 oz butter, melted
25 g/1 oz demerara sugar
15 g/½ oz gelatine
3 tablespoons hot water
225 g/8 oz pink marshmallows
300 ml/½ pint milk
75 g/3 oz chopped walnuts
150 ml/¼ pint double cream

**To decorate**
whipped cream
6-8 Maraschino cherries

Mix together the biscuit crumbs, melted butter and sugar and use to line the base and sides of an 18 cm/7 in springform tin. Chill.

Dissolve the gelatine in the hot water over a pan of simmering water. Roughly chop the marshmallows and place them in a pan with the milk. Heat gently, stirring until the marshmallows have melted. Remove from the heat, stir in the gelatine and chopped nuts, and allow to cool until it is just beginning to set. Whip the cream until it forms soft peaks, then fold it into the mixture. Pour into the biscuit base and chill for at least four hours.

Remove from the springform tin and decorate with piped cream rosettes and Maraschino cherries.

# 186 | Lace Baskets

**Preparation time**
30 minutes, plus 25
minutes to cool

**Cooking time**
10-12 minutes per batch

**Oven temperature**
180C, 350F, gas 4

**Makes 12**

**Calories**
83 per basket

**You will need**
50 g/2 oz butter or margarine
50 g/2 oz demerara sugar
50 g/2 oz golden syrup
50 g/2 oz plain flour, sifted

Place the butter or margarine, sugar and syrup in a large pan and heat gently until the fat has melted and the sugar dissolved. Cool slightly, then beat in the flour. Place 4 heaped teaspoonfuls of the mixture at least 10 cm/4 in apart in each of three baking trays. Bake each batch for 10-12 minutes, until golden.

Leave to cool slightly, then remove with a palette knife. If the mixture cools too much and becomes thick, spread it out thinly with the palette knife to flatten. Mould over the base of an inverted glass, with the top side of the biscuit touching the edge of the glass. Leave to set then remove carefully.

## Cook's Tip

*As a delicious treat, thread 4-6 marshmallows on to a skewer and grill on a high heat for 2-4 minutes until the marshmallows are toasted. Leave for a few minutes before eating.*

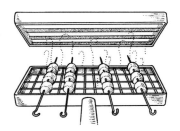

## Cook's Tip

*Do not make more than four lace baskets at a time or they will set before you can mould them. If they become too brittle to handle, soften them in the oven for 30 seconds.*

# 187 | Apple and Walnut Whirls

**Preparation time**
15 minutes

**Cooking time**
15-20 minutes

**Oven temperature**
180C, 350F, gas 4

**Serves 10**

**Calories**
274 per portion

**You will need**
75 g/3 oz butter
50 g/2 oz soft brown sugar
100 g/4 oz plain flour, sifted
75 g/3 oz walnuts, ground
chopped walnuts to decorate

**For the filling**
1 tablespoon apricot jam
500 g/1 lb dessert apples, peeled,
  cored and sliced
½ teaspoon ground cinnamon
250 ml/8 fl oz double cream,
  whipped

Cream the butter and sugar together until light and fluffy. Stir in the flour and walnuts, and mix to a firm dough. Turn on to a floured surface and knead lightly until smooth. Roll the dough out thinly; cut out ten 7.5 cm/3 in and ten 5 cm/2 in circles. Place on a baking tray and bake for 12-15 minutes, until golden. Transfer to a wire rack to cool.

Meanwhile, place the jam and apples in a pan, cover and cook gently for 15-20 minutes, until softened, stirring occasionally. Add the cinnamon and leave to cool.

Spread the cooled apple mixture over the larger rounds, pipe two-thirds of the cream over the apple and top with the small circles. Pipe the remaining cream on top and decorate with chopped walnuts.

# 188 | Creamy Guava Pie

**Preparation time**
25-30 minutes, plus 2
hours to rest and to set

**Cooking time**
30 minutes

**Oven temperature**
200C, 400F, gas 6

**Serves 6-8**

**Calories**
282 per portion

**You will need**
pâte sucrée, made with 175 g/6 oz
  plain flour (recipe 57)
2 tablespoons cornflour
450 ml/¾ pint milk
2 egg yolks
40 g/1½ oz granulated sugar
few drops vanilla essence
2 teaspoons gelatine
2 tablespoons hot water
150 ml/¼ pint whipped cream

**To decorate**
1 (400 g/14 oz) can guavas,
  drained and quartered
small pieces of angelica, cut
  into leaves

Make the pâte sucrée as recipe 57, chill for 30 minutes. Roll out and line a 23 cm/9 in flan ring. Bake blind for 20 minutes, then remove the beans and cook for a further 5 minutes or until the pastry is dry. Cool on a wire rack.

Blend the cornflour with a little of the milk and the egg yolks. Stir in the sugar. Heat the milk and pour a little of it on to the mixture. Mix well, return to the pan and bring to the boil, stirring. Dissolve the gelatine in the hot water over a pan of simmering water, then add to the custard. Mix well and add the vanilla essence, then strain into a bowl. Allow to cool, stirring frequently.

When the custard is beginning to thicken to a jelly-like consistency, whisk until quite smooth. Fold in the whipped cream and pour into the pastry case and leave to set. Decorate with the guavas and angelica leaves.

## Cook's Tip

*Walnuts are useful additions to both sweet and savoury dishes. They need to be used quite quickly after purchase as their fat content is quite high and this causes them to go rancid and bitter if they are kept for too long.*

## Cook's Tip

*The pastry case can be made 1-2 days in advance and stored in an airtight container. When the pie has been filled, however, it should be eaten on the same day or the filling will soften the pastry.*

# 189 | Chestnut Roulade

**Preparation time**
15 minutes, plus 45 minutes to cool

**Cooking time**
25-30 minutes

**Oven temperature**
180C, 350F, gas 4

**Serves 8**

**Calories**
424 per portion

**You will need**
3 eggs, separated
100 g/4 oz caster sugar
½ (439 g/15½ oz) can unsweetened chestnut purée
grated rind and juice of 1 orange
icing sugar, sifted for sprinkling
300 ml/½ pint double cream
2 tablespoons Grand Marnier
finely shredded orange rind to decorate

Whisk the egg yolks with the sugar until thick and creamy. Place the chestnut purée in a bowl with the orange juice and beat until blended, then whisk into the egg mixture. Whisk the egg whites until fairly stiff and fold in carefully. Turn into a greased and lined 20 × 30 cm/ 8 × 12 in Swiss roll tin. Bake for 25-30 minutes, until firm and springy to the touch.

Cool for 5 minutes, then cover with a clean damp cloth and leave until cold. Carefully turn the roulade on to a sheet of greaseproof paper, sprinkled thickly with icing sugar. Peel off the lining paper. Place the cream, orange rind and liqueur in a bowl and whip until stiff. Spread three-quarters over the roulade and roll up like a Swiss roll. Transfer to a serving dish, pipe the remaining cream along the top and decorate with the orange rind.

## Cook's Tip

*If you have some whipped cream left in your piping bag after decorating puddings, use it up by piping rosettes on to a baking tray and freezing. When frozen, pack into a rigid container and use to decorate cakes and trifles.*

# 190 | Nutty Profiteroles

**Preparation time**
15 minutes, plus 20 minutes to cool

**Cooking time**
40-45 minutes

**Oven temperature**
220C, 425F, gas 7 then 190C, 375F, gas 5

**Serves 4-6**

**Calories**
523 per portion

**You will need**

For the choux pastry
50 g/2 oz butter
150 ml/¼ pint water
65 g/2½ oz plain flour, sifted
2 eggs, beaten
50 g/2 oz blanched almonds, chopped
175 ml/6 fl oz double cream
2 tablespoons Tia Maria

For the sauce
150 ml/¼ pint double cream
50 g/2 oz unsalted butter
75 g/3 oz soft brown sugar

Melt the butter in a large pan, add the water and bring to the boil. Remove from the heat, add the flour all at once and beat until the paste leaves the sides of the pan. Cool slightly, then add the eggs a little at a time, beating vigorously to form a smooth shiny paste.

Put the mixture in a large piping bag fitted with a plain 1 cm/½ in nozzle and pipe small rounds on to a dampened baking tray. Sprinkle with the almonds. Bake for 10 minutes, then lower the temperature and bake for a further 20-25 minutes, until golden. Make a slit in the side of each bun and cool on a wire rack.

Whip the cream with the liqueur until stiff. Spoon a little into each bun and pile the profiteroles on a dish.

To make the sauce, heat the ingredients in a pan, stirring until the sugar has dissolved. Boil for 2 minutes until syrupy. Pour over the profiteroles and serve.

## Cook's Tip

*Making the slits in the choux buns as soon as they are cooked enables the steam to escape and keeps the pastry crisp.*

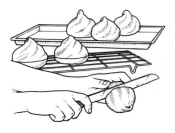

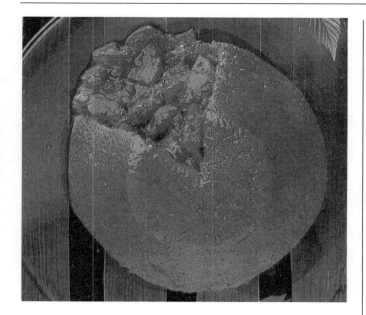

# 191 | Autumn Pudding

**Preparation time**
20 minutes, plus
overnight chilling

**Serves 6-8**

**Calories**
132 per portion

**You will need**
500 g/1 lb cooking apples, peeled,
    cored and sliced
350 g/12 oz blackberries
50 g/2 oz soft brown sugar
2 tablespoons water
3 tablespoons port
8 slices brown bread, crusts
    removed

Place the apples, blackberries and sugar in a heavy-based pan with the water. Cover and simmer gently until soft but not pulpy. Add the port and leave to cool. Strain, reserving the juice.

Cut three circles of bread to fit the base, middle and top of a 900 ml/1½ pudding basin. Shape the remaining bread to fit around the side of the basin. Soak the bread in the reserved fruit juice as you line the basin. Start with the small circle in the bottom of the basin, then the shaped bread round the side. Spoon in half the fruit and place the middle-sized circle of bread on top. Cover with the remaining fruit then top with the large bread circle. Fold over any bread protruding over the top of the basin. Cover with a saucer small enough to fit inside the basin and put a 500 g/1 lb weight on top. Chill overnight.

Turn on to a serving plate, pour over any remaining fruit juice and serve with whipped cream.

# 192 | Cream Cheese Mousse with Strawberries

**Preparation time**
10 minutes, plus 2-3
hours to chill

**Serves 6**

**Calories**
407 per portion

**You will need**
225 g/8 oz curd cheese
2 egg yolks
50 g/2 oz caster sugar
½ teaspoon vanilla essence
15 g/½ oz gelatine
3 tablespoons hot water
300 ml/½ pint whipping cream,
    whipped
350 g/12 oz strawberries, halved
2 tablespoons Cointreau

Place the cheese in a bowl with the egg yolks, sugar and vanilla essence and beat until smooth. Dissolve the gelatine in the hot water over a pan of simmering water, then stir into the cheese mixture with the cream. Turn into a greased 900 ml/1½ pint ring mould and chill until set. Sprinkle the strawberries with the liqueur and leave to soak for 1 hour.

Turn the mousse on to a serving plate and fill the centre with the strawberries.

## Cook's Tip

*Only late-season apples can be kept through the winter. Wrap these individually in newspaper and keep them in a cool place such as on a high shelf in a garage.*

## Cook's Tip

*To bring eggs to room temperature quickly, place them in a bowl standing in a large container of warm water.*

# Traditional Puddings and Pies

Bring back proper puddings like mother used to make and you will gain an unrivalled reputation as a first-class dessert cook. Tempt them with a selection of sponge and suet puddings; fruit-laden pies, cobblers and dumplings; sticky and sweet tarts and roly-polys or stuffed, fit-to-burst baked fruit.

## 193 | Apricot Toasts

**Preparation time**
10 minutes

**Cooking time**
15-20 minutes

**Serves 4**

**Calories**
155 per portion

**You will need**
2 eggs
2 tablespoons milk
8 small slices fruit, or plain bread, crusts removed
75 g/3 oz butter
4 tablespoons caster sugar
1 teaspoon ground cinnamon
2 (275 g/10 oz) cans apricot halves in juice, drained
whipped cream
2 tablespoons chopped pistachios or toasted almonds

Beat the egg and milk together and dip the bread slices in it until coated on both sides. Melt the butter and fry the slices of bread until crisp and golden on both sides. Drain on absorbent kitchen paper.

Mix the sugar and cinnamon together and sprinkle on to the bread. Top with the apricots, a whirl of whipped cream and the chopped nuts. Serve at once.

## 194 | Almond and Fig Sponge Pudding

**Preparation time**
15 minutes

**Cooking time**
1¾-2 hours

**Serves 6**

**Calories**
417 per portion

**You will need**
100 g/4 oz butter
75 g/3 oz caster sugar
2 eggs, beaten
grated rind of ½ lemon
100 g/4 oz self-raising flour, sifted
100 g/4 oz marzipan, diced
a little milk (if necessary)
1 (425 g/15 oz) can figs, drained

Grease a 1.2 litre/2 pint pudding basin. Cream the butter and sugar until light and fluffy, then beat in the eggs and lemon rind. Fold in the flour and moisten with milk, if necessary, to give a dropping consistency. Stir in the marzipan.

Arrange sufficient fig halves to cover the base of the prepared pudding basin. Spoon in half the sponge mixture and level the surface. Make a second layer of figs and finish with the remaining sponge mixture. Cover with greased foil, making a pleat across the centre to allow the pudding to rise. Steam for 1¾-2 hours until firm to the touch. Turn out on to a serving plate and serve with custard or cream.

## Cook's Tip

**This can be simply served sprinkled with sugar and topped with jam or cream or more sumptuously with brandied fruits. For a richer custard, substitute cream for the milk.**

## Cook's Tip

**Canned figs can make a delicious and quick pudding. Simply add a splash of marsala and serve with whipped cream.**

# 195 | Queen of Puddings

**Preparation time**
20 minutes, plus 15
minutes to soak

**Cooking time**
50-60 minutes

**Oven temperature**
180C, 350F, gas 4

**Serves 6**

**Calories**
335 per portion

**You will need**
300 ml/½ pint milk
200 g/7 oz caster sugar
3 eggs, separated
few drops vanilla essence
75 g/3 oz fresh white
  breadcrumbs
3 tablespoons raspberry jam
juice of ½ lemon
175 g/6 oz caster sugar

Grease a 900 ml/1½ pint ovenproof dish. Whisk together the milk, 25 g/1 oz of the sugar, the egg yolks and vanilla essence. Pour the mixture over the breadcrumbs and leave for 15 minutes. Transfer to the prepared dish and bake for 30 minutes. Remove from the oven and leave to cool slightly.

Mix the jam and lemon juice together and spread evenly over the surface of the pudding. Beat the egg whites until they are stiff. Add the remaining sugar 1 tablespoon at a time, whisking well between each addition until the mixture is thick and glossy. Pipe or spoon the meringue over the pudding and return to the oven for about 20 minutes until the meringue is crisp and lightly coloured. Serve hot.

## Cook's Tip

*If preparing this dish in advance, cook the breadcrumb mixture. Cool, cover and store overnight. Do not keep it longer than a day.*

# 196 | Treacle Pudding

**Preparation time**
15 minutes

**Cooking time**
1½-2 hours

**Serves 4**

**Calories**
472 per portion

**You will need**
100 g/4 oz butter or margarine
100 g/4 oz caster sugar
2 large eggs
100 g/4 oz self-raising flour, sifted
4 tablespoons golden syrup

For the sauce
2 tablespoons golden syrup
1 tablespoon water

Cream the butter or margarine with the sugar until light and fluffy. Beat in the eggs, one at a time, adding a little of the flour with the second egg. Beat thoroughly, then fold in the remaining flour.

Grease a 900 ml/1½ pint pudding basin and spoon in the syrup, then put the sponge mixture on top. Cover with greased foil, making a pleat across the centre to allow the pudding to rise. Steam for 1½-2 hours.

To make the sauce, heat the syrup and water in a small pan. Turn the pudding out on to a warmed serving dish and pour the hot sauce over before serving.

## Cook's Tip

*A spoonful of treacle or syrup won't dribble when you take it out of the tin if you keep turning the spoon over, as if using a screwdriver.*

# 197 | Jam Roly-Poly

**Preparation time**
20 minutes

**Cooking time**
45 minutes

**Oven temperature**
190C, 375F, gas 5

**Serves 4-6**

**Calories**
547 per portion

**You will need**
225 g/8 oz self-raising flour
50 g/2 oz caster sugar
100 g/4 oz shredded suet
1 egg, beaten
150 ml/¼ pint milk
100 g/4 oz strawberry or raspberry
  jam

**For the glaze**
1 tablespoon milk
caster sugar

Mix the flour, sugar and suet together. Add the egg and enough milk to form a soft dough. Roll the pastry out on a floured surface to make a 20 × 25 cm/8 × 10 in rectangle. Warm the jam a little and spread it over the pastry, leaving a narrow border. Fold the edges over to prevent the jam oozing out. Brush the edges with a little milk, and roll the dough up from the short edge.

Place the roll, seam side down, on a baking tray lined with greased foil. Fold the foil to make a box half-way up around the roll. Cut a few slanting slits on top of the roll, brush with a little milk and sprinkle with sugar. Bake in the oven for 45 minutes or until golden brown. Serve with hot custard.

# 198 | Eve's Pudding

**Preparation time**
15 minutes

**Cooking time**
40-45 minutes

**Oven temperature**
180C, 350F, gas 4

**Serves 4**

**Calories**
557 per serving

**You will need**
500 g/1 lb cooking apples, peeled,
  cored and thinly sliced
50 g/2 oz soft brown sugar
100 g/4 oz butter or margarine
100 g/4 oz caster sugar
2 eggs
100 g/4 oz self-raising flour, sifted
1 tablespoon hot water

Place the apples in a greased 1.2 litre/2 pint shallow oven-proof dish and sprinkle with the brown sugar. Cream the butter or margarine with the caster sugar until light and fluffy. Add the eggs, one at a time, adding a little flour with the second egg. Fold in the remaining flour, then the hot water.

Spread the mixture evenly over the apples and bake for 40-45 minutes until golden brown. Serve with cream or custard.

## Cook's Tip

**Glaze sweet pies and puddings with milk or egg white and dust with caster sugar. Savoury pies are brushed with beaten egg or egg yolk diluted in milk.**

## Cook's Tip

**If the fat and sugar begin to curdle after the addition of the whisked eggs in this or any similar recipe, try adding a little of the measured amount of flour and beating it in gently to correct the curdling.**

# 199 | *Baked Pears in White Wine*

**Preparation time**
15 minutes

**Cooking time**
20-30 minutes

**Oven temperature**
180C, 350F, gas 4

**Serves 6**

**Calories**
219 per portion

**You will need**
50 g/2 oz butter
6 large ripe pears (preferably
  Conference), peeled, halved
  and cored
6 tablespoons ginger marmalade
6 tablespoons roughly crushed
  macaroons
300 ml/½ pint sweet white wine

Use 15 g/½ oz of the butter to grease a large shallow ovenproof dish, just big enough to hold the pears in a single layer. Place the pear halves in the dish, cut side up, and fill the hollows with the ginger marmalade and crushed macaroons. Pour the wine around the pears, dot them with the remaining butter and bake for 20-30 minutes until just tender when tested with a skewer.

# 200 | *Apricot Upside-down Pudding*

**Preparation time**
15 minutes

**Cooking time**
55-60 minutes

**Oven temperature**
180C, 350F, gas 4

**Serves 6**

**Calories**
484 per portion

**You will need**
175 g/6 oz butter or margarine
50 g/2 oz soft brown sugar
1 (425 g/15 oz) can apricot halves,
  or cooked fresh apricots, halved
  and stoned
100 g/4 oz caster sugar
2 eggs
100 g/4 oz self-raising flour, sifted
1 teaspoon ground mixed spice

Cream 50 g/2 oz of the fat, mix with the brown sugar and spread over the bottom of a 1.2 litre/2 pint ovenproof dish. Drain the apricots, reserving 1 tablespoon of the juice. Arrange in the dish.

Cream the remaining fat with the caster sugar until light and fluffy. Add the eggs, one at a time, adding 1 tablespoon of the flour with each egg. Beat thoroughly, then fold in the remaining flour, mixed spice and reserved apricot juice. Spread over the apricots and bake for 55-60 minutes, until the sponge is springy to the touch. Turn out on to a warmed serving dish and serve with cream.

## Cook's Tip

**Keep any leftover wine for cooking purposes. Pour it into a small container, seal and use for deglazing pans after roasting and frying, to tenderise tough meats in a marinade, and to improve the flavour of bland dishes.**

## Cook's Tip

**Mixed spice usually consists of four parts each of ground nutmeg and cinnamon to two parts ginger and one part cloves. Experiment with different brands, or mix your own to taste.**

## 201 | Bread and Butter Pudding

**Preparation time**
10 minutes, plus 30 minutes to soak

**Cooking time**
50-60 minutes

**Oven temperature**
160C, 325F, gas 3

**Serves 4**

**Calories**
421 per portion

**You will need**
9 slices white bread, crusts removed
50 g/2 oz butter
50 g/2 oz sultanas or currants
50 g/2 oz caster sugar
2 large eggs
600 ml/1 pint milk
grated nutmeg

Spread the bread thickly with butter and cut each slice into four. Arrange half in a greased 1.2 litre/2 pint ovenproof dish, buttered side down. Sprinkle with the fruit and half the sugar. Cover with the remaining bread, butter side up.

Beat the eggs and milk together and strain over the pudding. Sprinkle with the remaining sugar and nutmeg to taste and leave for 30 minutes. Bake for 50-60 minutes, until the top is golden. Serve with custard or cream.

## 202 | Apricot Brown Betty

**Preparation time**
20 minutes

**Cooking time**
40 minutes

**Oven temperature**
190C, 375F, gas 5

**Serves 4-6**

**Calories**
355 per portion

**You will need**
500 g/1 lb fresh apricots or 225 g/8 oz dried apricots, soaked overnight
100 g/4 oz fresh white breadcrumbs
75 g/3 oz butter, melted
75 g/3 oz caster sugar
grated rind of 1 orange

**To serve**
2 tablespoons demerara sugar
1 quantity fruit coulis (recipe 157) made with stewed or poached apricots
150 ml/¼ pint single cream

Grease a 1.2 litre/2 pint ovenproof dish. If using fresh apricots, halve them and remove the stones. Toss the breadcrumbs in the melted butter, then spread a thin layer of crumbs in the prepared dish. Cover with a shallow layer of fruit, sprinkled with the sugar and orange rind. Continue to layer the fruit and crumbs alternately, finishing with a layer of crumbs and a sprinkling of sugar. Bake for 40 minutes until crisp and golden.
Make the fruit coulis as instructed in recipe 157. Sprinkle the pudding with the demerara sugar and serve with the fruit coulis and cream.

## Cook's Tip

**Try substituting stale tea breads and tea cakes for some of the crustless white bread. Add rinsed and chopped glacé cherries to the sultanas or currants as well.**

## Cook's Tip

**If brown sugar has gone hard put it in a bowl and cover with a clean cloth wrung out in water. Leave overnight, it will have softened by the morning.**

# 203 | Plum Dumplings

**Preparation time**
15 minutes

**Cooking time**
20-25 minutes

**Oven temperature**
200C, 400F, gas 6

**Serves 4**

**Calories**
226 per portion

**You will need**
8 firm red plums
8 teaspoons caster sugar
225 g/8 oz shortcrust pastry
  (recipe 58)
milk
caster sugar to glaze

Carefully split each plum and remove the stone. Fill one half with a teaspoon of caster sugar and replace the other half. Make the shortcrust pastry as instructed in recipe 58. Divide the pastry into eight pieces and on a lightly floured surface roll out each piece to form a square large enough to enclose a plum. Trim the edges. Draw the corners of the pastry to the centre and seal the edges well with water. Decorate each dumpling with pastry leaves made from the trimmings.

Place the dumplings upright on a greased baking tray. Brush with milk and sprinkle with caster sugar. Bake for 20-25 minutes until crisp and golden on the outside and just tender in the centre when tested with a skewer. Serve at once with single cream.

# 204 | Plum and Almond Crisp

**Preparation time**
10 minutes, plus 1 hour to cool

**Cooking time**
35-40 minutes

**Oven temperature**
180C, 350F, gas 4

**Serves 4**

**Calories**
325 per portion

**You will need**
50 g/2 oz butter
100 g/4 oz soft white
  breadcrumbs
50 g/2 oz soft brown sugar
50 g/2 oz flaked almonds
½ teaspoon ground cinnamon
500 g/1 lb plums, stoned and
  lightly poached
whipping or double cream,
  whipped, to serve

Melt the butter in a pan. Stir in the breadcrumbs, sugar, almonds and cinnamon. Place the plums in a 900 ml/1½ pint pie dish, then sprinkle the breadcrumb mixture over the top. Bake for 30-35 minutes. Serve cold with the whipped cream.

## Cook's Tip

*Roll each plum briefly between your palms to loosen the stone from the flesh, before cutting in half.*

## Cook's Tip

*This is a very versatile recipe with many variations. The plums can be replaced by lightly poached apples or rhubarb, and finely chopped walnuts or Brazil nuts instead of flaked almonds.*

# 205 | Almond and Apricot Puddings

**Preparation time**
15 minutes

**Cooking time**
40 minutes

**Serves 4**

**Calories**
279 per portion

**You will need**
4 tablespoons apricot jam
50 g/2 oz butter
1 tablespoon caster sugar
100 g/4 oz ground almonds
few drops almond essence
2 eggs, separated

Lightly grease four ramekin dishes with butter. Place a tablespoon of jam in each. Cream the butter and sugar until light and fluffy. Add the ground almonds, almond essence and egg yolks and mix together. Whisk the egg whites until they are stiff, then gently fold them into the almond mixture.

Divide the mixture between the four ramekin dishes and cover each one with greased foil, making a pleat across the centre. Tie with string. Place the dishes in a heavy pan and pour in enough boiling water to come half-way up the sides of the dishes. Cover the pan and simmer for 30-40 minutes, topping up with hot water if necessary. To serve, remove the string and foil and turn the puddings out on to warmed plates. Serve with whipped cream if wished.

# 206 | Almond and Fig Baked Apples

**Preparation time**
15 minutes

**Cooking time**
30-35 minutes

**Oven temperature**
180C, 350F, gas 4

**Serves 6**

**Calories**
326 per portion

**You will need**
6 Bramley cooking apples, cored
50 g/2 oz butter
400 g/14 oz dried figs, chopped
6 tablespoons ground almonds
3 tablespoons sherry

Make a circular cut around the waist of each apple and place in a roasting tin. Melt half the butter in a small pan and add the figs, half the almonds and the sherry. Stir over a high heat for 5 minutes. Fill the apples with this mixture and top each one with a little of the remaining butter. Bake for 25-30 minutes, depending on the size of the apples. Serve with cream or custard.

## Cook's Tip

**To make hazelnut and raspberry puddings, replace the apricot jam with raspberry jam and the ground almonds with freshly ground hazelnuts. Omit the almond essence.**

## Cook's Tip

**There are endless stuffings for baked apples. Keep the filling tasty but reasonably dry then use honey, golden syrup, treacle or maple syrup to pour over the apples during cooking. Baste regularly during the cooking time.**

# 207 | Pineapple Pudding

**Preparation time**
15 minutes

**Cooking time**
1½-2 hours

**Serves 4**

**Calories**
553 per portion

**You will need**
1 (439 g/15½ oz) can pineapple
　slices, drained
15 g/½ oz angelica
100 g/4 oz butter or margarine
100 g/4 oz caster sugar
grated rind and juice of 1 lemon
2 eggs
150 g/5 oz self-raising flour, sifted

Grease a 900 ml/1½ pint pudding basin and arrange the pineapple slices around the base and sides. Place a piece of angelica in the centre of each. Cream the butter or margarine, sugar and lemon rind together until light and fluffy. Add the eggs, one at a time, adding a little flour with the second egg. Beat thoroughly, then fold in the remaining flour with the lemon juice.

Turn the mixture into the prepared basin. Cover with greased foil, making a pleat across the centre to allow the pudding to rise. Steam for 1½-2 hours. Turn out on to a warmed serving dish. Serve with cream or custard.

# 208 | Baked Stuffed Peaches

**Preparation time**
15 minutes

**Cooking time**
15-20 minutes

**Oven temperature**
180C, 350F, gas 4

**Serves 4**

**Calories**
285 per portion

**You will need**
50 g/2 oz sponge cake, crumbled
75 g/3 oz ground almonds
grated rind and juice of 1 medium
　orange
4 large ripe peaches or nectarines
2 tablespoons caster sugar
25 g/1 oz butter
150 ml/¼ pint sweet white wine

Mix the sponge cake, ground almonds, orange rind and juice together to a paste. Halve and stone the peaches and pipe or spoon some almond mixture on top of each peach half. Place in a single layer, in a greased ovenproof dish, sprinkle with the sugar and dot with the butter. Pour the wine into the dish and bake for 15-20 minutes. Serve at once.

## Cook's Tip

**Don't confine yourself to using canned pineapple slices for this steamed pudding. A can of either apricots, peaches, plums or pears could be used instead.**

## Cook's Tip

**For an attractive lemon or orange garnish, run a potato peeler or canelle knife down the fruit from top to bottom several times before slicing, to give a floral effect.**

# 209 | *Multi-coloured Marble Cake*

**Preparation time**
30 minutes

**Cooking time**
50-60 minutes

**Oven temperature**
180C, 350F, gas 4

**Serves 6**

**Calories**
457 per portion

**You will need**
175 g/6 oz butter
175 g/6 oz caster sugar
3 eggs, beaten
175 g/6 oz self-raising flour, sifted
grated rind and juice of 1 lemon
grated rind and juice of 1 orange
grated rind and juice of 1 lime
few drops yellow food colouring
few drops orange food colouring
few drops green food colouring

Grease and flour a 20 cm/8 in loose-bottomed cake tin. Cream the butter and sugar until light and fluffy. Gradually add the eggs, beating well between each addition, then fold in the flour.

Divide the mixture equally between three bowls. To the first add the rind and juice of a lemon with a few drops of yellow food colouring; to the second, add the orange rind and juice and orange food colouring; to the third add the lime rind and juice and green food colouring. Place spoonfuls of each coloured mixture in the prepared tin, keeping each colour apart. Bake for 50-60 minutes until risen and springy to the touch. Turn out and leave to cool on a wire rack.

## Cook's Tip

*Divide the cake mixture as above and choose the three flavours and colours from the following; peppermint essence/green colouring, chocolate essence/1 tablespoon cocoa powder blended with 2 tablespoons*
*hot water/vanilla essence/no colouring added.*

# 210 | *Apricot and Almond Sponge Pudding*

**Preparation time**
15 minutes

**Cooking time**
1¾-2 hours

**Serves 6**

**Calories**
327 per portion

**You will need**
75 g/3 oz butter or margarine, softened
100 g/4 oz caster sugar
2 eggs, beaten
few drops almond essence
100 g/4 oz self-raising flour, sifted
50 g/2 oz ground almonds
a little milk (if necessary)
1 (425 g/15 oz) can apricot halves, drained
6 whole blanched almonds

Grease a 1.2 litre/2 pint pudding basin. Cream the butter and sugar until light and fluffy, then beat in the eggs and almond essence. Fold in the flour and ground almonds, and moisten with milk, if necessary, to give a dropping consistency.

Place six apricot halves, cut side up, with an almond in the centre of each, in a single layer in the prepared basin. Roughly chop the remaining apricots and fold into the sponge mixture. Spoon into the basin and cover with greased foil, making a pleat across the centre to allow the pudding to rise. Steam for 1¾-2 hours until firm to the touch. Turn out on to a serving plate and serve with custard or cream.

## Cook's Tip

*Mark fats such as butter, hard margarine and lard into 25 g/ 1 oz portions before use to eliminate the need to weigh them while you are preparing a dish.*

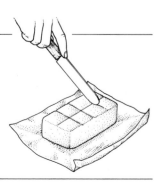

# 211 | Apple and Date Pudding

**Preparation time**
15 minutes

**Cooking time**
1½-2 hours

**Serves 6**

**Calories**
271 per portion

**You will need**
100 g/4 oz self-raising flour
50 g/2 oz fresh white
 breadcrumbs
pinch of salt
75 g/3 oz shredded suet
25 g/1 oz caster sugar
100 g/4 oz apple, peeled and finely
 chopped
100 g/4 oz dates, chopped
grated rind of 1 lemon
about 150 ml/¼ pint milk

Mix together the flour, breadcrumbs, salt, suet and sugar. Stir in the apple, dates and lemon rind. Make a well in the centre and add enough milk to give a soft dropping consistency. Transfer to a greased 900 ml/1½ pint pudding basin, cover with greased foil making a pleat across the centre to allow the pudding to rise, and tie up with string.

Place the basin in a steamer or large pan half-filled with boiling water. Cover and cook for 1½-2 hours, topping up the water as necessary. Remove the foil and turn the pudding out on to a plate. Serve with custard.

# 212 | Spotted Dick

**Preparation time**
15 minutes, plus 15
minutes to make the
crème anglaise

**Cooking time**
2 hours

**Serves 4-6**

**Calories**
338 per portion

**You will need**
100 g/4 oz self-raising flour
100 g/4 oz shredded suet
50 g/2 oz sugar
pinch of salt
100 g/4 oz fresh white
 breadcrumbs
150 g/5 oz currants
85-120 ml/3-4 fl oz water

For the crème anglaise
6 egg yolks
120 g/4½ oz vanilla sugar
500 ml/18 fl oz milk

Grease a 900 ml/1½ pint pudding basin. Mix all the ingredients together to form a soft dough. Turn out on to a floured board and knead gently into a ball. Place the dough in the prepared basin, pushing it gently to fit. Cover with greased foil, making a pleat across the centre to allow the pudding to rise. Tie with string.

Place the basin in a large pan and add enough boiling water to come half-way up the side. Cover the pan and steam over a low heat for 2 hours, topping up with hot water if necessary. Turn out on to a warmed serving dish and serve with crème anglaise.

To make the sauce, whisk the egg yolks and sugar until creamy. Heat the milk to simmering point, then pour over the egg yolk mixture. Return to the rinsed pan and heat gently, stirring constantly until the sauce coats the back of a spoon. (It will curdle if boiled.) Pour into a clean serving jug.

## Cook's Tip

*Place the pudding basin on a trivet or inverted saucer in the pan when making a steamed pudding.*

## Cook's Tip

*Crème anglaise will keep in the refrigerator for 2-3 days. It can be used with a number of dishes (including recipe 117).*

# 213 | Rhubarb and Apple Cobbler

**Preparation time**
20 minutes

**Cooking time**
30 minutes

**Oven temperature**
200C, 400F, gas 6

**Serves 4**

**Calories**
415 per portion

**You will need**
500 g/1 lb rhubarb, chopped
500 g/1 lb cooking apples, peeled,
    cored and sliced
100 g/4 oz caster sugar
1 teaspoon ground cinnamon
175 g/6 oz self-raising flour
50 g/2 oz butter or margarine
about 120 ml/4 fl oz milk

Place the rhubarb and apples in a pan with just enough water to cover the bottom of the pan. Add half the sugar and simmer for about 15 minutes until tender. Stir in the cinnamon and transfer to an ovenproof dish.

Sift the flour into a bowl and rub in the fat until the mixture resembles breadcrumbs. Add the remaining sugar, then stir in enough milk, a little at a time, to give a fairly soft dough. Turn on to a lightly floured board and pat out to a 1 cm/½ in thickness. Cut into 3.5 cm/1½ in rounds, using a biscuit cutter, and arrange over the fruit. Brush with milk and bake for 15 minutes, or until the topping is golden.

# 214 | Rice and Raisin Pudding

**Preparation time**
10 minutes

**Cooking time**
2 hours

**Oven temperature**
150C, 300F, gas 2

**Serves 4**

**Calories**
259 per portion

**You will need**
600 ml/1 pt milk
50 g/2 oz short-grain rice, rinsed
    under cold water
15 g/½ oz butter
25 g/1 oz vanilla sugar
150 ml/¼ pint double cream,
    whipped
75 g/3 oz raisins
raspberry jam to decorate

Lightly grease a 900 ml/1½ pint ovenproof dish. Bring the milk to the boil in a pan and stir in the rice. Pour into the prepared dish, dot with butter and sprinkle with the vanilla sugar. Bake for 2 hours until set. Half-way through the cooking time, stir the pudding to separate the grains. Leave to cool a little. Stir in the cream and raisins and serve topped with a swirl of raspberry jam.

## Cook's Tip

*Substitute a spoonful of
natural yogurt for some of the
milk when making the scones.*

## Cook's Tip

*Use short-grain rice for
puddings and sweet dishes
and long-grain for savoury
ones. Short grain is best for
rice puddings such as this
because it is absorbent and
becomes deliciously creamy
during cooking.*

# 215 | Treacle Tart

**Preparation time**
15 minutes, plus 15
minutes to chill

**Cooking time**
30-35 minutes

**Oven temperature**
200C, 400F, gas 6

**Serves 4-6**

**Calories**
347 per portion

**You will need**
175 g/6 oz plain flour
75 g/3 oz butter or margarine
1-2 tablespoons iced water

**For the filling**
225 g/8 oz golden syrup
75 g/3 oz fresh white
  breadcrumbs
grated rind of ½ lemon

Sift the flour into a bowl. Rub in the butter or margarine until the mixture resembles fine breadcrumbs. Add the water gradually and mix to a firm dough. Turn out on to a floured surface and knead lightly. Roll out thinly to a 23 cm/9 inch circle. Use to line an 18 cm/7 inch flan ring placed on a baking tray. Chill the flan and pastry trimmings for 15 minutes.

Mix the syrup, breadcrumbs and lemon rind together and spread over the pastry. Roll out the trimmings, cut into long narrow strips and make a lattice pattern over the filling. Bake for 30-35 minutes. Serve warm with cream.

# 216 | Baked Custard Tart

**Preparation time**
10 minutes, plus 30
minutes to chill

**Cooking time**
1 hour 10 minutes

**Oven temperature**
200C, 400F, gas 6
(pastry case) then
160C, 325F, gas 3
(custard tart)

**Serves 6**

**Calories**
300 per portion

**You will need**
1 quantity shortcrust pastry (recipe
  58)
4 eggs
25 g/1 oz caster sugar
½ teaspoon vanilla essence
450 ml/¾ pint milk
grated nutmeg

Make the pastry as instructed in recipe 58. Use it to line a 20 cm/8 in flan ring or tin. Bake blind for 15-20 minutes. Remove the beans and paper and cook for a further 5 minutes.

Lightly whisk the eggs with the sugar and vanilla essence in a bowl. Heat the milk until lukewarm and whisk in the eggs. Strain into the pastry case and sprinkle with nutmeg. Bake for 45-50 minutes, until set and lightly browned. Serve warm or cold.

## Cook's Tip

*Make a batch of pastry flan cases to be baked blind and frozen all on the same day. They are an invaluable standby and, if you use a plain shortcrust pastry, you can fill with sweet or savoury fillings as you need them.*

## Cook's Tip

*Check that the surface of the baked custard is not browning too much during the cooking period. You may need to cover it with greased butter papers or foil if it is.*

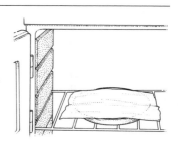

## 217 | Spiced Apple Pie

**Preparation time**
20 minutes

**Cooking time**
30-40 minutes

**Oven temperature**
200C, 400F, gas 6

**Serves 4-6**

**Calories**
350 per portion

**You will need**
750 g/1½ lb cooking apples,
   peeled, cored and thinly sliced
75 g/3 oz soft brown sugar
1 teaspoon mixed spice
4 cloves

For the shortcrust pstry
175 g/6 oz plain flour
75 g/3 oz butter or margarine
1-2 tablespoons iced water
water and caster sugar, to glaze

For the crème à la vanille
2 egg yolks
1 teaspoon cornflour
25 g/1 oz caster sugar
300 ml/½ pint milk
½ teaspoon vanilla essence

Layer the apples with the sugar and spices in a 900 ml/1½ pint pie dish. Make the shortcrust pastry as in recipe 58. Roll it out to a circle about 5 cm/2 in larger than the dish. Cut a strip all round and use to cover the dampened rim of the dish; brush with water. Place the pastry over the apples, sealing the edges. Trim and flute the edges; make a hole in the centre. Brush with water, sprinkle with sugar and bake for 30-40 minutes.

To make the crème à la vanille, cream the egg yolks with the cornflour and sugar. Bring the milk to the boil, pour on to the egg yolk mixture and stir well. Return to the pan and heat gently, stirring until the mixture is thick enough to coat the back of a spoon. Add the vanilla essence, then strain. Serve hot or cold with the pie.

## Cook's Tip

**Place the utensils – rolling pin, board, cutters – in the refrigerator or freezer for a short time before making pastry. The cooler the conditions, the better the finished pastry will be.**

## 218 | Apple Plate Pie

**Preparation time**
25 minutes

**Cooking time**
35 minutes

**Oven temperature**
200C, 400F, gas 6

**Serves 6**

**Calories**
333 per portion

**You will need**

For the shortcrust pastry
175 g/6 oz plain flour
pinch of salt
40 g/1½ oz hard margarine, diced
40 g/1½ oz lard, diced
4 tablespoons milk

For the filling
25 g/1 oz unsalted butter
1 teaspoon ground semolina
250 g/9 oz cooking apples, peeled,
   cored and chopped
2 Cox's Orange Pippin apples,
   peeled, cored and chopped
65 g/2½ oz sugar
milk and caster sugar to glaze

Make the shortcrust pastry as instructed in recipe 58. Roll out two-thirds of it on a floured surface and use it to line a 20 cm/8 in pie plate or tin. Prick with a fork. Melt half the butter and brush over the pastry base, covering it completely. Sprinkle with the semolina.

Stew the cooking apples in the remaining butter. Mash with a fork, mix with the eating apples and sugar and pour on to the pastry base. Roll out the remaining pastry to a 20 cm/8 in circle. Brush the edges with water and place over the apple, sealing the edges. Trim and crimp the edges and make a hole in the centre. Brush with milk and sprinkle with sugar. Bake for 35 minutes.

## Cook's Tip

**If you have time, put pastry in the refrigerator for 30 minutes to allow it to relax. it also helps prevent shrinkage occurring during cooking.**

# 219 | Pecan Pie

**Preparation time**
15 minutes, plus 20-30 minutes to chill

**Cooking time**
1 hour-1 hour 10 minutes

**Oven temperature**
200C, 400F, gas 6 then 220C, 425F, gas 7 (pastry case) then 180C, 350F, gas 4 (pie)

**Serves 6-8**

**Calories**
320 per portion

**You will need**
25 g/1 oz butter
100 g/4 oz caster sugar
175 g/6 oz maple or golden syrup
4 large eggs
1 teaspoon vanilla essence
50 g/2 oz pecan nuts or walnuts, chopped

**For the rich shortcrust pastry**
175 g/6 oz plain flour
100 g/4 oz butter
1 egg yolk
2-3 tablespoons cold water

Make the rich shortcrust pastry as instructed in recipe 55 omitting the sugar. Use it to line a 20 cm/8 in fluted flan ring or pie dish. If possible, chill for 20-30 minutes. Bake blind (see Cook's Tip 52) on the top shelf for 15-20 minutes. Remove the beans and paper and cook for a further 5 minutes. Cool and remove the flan ring, if used.

Cream the butter and sugar until light and fluffy. Gradually beat in the syrup, then the eggs, one at a time, and vanilla essence. Pour into the pastry case and sprinkle over the nuts. Bake for 10 minutes, then lower the temperature and cook for 30-35 minutes. Serve cool.

# 220 | Mince Pies

**Preparation time**
20 minutes, plus 15 minutes to chill

**Cooking time**
15-20 minutes

**Oven temperature**
200C, 400F, gas 6

**Makes 10-12**

**Calories**
206 per portion

**You will need**
4-5 tablespoons mincemeat
1 tablespoon brandy
sifted icing sugar to serve

**For the rich shortcrust pastry**
225 g/8 oz plain flour
150 g/5 oz butter
1 tablespoon caster sugar
1 egg yolk
1-2 tablespoons cold water
milk to glaze

Make the rich shortcrust pastry as instructed in recipe 55. Chill for 15 minutes. Roll out half the pastry fairly thinly on a floured surface and cut out ten to twelve rounds, using a 6 cm/2½ in fluted cutter. Roll out the other half of the pastry a little thinner than the first, cut out ten to twelve 7.5 cm.3 in rounds and use to line ten to twelve patty tins.

Mix the mincemeat with the brandy and divide between the patty tins. Dampen the edges of the pastry, place the smaller rounds on top and press the edges together. Make a hole in the centre of each and brush with milk. Bake for 15-20 minutes until golden. Sprinkle with icing sugar and serve warm.

## Cook's Tip

*The choice of fat for pastry-making depends on personal preference. Try using either half quantities of lard and margarine, or half a quantity of lard and a quarter each of margarine and butter.*

## Cook's Tip

*To make brandy butter, cream 100 g/4 oz butter with 75 g/3oz sieved icing sugar. Slowly beat in about 2 tablespoons brandy, blending well, then add a further 25 g/1 oz sugar. Serve chilled.*

# Gâteaux and Exotic Desserts

In this chapter you will find more than a bakers dozen of delicious recipes for gâteaux and exotic desserts. Many use rich and tempting ingredients and take a little time and patience to prepare so use these as the mainstay of your repetoire for entertaining with the special occasion recipes that follow.

## 221 | Peach Gâteau

**Preparation time**
40 minutes

**Cooking time**
35-40 minutes

**Oven temperature**
180C, 350F, gas 4

**Serves 8**

**Calories**
278 per portion

**You will need**
3 eggs separated
100 g/4 oz caster sugar
finely grated rind and juice of ½ lemon
50 g/2 oz semolina
25 g/1 oz ground almonds

**To serve**
4 ripe peaches, stoned and thinly sliced
300 ml/½ pint double cream, whipped
4 tablespoons apricot jam
2 teaspoons lemon juice
50 g/2 oz ground hazelnuts, toasted

Grease and line a deep 20 cm/8 in cake tin. Place the egg yolks, sugar, lemon rind and juice in a bowl and whisk until thick. Stir in the semolina and ground almonds. Whisk the egg whites until stiff, then fold in. Turn the mixture into the tin. Bake for 35-40 minutes until the cake is springy to the touch. Turn out on to a wire rack, turn the cake the right way up and leave to cool.

Split the cake in half. Fold half the peach slices into three-quarters of the cream and sandwich the layers together. Put the jam and lemon juice in a small pan and heat gently, stirring until the jam has melted. Sieve and reheat. Arrange the remaining peach slices on top of the cake. Brush the peaches and the sides of the cake with the warm glaze. Press the hazelnuts around the sides, then decorate with the remaining cream. Serve chilled.

## Cook's Tip

*To test a cake is 'springy to the touch', gently press it in the centre. If the cake is cooked the indentation will disappear as the cake springs back into shape.*

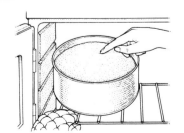

## 222 | Pear and Ginger Gâteau

**Preparation time**
40-45 minutes

**Cooking time**
30-40 minutes

**Oven temperature**
180C, 350F, gas 4

**Serves 6**

**Calories**
447 per portion

**You will need**
3 eggs
90 g/3½ oz caster sugar
90 g/3½ oz plain flour, sifted
1 (400 g/14 oz) can pear quarters
600 ml/1 pint double or whipping cream, whipped
50 g/2 oz crystallised ginger
small cone-shaped brandy snaps

Grease and line a 19 cm/7½ in cake tin. Whisk the eggs and sugar in a bowl over a pan of hot water until the mixture is thick and creamy. Remove from the heat and beat until cool. Fold in the flour. Pour the mixture into the tin and bake for 30 minutes, until golden and springy to the touch. Turn out on to a wire rack and cool.

Slice the sponge in half. Reserve eight pear quarters and chop the rest. Reserve some ginger for decoration, chop the remainder and mix with the pears and 3-4 tablespoons of the cream. Sandwich the sponge with the ginger cream mixture. Coat the outside of the sponge with most of the cream. Pipe cream into the brandy snaps. Arrange them with the reserved pear quarters on top of the sponge. Crush enough brandy snaps to coat the sides of the gâteau. Press on the pieces with a palette knife. Pipe around the top of the sponge with rosettes of cream and decorate with the reserved pieces of ginger.

## Cook's Tip

*This type of sponge is best eaten as fresh as possible so do not store it for more than one night. You can fill and coat it with cream some time before serving, but do not decorate it until a short time before.*

## 223 | Black Forest Gâteau

**Preparation time**
50 minutes, plus
overnight soaking

**Cooking time**
30-40 minutes

**Oven temperature**
190C, 375F, gas 5

**Serves 8-10**

**Calories**
480 per portion

**You will need**
6 eggs
175 g/6 oz caster sugar
175 g/6 oz plain flour, sifted
50 g/2 oz cocoa powder, sifted
8 tablespoons Kirsch
2 (450 g/15 oz) cans black
   cherries, drained, stoned and
   halved, with 150 ml/¼ pint juice
   reserved
600 ml/1 pint double cream,
   whipped
2 teaspoons arrowroot
75 g/3 oz plain dark chocolate

Grease and flour two 20 cm/8 in round cake tins. Whisk the eggs and sugar over simmering water until pale and thick. Remove from the heat. Continue to whisk until the mixture is cool. Gently fold in the flour and cocoa.

Divide the mixture between the two tins and bake for 30-40 minutes or until firm and spongy. Cool in the tins, then turn out on to a wire rack. Split the cakes in half when cold. Sprinkle 2 tablespoons of Kirsch and 4 tablespoons of cherry juice on each layer. Soak overnight.

Sandwich a third of the cream and half the black cherries between each layer of cake. Spread half the remaining cream around the sides of the cake. Arrange the remaining cherries on top. Mix the arrowroot with a little water and stir into the reserved cherry juice. Bring the juice to the boil, stirring until it thickens. Pour over the cherries. Decorate with cream and grated chocolate.

## Cook's Tip

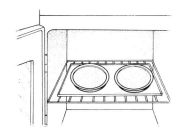

**When baking two cakes at the same time, do not let the tins touch the sides of the oven or they will burn. If, to avoid this, they have to be baked on different shelves in the oven, change them over half way through the cooking time.**

## 224 | Strawberry Gâteau

**Preparation time**
45 minutes, plus 1½
hours to set

**Cooking time**
20 minutes

**Oven temperature**
180C, 350F, gas 4

**Serves 4-6**

**Calories**
526 per portion

**You will need**
50 g/2 oz soft margarine
50 g/2 oz self-raising flour, sifted
½ teaspoon baking powder
1 egg
150 g/5 oz caster sugar
225 g/8 oz strawberries
350 g/12 oz curd cheese
15 g/½ oz gelatine
3 tablespoons hot water
1 teaspoon vanilla essence
375 ml/13 fl oz double or whipping
   cream, whipped
3 egg whites
1 tablespoon icing sugar

Grease and line an 18 cm/7 in sandwich tin. Beat the margarine, flour, baking powder, egg and 50 g/2 oz of the sugar in a bowl until light. Turn into the tin and bake for 20 minutes. Turn out on to a wire rack to cool.

Mix the cheese with the remaining sugar. Dissolve the gelatine in the hot water over a pan of simmering water and add to the cheese with the vanilla essence. Fold in 200 ml/⅓ pint of the cream. Whisk the egg whites and fold into the cheese mixture.

Lightly grease the sides of a 17 cm/6½ in loose-bottomed cake tin. Cut the sponge in half and place one half in the tin. Reserve six strawberries and slice the rest on to the sponge base. Pour in the cheesecake mixture and top with the reserved sponge. Chill. Decorate with icing sugar the remaining cream and strawberries.

## Cook's Tip

**There are many types of soft cheese available and most are suitable for cheesecakes. Curd cheese, cottage cheese and low-fat soft cheese are all good for keeping the calories down. If full-fat soft cheese is used, keep the fat content down by replacing half the cream in the recipe with natural yogurt.**

# 225 | *Praline and Peach Gâteau*

**Preparation time**
30-40 minutes

**Cooking time**
30-35 minutes

**Oven temperature**
190C, 375F, gas 5

**Serves 6**

**Calories**
526 per portion

**You will need**
3 eggs
150 g/5 oz caster sugar
grated rind of 1 lemon
75 g/3 oz plain flour, sifted

For the praline
50 g/2 oz whole almonds
50 g/2 oz caster sugar

To finish
300 ml/½ pint double cream,
    whipped
4 tablespoons apricot jam
2 teaspoons water
2 peaches, stoned and sliced

Place the eggs, sugar and lemon rind in a bowl and whisk until thick and mousse-like. Fold in the flour, then turn into a greased, lined and floured deep 20 cm/8 in cake tin. Bake for 30-35 minutes, until the cake springs back when lightly pressed. Turn out on to a wire rack to cool.

Make the praline as instructed in recipe 22 and fold half of it into two-thirds of the cream. Split the cake in half and sandwich together with the praline cream. Heat the jam with the water; sieve, reheat and use three-quarters to glaze the sides of the cake. Press the remaining praline around the sides. Arrange the peaches, overlapping, in a circle on top, leaving a border around the edge. Reheat the remaining glaze and brush over the peaches. Pipe with the remaining cream to decorate.

## Cook's Tip

*If using an electric whisk to whip cream or whisk egg whites, switch it off from time to time during the whisking process to scrape the mixture from the sides of the bowl.*

# 226 | *Gâteau Regent*

**Preparation time**
50 minutes

**Cooking time**
25 minutes

**Oven temperature**
190C, 375F, gas 5

**Serves 6-8**

**Calories**
286 per portion

**You will need**
4 eggs
100 g/4 oz caster sugar
75 g/3 oz flour
25 g/1 oz cocoa powder
25 g/1 oz butter melted

To finish
250 g/9 oz chestnuts, peeled
1 egg, plus 1 egg yolk
75 g/3 oz caster sugar
15 g/½ oz flour
250 ml/8 fl oz milk
200 g/7 oz apricot jam
1 tablespoon water
8 apricot halves, sliced

Grease a 20 cm/8 in cake tin. Whisk the eggs and sugar over a pan of simmering water until trebled in volume. Sift the flour with the cocoa and fold half into the eggs. Stir in the butter and fold in the remaining flour and cocoa. Pour the mixture into the prepared tin. Bake for 25 minutes, then cool on a wire rack.

Poach all but eight of the chestnuts for 20 minutes, until tender. Purée them in a liquidiser or rub through a sieve. Beat the egg, egg yolk, sugar and flour together. Heat the milk and pour it into the egg mixture, stirring well. Cook the sauce gently until thickened, stirring, then add to the chestnut purée and mix well. Cut the sponge in three and sandwich together with the chestnut filling. Heat the apricot jam and water, then sieve it and use to glaze the gâteau. Decorate with chestnuts and apricot slices.

## Cook's Tip

*Redcurrant jelly is a fast alternative to sieved apricot jam in any recipe because it requires no sieving. Alternatively, make a quantity of sieved apricot jam and keep the surplus stored in a screw-topped jar.*

# 227 | Gâteau Ambassadrice

**Preparation time**
45-50 minutes

**Cooking time**
40-50 minutes

**Oven temperature**
180C, 350F, gas 4

**Serves 6-8**

**Calories**
374 per portion

**You will need**
90 g/3½ oz plain flour
50 g/2 oz cornflour
few drops vanilla essence
4 eggs, separated
120 g/4½ oz caster sugar

For the filling and coating
15 g/½ oz plain flour
20 g/¾ oz caster sugar
2 egg yolks
few drops vanilla essence
150 ml/¼ pint milk
75 g/3 oz glacé fruits, chopped
300 ml/½ pint whipped cream

Grease and line a 17 cm/6½ in charlotte or cake tin. Sift the flours and mix with the egg yolks, sugar and vanilla essence. Whisk the egg whites until stiff and fold into the mixture. Pour into the prepared tin and bake for 40-50 minutes, until golden brown. Cool on a wire rack.

For the filling, mix the flour, sugar, egg yolks and vanilla essence. Heat the milk and pour on to the mixture. Return to the pan, boil, and cook for a few minutes. Pour into a bowl and cool. Fold in the glacé fruit, reserving a few pieces with 3-4 tablespoons of cream. Chill.

Slice 1 cm/½ in off the sponge and scoop out the centre of the other piece. Return to the tin and fill with the prepared cream. Cover with the slice of sponge and turn out on to a plate (the slice forms the base). Decorate with the remaining cream and glacé fruit.

# 228 | Charlotte Malakoff

**Preparation time**
20-30 minutes, plus 2-3 hours to chill

**Serves 6-8**

**Calories**
605 per portion

**You will need**
20-24 sponge finger biscuits
175 g/6 oz unsalted butter
175 g/6 oz caster sugar
1 teaspoon vanilla sugar or a few drops vanilla essence
225 g/8 oz ground almonds
450 ml/¾ pint double cream, whipped
2-3 tablespoons rum or Kirsch
lemon twist to decorate

Line the base of a 15 cm/6 in charlotte mould with a circle of greaseproof paper. Cut a small piece off the end of each biscuit and arrange them, cut end down, sugar side out, around the inside of the tin, shaping them if necessary so that there are no gaps.

Cream the butter and sugar with the vanilla sugar or essence until light and fluffy. Stir in the ground almonds and fold in three-quarters of the cream with the rum or Kirsch. Spoon the mixture into the prepared tin, taking care that it is even on the base. Smooth the top. Chill for at least 2-3 hours.

Trim the sponge biscuits level with the filling and unmould the charlotte on to a serving dish. Whip the remaining cream until stiff. Decorate with the lemon twist and small rosettes of cream. Chill until required.

## Cook's Tip

**To prevent a wire rack indenting the top of a cake with the outline of the mesh, place a clean tea-towel over the rack before turning the cake out.**

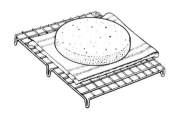

## Cook's Tip

**For a less rich charlotte, use 100 g/4 oz ground almonds and 100 g/4 oz Madeira cake crumbs instead of 225 g/8 oz ground almonds by themselves.**

# 229 | *Zucotto*

**Preparation time**
15-20 minutes, plus
2½-3½ hours to cool
and to chill

**Cooking time**
35-40 minutes

**Oven temperature**
180C, 350F, gas 4

**Serves 6-8**

**Calories**
370 per portion

**You will need**
3 large eggs
75 g/3 oz caster sugar
50 g/2 oz plain flour
1 tablespoon cocoa powder
1 tablespoon oil

For the filling
4 tablespoons brandy
450 ml/¾ pint double cream
40 g/1½ oz icing sugar, sifted
50 g/2 oz plain chocolate, chopped
25 g/1 oz almonds, chopped and
    toasted
175 g/6 oz cherries, stoned
2 tablespoons Kirsch
1 tablespoon cocoa powder, sifted

Place the eggs and sugar in a bowl and whisk over a pan of hot water until thick. Sift the flour and cocoa and fold in, then fold in the oil. Spoon into a greased 20 cm/8 in cake tin. Bake for 35-40 minutes. Turn on to a wire rack.

Cut the sponge in half and line a 1.2 litre/2 pint basin with one layer. Sprinkle with brandy. Whip the cream to soft peaks. Fold in 25 g/1 oz of the icing sugar, the chocolate, almonds, cherries and Kirsch. Spoon into the basin and top with the remaining sponge. Cover with a plate and chill.

Turn out on to a plate, sprinkle with the remaining icing sugar and cocoa powder to make a pattern.

## Cook's Tip

*When storing, chocolate requires a cool, dry shelf to keep it in good condition. Leave in its foil wrapper as this will protect it better than re-wrapping it in cling film.*

# 230 | *Baclava*

**Preparation time**
45 minutes, plus at
least 6 hours to soak

**Cooking time**
55 minutes

**Oven temperature**
220C, 425F, gas 7
then 190C, 375F, gas 5

**Makes 8-12
pieces**

**Calories**
491 per serving

**You will need**
75 g/3 oz almonds
75 g/3 oz walnuts
40 g/1½ oz pistachio nuts
1 tablespoon pine kernels
1 teaspoon cinnamon
65 g/2½ oz unsalted butter
65 g/2½ oz sugar
50 ml/2 fl oz water
1½ (212 g/7½ oz) packet frozen
    puff pastry, defrosted

For the syrup
100 g/4 oz sugar
100 g/4 oz honey
120 ml/4 fl oz water
juice of ½ lemon

Finely chop the almonds, walnuts, pistachios and pine kernels by hand and mix with the cinnamon. Place the butter, sugar and water in a pan and boil for 3 minutes. Line a 20 × 30 cm/8 × 12 in baking tin with foil. Divide the pastry into four equal pieces and roll each one into a rectangle 20 × 30 cm/8 × 12 in. Line the base of the tin with one sheet of pastry, then brush with the butter and sugar mixture. Cover with a third of the nuts. Repeat the layers, ending with a sheet of pastry. Bake for 15 minutes. Reduce the temperature and bake for a further 40 minutes.

Meanwhile, make the syrup. Place the sugar, honey, water and lemon juice in a pan. Boil until the sugar dissolves. Remove the baclava from the oven and cut it into 8-12 equal squares. Pour over the syrup and leave to soak in the tin for at least 6 hours.

## Cook's Tip

*Filo pastry can be used too. Cut the filo sheets to fit the tin. Place 2 or 3 sheets in the base, brushing each sheet with melted mixture. Layer as above, ending with 3 layers of buttered pastry. Bake at 180C, 350F, gas 4 for 30 minutes.*

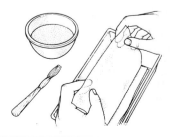

# 231 | Hungarian Crêpe Cake

**Preparation time**
35 minutes

**Cooking time**
20 minutes

**Oven temperature**
180C, 350F, gas 4

**Serves 6**

**Calories**
342 per portion

**You will need**
12 pancakes (recipe 154)

For the filling
1 kg/2 lb cooking apples, peeled, cored and sliced
50 g/2 oz unsalted butter
75 g/3 oz brown sugar
1 teaspoon ground cinnamon
grated rind of 1 lemon

For the glaze
6 tablespoons apricot jam
2 tablespoons rum
grated rind and juice of 1 lemon
50 g/2 oz flaked almonds

Prepare and cook the pancakes as instructed in recipe 128. To make the filling, fry the apples gently in the butter until they soften and colour. Add the sugar, cinnamon and lemon rind. Place one pancake on a greased baking dish. Cover with a little of the apple, then another pancake. Continue the layering in this way, ending with a pancake.

To make the glaze, combine the jam, rum, lemon rind and juice. Spoon a little glaze on top of the pile of pancakes. Scatter with almonds. Bake for 10 minutes. Serve immediately with whipped cream and the remainder of the apricot glaze.

# 232 | Austrian Cheese-stuffed Pancakes

**Preparation time**
30-35 minutes, including pancakes

**Cooking time**
45-50 minutes

**Oven temperature**
180C, 350F, gas 4

**Serves 5-6**

**Calories**
459 per portion

**You will need**
100 g/4 oz curd or cottage cheese
50 g/2 oz caster sugar
2 egg yolks
25 g/1 oz sultanas
2 teaspoons vanilla sugar or a few drops vanilla essence
100 ml/3½ fl oz double cream, stiffly whipped
10-12 small pancakes (recipe 154)

To serve
150 ml/¼ pint milk
150 ml/¼ pint soured cream
1 egg, beaten
2-3 teaspoons caster sugar
powdered cinnamon

If cottage cheese is used in this recipe, it should first be sieved or beaten until smooth in a liquidiser or food processor. Cream the cheese and sugar together until smooth, then beat in the egg yolks, one at a time. Fold in the sultanas, vanilla sugar or essence and the double cream. Spread a spoonful of the mixture on each pancake. Roll up and cut in half. Arrange the pancakes in a well-buttered deep 15 cm/6 in ovenproof dish.

Beat the milk and soured cream with the egg and sugar. Strain the mixture over the top of the pancakes and cook for 45-50 minutes. Sprinkle with cinnamon and serve hot, cut into wedges.

## Cook's Tip

**An omelette pan can also be used for making pancakes. Unless it has a non-stick surface it should not be washed, but cleaned after each use with salt on a piece of absorbent kitchen paper or a damp cloth.**

## Cook's Tip

**To keep pancakes hot, place a saucer, rounded-side up, on a large plate over a pan of simmering water. As the pancakes are cooked, drape them over the saucer.**

# 233 | Profiteroles au Caramel

**Preparation time**
15 minutes, plus 20 minutes to cool

**Cooking time**
25-30 minutes

**Oven temperature**
200C, 400F, gas 6

**Serves 6**

**Calories**
469 per portion

**You will need**

For the choux pastry
150 ml/¼ pint water
50 g/2 oz butter
65 g/2½ oz plain flour
pinch of salt
2 eggs, lightly beaten

For the filling
250 ml/8 fl oz double cream, lightly whipped

For the caramel sauce
75 g/3 oz granulated sugar
4 tablespoons cold water
150 ml/¼ pint double cream

Make the choux pastry as instructed in recipe 190. Spoon it into a piping bag fitted with a 2.5 cm/1 in plain nozzle and pipe small mounds on greased baking trays. Bake for 15-20 minutes, until risen and golden-brown. Transfer the profiteroles to a wire rack and split each one. Cool, then fill with the cream.

To make the sauce, heat the sugar in a pan over a low heat until dissolved. Increase the heat and cook to a golden-brown caramel. Remove from the heat and carefully add the water. Return to the heat and stir until the caramel dissolves. Cool, then whip into the cream. Arrange the profiteroles on a dish and spoon over the sauce. Serve chilled.

## Cook's Tip

*Make the caramel and pour it over fresh fruit such as pears, oranges or bananas. Serve with vanilla ice cream sprinkled with chopped hazelnuts or walnuts for a quick dessert.*

# 234 | Charlotte Royale

**Preparation time**
20-30 minutes, plus 1½ hours to infuse and to set

**Cooking time**
5-10 minutes

**Serves 5-6**

**Calories**
490 per portion

**You will need**
450 ml/¾ pint milk
1 vanilla pod
5 egg yolks
25 g/1 oz gelatine
2-3 tablespoons hot water
75 g/3 oz caster sugar
3-4 tablespoons Kirsch (optional)
1 packet miniature Swiss rolls
200 ml/⅓ pint double or whipping cream, whipped
3-4 tablespoons double or whipping cream, whipped

Bring the milk to the boil with the vanilla pod, then remove from the heat and leave for 15-20 minutes. Beat the egg yolks with the sugar. Reheat the milk, remove the vanilla pod and pour the milk on to the eggs. Mix well, return to the pan and heat gently, stirring until the mixture coats the back of a spoon. Remove from the heat. Dissolve the gelatine in the hot water over a pan of gently simmering water and add to the custard. Mix well, strain into a large bowl and leave until almost set, stirring occasionally. Stir in the Kirsch, if using, when the mixture is cool.

Slice the Swiss rolls and use to line a 600 ml/1 pint pudding basin; do not leave any spaces. Whip the custard, then carefully fold in the cream. Pour into the prepared mould and leave to set. Turn out and decorate with the whipped cream.

## Cook's Tip

*To test if custard is cooked, take the stirring spoon out of the pan and draw a finger across the back of the spoon; if the custard holds the line without running, it is ready to use.*

# 235 | Gulab Jaman

**Preparation time**
20 minutes, plus
overnight steeping

**Cooking time**
about 12 minutes

**Serves 4**

**Calories**
176 per portion

**You will need**
175 g/6 oz sugar
350 ml/12 fl oz water
2 drops rosewater
40 g/1½ oz low-fat milk powder
20 g/¾ oz self-raising flour
1 teaspoon semolina
15 g/½ oz unsalted butter, melted
4 small green cardamoms, shelled
  and ground
generous pinch of saffron powder
25 g/1 oz milk
oil for deep frying

Place the sugar and water in a pan and bring to the boil slowly, stirring constantly until the sugar has completely dissolved. Boil for 2 minutes. Add the rosewater. Pour the syrup into a serving bowl and leave to cool.

Put the milk powder, flour, semolina, butter, cardamoms and saffron in a mixing bowl. Work in the milk. Knead to a smooth dough and divide into 16 small balls, each about the size of a large hazelnut.

Heat the oil in a saucepan to 190C, 375F and fry the balls gently for 10 minutes until cooked through. Lift out with a slotted spoon and drain on absorbent kitchen paper. Put the balls into the syrup and leave to steep overnight. To serve, spoon the balls and some syrup into individual dishes.

# 236 | Nid d'Abeilles

**Preparation time**
30 minutes, plus 1½
hours to rise and prove

**Cooking time**
30 minutes

**Oven temperature**
200C, 400F, gas 6

**Serves 8**

**Calories**
410 per portion

**You will need**
300 g/11 oz flour
100 g/4 oz butter
120 ml/4 fl oz milk
10 g/¼ oz dried yeast
1 egg, lightly beaten
50 g/2 oz unsalted butter
75 g/3 oz caster sugar
25 g/1 oz honey
25 g/1 oz flaked almonds
1 tablespoon Kirsch
300 g/11 oz crème pâtissière
  (Cook's Tip 245)

Grease a 20 cm/8 in cake tin. Sift the flour and rub in the butter. Heat the milk to body temperature. Dissolve the yeast in the milk. Add the egg and milk to the flour and knead to a smooth dough. Leave the dough to rise in a warm place until it doubles in volume, Knock back the dough. Put it in the prepared tin and leave to prove again until well risen.

Melt the remaining butter over a gentle heat with the sugar and honey, stirring until the sugar dissolves. Spread the mixture over the risen dough and sprinkle the almonds on top. Bake for 30 minutes, covering with greased foil after 20 minutes of the cooking time. Remove from the tin and cool on a wire rack. When the cake is cold, split it in half. Beat the Kirsch into the cold crème pâtissière. Spread the filling and sandwich the cake together.

## Cook's Tip

*If using the dried flower saffron rather than the powdered variety, soak a few strands in a little of the cooking liquor for about 15 minutes then add to the dish with the soaking water.*

## Cook's Tip

*To store crème pâtissière, rub the surface with a lump of butter while still hot to prevent a crust from forming.*

# 237 | *Anjou Plum Pudding*

**Preparation time**
15 minutes

**Cooking time**
30-35 minutes

**Oven temperature**
200C, 400F, gas 6

**Serves 6-8**

**Calories**
322 per portion

**You will need**
175 g/6 oz plain flour
175 g/6 oz butter
75 g/3 oz caster sugar
50 g/2 oz ground almonds
1 egg yolk
1 tablespoon cold water
750 g/1½ lb plums, halved and
    stoned

Sift the flour into a bowl and rub in two-thirds of the butter. Stir in 25 g/1 oz of the sugar and the ground almonds. Mix to a firm dough with the egg yolk and water. Chill until required.

Melt the remaining butter in a 23 cm/9 in round flame-proof dish. Add the remaining sugar and stir well until caramelised. Remove from the heat and arrange the plums, skin side down, on the base of the dish.

Roll out the pastry on a lightly floured surface, into a round just over 23 cm/9 in. Place on top of the plums, pressing down gently and tucking in at the edges. Bake for 30-35 minutes until golden. Cool in the dish for 5 minutes, then turn out on to a large serving dish. Serve at once.

# 238 | *Austrian Curd Cake*

**Preparation time**
20 minutes, plus 2
hours 10 minutes to
chill

**Serves 8**

**Calories**
566 per portion

**You will need**
75 g/3 oz butter
175 g/6 oz digestive biscuits,
    crushed
50 g/2 oz demerara sugar
350 g/12 oz curd cheese
50 g/2 oz caster sugar
3 eggs, separated
grated rind of 1 lemon
15 g/½ oz gelatine
3 tablespoons hot water
450 ml/¾ pint whipping cream,
    whipped

Melt the butter in a pan, add the biscuit crumbs and demerara sugar and mix well. Spread half the mixture over the base of a 20 cm/8 in loose-bottomed cake tin and chill until firm.

Meanwhile, place the cheese in a bowl and beat in the sugar, egg yolks and lemon rind. Dissolve the gelatine in the hot water over a pan of simmering water, then stir into the cheese mixture. Fold two-thirds of the whipped cream into the cheese mixture. Whisk the egg whites until stiff and fold into the mixture. Spoon over the biscuit base and chill for 10 minutes. Spread the remaining crumbs over the top and chill for a further 2 hours. Remove from the tin and decorate with piped cream.

## Cook's Tip

*Make this cake with any plums that are available, from early imported ones right through to the autumn varieties. Vary the look of the pudding by using damsons or greengages.*

## Cook's Tip

*Cream achieves more volume if you add 1 tablespoon of milk to 150 ml/¼ pint double cream before whipping it.*

# 239 | Flemish Baked Apples

**Preparation time**
15-20 minutes

**Cooking time**
20-25 minutes

**Oven temperature**
160C, 325F, gas 3

**Serves 4**

**Calories**
503 per portion

**You will need**
225 g/8 oz plain flour
pinch of salt
100 g/4 oz butter
1 tablespoon caster sugar
3-5 tablespoons iced water
4 large dessert apples, peeled and
cored
4 tablespoons quince or plum jam
beaten egg to glaze

Sift the flour and salt into a bowl. Rub in the butter until the mixture resembles fine breadcrumbs, then stir in the sugar. Add enough water to mix to a smooth, pliable dough. Divide the dough into four pieces and roll each into a square. Fill the centres of the apples with the jam and place on the squares.

Brush the edges of the squares with water and wrap the pastry around the apples. Trim any excess pastry and press the edges firmly to seal. Decorate with pastry leaves cut from the trimmings. Place on a baking sheet and brush with beaten egg. Bake for 20-25 minutes until golden. Serve hot, with cream.

## Cook's Tip

*The flavour of quinces goes particularly well with that of apples. Use them together in pies, pancakes and purées as well as jams, wines and compotes.*

# 240 | French Christmas Pudding

**Preparation time**
30 minutes

**Cooking time**
2 hours

**Oven temperature**
180C, 350F, gas 4

**Serves 8**

**Calories**
593 per portion

**You will need**
1 (425 g/15 oz) can chestnut purée
100 g/4 oz unsalted butter,
softened
4 eggs, separated
175 g/6 oz caster sugar
2 tablespoons brandy (optional)

**For the chocolate sauce**
150 ml/¼ pint double cream
225 g/8 oz plain dark chocolate,
broken into pieces
2 tablespoons brandy
4 marrons glacés, sliced, to
decorate (optional)

Grease and line a 1.2 litre/2 pint non-stick or enamel loaf tin. Cream the chestnut purée and butter, then beat in the egg yolks and sugar. Whisk the egg whites until stiff and fold them into the chestnut mixture, then pour into the prepared tin. Place the tin in a water bath and bake for 2 hours until set. Cover with a piece of buttered foil if necessary during cooking. Meanwhile, prepare the sauce. Heat the cream in a small heavy pan over a gentle heat; do not let it boil. Add the chocolate and brandy. Stir over a very gentle heat until the chocolate has melted and the sauce is smooth. Remove the pudding from the oven and cool in the tin for 5-10 minutes. Loosen it with a knife and turn out on to a warmed dish. Coat with a little chocolate sauce and decorate with the marrons glacés, if using. Hand the remaining sauce separately.

## Cook's Tip

*Chestnuts are a versatile food suitable for use in savoury stuffings, soups and pies, as well as a basis for sweet flans and puddings. Their flavour is enhanced by chocolate.*

# 241 | Polish Plum Cake

**Preparation time**
20 minutes

**Cooking time**
45 minutes

**Oven temperature**
190C, 375F, gas 5
then 200C, 400F, gas 6

**Serves 6-8**

**Calories**
268 per portion

**You will need**
175 g/6 oz plain flour
65 g/2½ oz unsalted butter
40 g/1½ oz caster sugar
1 egg
3 tablespoons soured cream
225 g/8 oz plums
4 teaspoons vanilla sugar
200-300 ml/⅓-½ pint whipping
    cream, whipped (optional)

Grease a 20 cm/8 in springform tin. Sift the flour into a bowl and rub in the butter until the mixture resembles fine breadcrumbs. Stir in the sugar and add the egg and soured cream. Stir to form a moderately firm dough, then turn into the prepared tin and spread in an even layer.

Cut the plums in half, twist to remove the stones and press them, cut side up, as closely together as possible, to form neat circles on top of the dough. Sprinkle with half the vanilla sugar and bake for 35 minutes, then increase the temperature, if necessary, and bake for a further 10 minutes to brown. When the cake is golden-brown and the fruit cooked, remove from the oven and cool slightly. Remove from the tin and cool on a wire rack. Sprinkle with the remainder of the vanilla sugar and serve warm or cold with whipped cream, if desired.

# 242 | Tuiles d'Oranges

**Preparation time**
15 minutes

**Cooking time**
6-8 minutes per batch

**Oven temperature**
190C, 375F, gas 5

**Makes about 15**

**Calories**
38 per biscuit

**You will need**
1 egg white
50 g/2 oz caster sugar
25 g/1 oz plain flour
grated rind of ½ orange
25 g/1 oz butter, melted

Place the egg white in a bowl and beat in the sugar. Add the remaining ingredients and mix well. Place teaspoonfuls of the mixture well apart on greased baking trays and spread out thinly with a palette knife. Bake, not more than four at a time, for 6-8 minutes per batch, until pale golden-brown. If you bake more than four per batch, they will set before you have time to shape them.

Leave on the baking trays for a few seconds, then remove with a palette knife, and place on a rolling pin to curl. Leave until cool then remove carefully.

## Cook's Tip

**You can make your own whipping cream if necessary by mixing together double and single cream in equal proportions.**

## Cook's Tip

**These biscuits are quite delicious as they are, but add a hint of luxury when served with ice creams or creamy desserts.**

# 243 | *Poires en Douillons*

**Preparation time**
*20 minutes*

**Cooking time**
*40 minutes*

**Oven temperature**
*220C, 425F, gas 7
then 190C, 375F, gas 5*

**Serves 4**

**Calories**
*817 per portion*

**You will need**
*1½ (212 g/7½ oz) packets frozen
    puff pastry, defrosted
1 tablespoon semolina
1 tablespoon caster sugar
1 teaspoon ground cinnamon
4 dessert pears, peeled and cored
1 egg yolk, beaten with 1
    teaspoon water*

Roll the puff pastry out into a square on a floured surface to a thickness of 5 mm/¼ in. Divide into four equal squares. Mix the semolina, sugar and cinnamon. Level the rounded bases of the pears so they will stand upright, then roll them in the semolina mixture. Wrap each pear in a square of pastry. Seal by brushing the pastry edges with water and pressing them together. Trim the pastry to obtain a neat finish.

Roll out the pastry trimmings and cut out eight long strips with a pastry cutter. Moisten the strips with a little water and wind them in a spiral around the wrapped pears to decorate. Stand the pears on a baking tray and brush with egg yolk. Bake for 30 minutes, then reduce the temperature and bake for a further 10 minutes. Serve hot with whipped cream or chocolate sauce.

## Cook's Tip

*Pears deteriorate very quickly once they have ripened. If you keep them in the fridge, allow them to reach room temperature before you serve them to allow the flavour to develop.*

# 244 | *Caribbean Sponge*

**Preparation time**
*30 minutes*

**Cooking time**
*1½ hours*

**Serves 4-6**

**Calories**
*377 per portion*

**You will need**
*100 g/4 oz butter
100 g/4 oz caster sugar
grated rind and juice of 1 lime
2 eggs, beaten
150 g/5 oz self-raising flour
50 g/2 oz desiccated coconut
1 tablespoon dark rum (optional)*

Grease a 900 ml/1½ pint pudding basin. Cream the butter, sugar and lime rind until they are light and fluffy. Add the eggs gradually and beat well between each addition. Sift in the flour and fold in the desiccated coconut. Add the lime juice and a little rum, if using.

Pour the mixture into the prepared pudding basin. Cover with a sheet of greased foil, pleated across the centre to allow for expansion, and tie with string. Place in a large pan and pour in enough boiling water to come half-way up the sides of the basin. Cover the pan and steam over a gentle heat for 1½ hours, topping up with hot water if necessary.

Remove the foil and string and turn the sponge out on to a warmed serving dish. Serve with rum-flavoured whipped cream if desired.

## Cook's Tip

*Desiccated coconut can be browned under the grill or in a cool oven and used in various recipes for cakes, biscuits, salads and curries. Turn it from time to time while browning.*

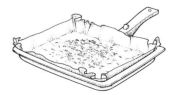

## 245 | Tarte St-Tropez

**Preparation time**
45 minutes, plus 1½ hours to rise

**Cooking time**
20 minutes

**Oven temperature**
220C, 425F, gas 7

**Serves 8**

**Calories**
515 per portion

**You will need**
250 g/9 oz flour
165 g/5½ oz unsalted butter
75 g/3 oz caster sugar
2 teaspoons dried yeast
120 ml/4 fl oz milk, heated to body temperature
3 eggs, lightly beaten, plus 2 yolks
5 teaspoons water
pinch of cream of tartar
250 g/9 oz crème pâtissière (see Cook's Tip below)
icing sugar to dust

Butter and flour a 25 cm/10 in flan dish. Sift the flour and rub in 75 g/3 oz of the butter. Add 15 g/½ oz of the sugar. Dissolve the yeast in the warm milk, then add to the flour with the eggs. Knead to a smooth, slightly sticky dough. Spread the dough over the base of the prepared flan dish. Cover and leave in a warm place to rise, until it doubles in size. Bake for 20 minutes. Cover with foil half-way through cooking. Turn on to a tray. Cool.

Whisk the egg yolks until light and creamy. Place the remaining sugar, the water and cream of tartar in a pan and boil hard for 3 minutes to the soft ball stage (see Cook's Tip 22). Whisk the yolks again, at the same time pouring the sugar into them in a steady stream. Whisk for a further 5 minutes. Gradually beat in the remaining butter and continue beating until the mixture is smooth and creamy. Beat the crème pâtissière into the butter cream 1 tablespoon at a time. Split the tart in half, spread with the filling and sandwich together. Dust with icing sugar.

## 246 | Scandinavian Raspberry Flummery

**Preparation time**
10 minutes

**Cooking time**
20 minutes

**Serves 6**

**Calories**
245 per portion

**You will need**
500 g/1 lb raspberries
300 ml/½ pint water
175 g/6 oz caster sugar
50 g/2 oz semolina

Reserve 12 of the best raspberries for decoration. Place the remainder in a pan with the water and 50 g/2 oz of the sugar. Simmer for 5 minutes until very soft. Sieve to remove the seeds and make up to 600 ml/1 pint with water.

Return the raspberry purée to the rinsed pan. Bring to the boil, stir in the remaining sugar and the semolina and simmer for 10 minutes, stirring frequently. Turn the mixture into a large bowl and whisk until light and fluffy. Serve warm in individual dishes. Decorate with the reserved raspberries and serve with single cream.

## Cook's Tip

To make crème pâtissière, whisk 2 eggs with 75 g/3 oz vanilla sugar until light and creamy, then whisk in 25 g/1 oz cornflour. Heat 250 ml/8 fl oz milk to simmering point, then pour over the egg mixture. Return to the pan and, stirring constantly, heat until the sauce thickens. Cool.

## Cook's Tip

This can be made with any soft fruit, including loganberries, blackberries and blueberries. Ring the changes by using wholewheat semolina, too.

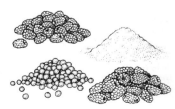

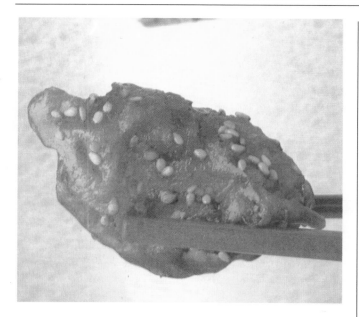

# 247 | *Chinese Toffee Apples*

**Preparation time**
15 minutes

**Cooking time**
15 minutes

**Serves 4**

**Calories**
384 per portion

**You will need**
100 g/4 oz plain flour
1 tablespoon cornflour
pinch of salt
2 eggs, beaten
150 ml/¼ pint water
4 dessert apples, peeled and
    cored
a little cornflour, for coating
oil for deep frying

For the toffee
225 g/8 oz sugar
300 ml/½ pint water
2 tablespoons groundnut oil
50 g/2 oz sesame seeds

Sift the flour, cornflour and salt into a bowl. Mix in the eggs, and whisk in the water to form a smooth batter.

Cut each apple into six, then toss in a little cornflour. In a large saucepan heat the fat to 190C, 375F, or until a cube of bread browns in 30 seconds. Coat the apple wedges with the batter and fry until golden. Drain on absorbent paper and keep warm.

To make the toffee, stir the sugar into the water in a heavy pan over a low heat. When the sugar has dissolved, add the oil and increase the heat. Boil until golden caramel. Remove from the heat. Tip in the apple wedges and sesame seeds and turn the pieces of apple until coated with toffee. Dip the toffee apples quickly in iced water and serve immediately. The toffee should be crisp.

## Cook's Tip

*Toffee apples of any kind should be eaten on the day they are made or the crisp caramel coating may soften if it is in prolonged contact with the fruit.*

# 248 | *German Apple Pudding*

**Preparation time**
20 minutes

**Cooking time**
1-1¼ hours

**Oven temperature**
180C, 350F, gas 4

**Serves 4**

**Calories**
672 per portion

**You will need**
100 g/4 oz self-raising flour
25 g/1 oz ground almonds
75 g/3 oz butter
50 g/2 oz soft brown sugar
1 teaspoon lemon juice
1 egg yolk

For the filling
500 g/1 lb cooking apples, peeled,
    cored and thinly sliced
75 g/3 oz soft brown sugar
grated rind of 1 lemon
1 teaspoon lemon juice

For the topping
50 g/2 oz plain flour
50 g/2 oz butter
150 g/5 oz soft brown sugar
1 teaspoon ground cinnamon

Sift the flour into a bowl and add the ground almonds and butter. Rub in until the mixture resembles fine breadcrumbs. Stir in the sugar, lemon juice and egg yolk and mix together. Press firmly into a greased 20 cm/8 in loose-bottomed cake tin. Mix the apples with the remaining filling ingredients and arrange over the mixture.

To make the topping, sift the flour into a bowl and rub in the butter until evenly combined. Stir in the sugar and cinnamon. Sprinkle on top of the apples. Bake for 1-1¼ hours, until golden. Cool slightly in the tin before turning out. Serve hot or cold.

## Cook's Tip

*If you have run out of brown sugar and a recipe calls for it specifically, you can cheat by adding 1 teaspoon of black treacle to about 75 g/3 oz white sugar.*

# Special Occasion Desserts

*Whether you're cooking for a special dinner party, celebration meal or simply dinner for two here are some recipes that will give the crowning glory to a special occasion meal. Add your own touch of class to these ideas with imaginative decorations and personal finishing touches to make a memorable sweet finale.*

## 249 | Apple Shortcake

**Preparation time**
35 minutes

**Cooking time**
40 minutes

**Oven temperature**
160C, 325F, gas 3
then 190C, 375F, gas 5

**Serves 6**

**Calories**
315 per portion

**You will need**
100 g/4 oz butter or margarine
50 g/2 oz plus 1 tablespoon caster
  sugar
175 g/6 oz plain flour
1 teaspoon ground cinnamon
1 dessert apple, quartered, cored
  and thinly sliced

**To glaze**
3 tablespoons apricot jam
2 teaspoons lemon juice

Cream the butter or margarine and 50 g/2 oz of the sugar until light and fluffy. Sift the flour and cinnamon together and add to the creamed mixture. Stir until the shortcake mixture binds together. Turn the dough on to a lightly floured surface and knead until smooth. Roll out to a 20 cm/8 in round and place on a baking tray. Pinch the edges firmly with your fingers and prick well with a fork. Bake for 20 minutes. Remove from the oven and increase the temperature.

Arrange the apples in overlapping circles on top of the shortbread, sprinkle with the remaining 1 tablespoon of sugar and cook for a further 20 minutes. Remove from the oven, transfer to a wire rack and leave to cool.

Heat the apricot jam with the lemon juice, stirring until the jam has melted. Sieve, reheat and brush over the apples. Leave the apple shortcake to cool before serving.

## 250 | Orange Ice Cream

**Preparation time**
20 minutes, plus 5-6
hours to freeze

**Serves 6-8**

**Calories**
297 per portion

**You will need**
4 large oranges
4 egg yolks
100 g/4 oz caster sugar
300 ml/½ pint single cream
150 ml/¼ pint double cream,
  whipped
6-8 chocolate triangles (Cook's Tip
  142) to decorate

Halve two of the oranges, carefully scoop out the flesh and juice and sieve to extract all juices; keep on one side. Freeze the orange shells.

Finely grate the rind of the remaining oranges and place in a heatproof bowl with the egg yolks and sugar. Beat until thoroughly blended. Heat the single cream to just below boiling point, then stir into the egg yolk mixture. Place the bowl over a pan of simmering water and stir until thickened. Add the orange juice, strain and cool.

Fold the orange custard into the double cream and turn into a rigid freezerproof container. Cover, seal and freeze until firm. Scoop the ice cream into the reserved orange shells, piling up well. Return the leftover ice cream to the freezer for another occasion or scoop into extra shells or individual glasses. Decorate each orange ice with a chocolate triangle and serve immediately, or return to the freezer until required.

# 251 | Ginger Charlotte Russe

**Preparation time**
25 minutes, plus about
5 hours to chill

**Cooking time**
15 minutes

**Serves 6-8**

**Calories**
320 per portion

**You will need**
1 teaspoon powdered gelatine
65 ml/2½ fl oz hot water
65 ml/2½ fl oz ginger wine
1 half Maraschino cherry
5 crystallised orange segments
1 strip angelica, 5 cm/2 in long
about 20 boudoir biscuits

For the Bavarois
2 eggs, separated
50 g/2 oz caster sugar
250 ml/8 fl oz milk
50 g/2 oz bitter or plain chocolate
15 g/½ oz powdered gelatine
50 ml/2 fl oz ginger wine
300 ml/½ pint whipped cream

Dissolve the gelatine in the hot water over a pan of hot water. Stir in the ginger wine. Use enough gelatine to coat the base of a deep 15 cm/6 in cake tin, reserving the surplus gelatine in a bowl standing in warm water. Use the cherry, orange and angelica to decorate the base. Chill for 30 minutes. Pour over the remaining gelatine. Line the sides of the tin with the biscuits.

Make the Bavarois as recipe 111, adding the chocolate with the milk. Remove from the heat. Dissolve the gelatine in the ginger wine over a pan of hot water. Stir into the custard. Cool, then chill for 1 hour. Fold half the cream and the stiffly beaten egg whites into the Bavarois mixture. Pour into the prepared tin and chill for 3 hours. Unmould, then decorate with the remaining cream.

## Cook's Tip

*Ensure the biscuits stand upright by pushing one end into the jelly. If necessary, trim the biscuits level with the filling before unmoulding the charlotte russe.*

# 252 | Honey Soufflé Pudding

**Preparation time**
35 minutes

**Cooking time**
30-35 minutes

**Oven temperature**
190C, 375F, gas 5

**Serves 4**

**Calories**
366 per portion

**You will need**
60 g/2¼ oz unsalted butter
2 tablespoons caster sugar
50 g/2 oz honey
50 g/2 oz flour
grated rind of 1 lemon
150 ml/¼ pint milk
2 eggs, separated

For the sabayon
2 egg yolks
20 g/¾ oz caster sugar
20 g/¾ oz honey
1 tablespoon rum
4 tablespoons milk

Melt 10 g/¼ oz of the butter and brush the insides of four 150 ml/¼ pint soufflé dishes. Dust with the sugar. Cream the remaining butter, honey, flour and lemon rind. Heat the milk, pour over the mixture and blend. Return to the pan and heat until thickened. Beat in the egg yolks. Whisk the egg whites until stiff and fold into the mixture. Pour into the soufflé dishes and smooth the tops.

Stand the dishes in a roasting tin containing hot water to come half-way up the dishes. Bake for 30-35 minutes, covering with greased foil after 20 minutes.

For the sabayon, whisk the egg yolks, sugar and honey in a bowl until creamy. Add the rum and milk, then stand the bowl over a pan of hot water. Whisk until the sabayon has increased its volume. Remove the puddings from the oven, loosen the edges and turn out on to four plates. Pour some of the sabayon over. Serve.

## Cook's Tip

*Honey will keep almost indefinitely if kept in a screw-topped jar in a cool, dark place.*

# 253 | Passionfruit Sorbet

**Preparation time**
15 minutes, plus 3-5 hours to freeze

**Serves 4**

**Calories**
169 per portion

**You will need**
10 passionfruit
juice of ½ lime
400 ml/14 fl oz water
300 g/11 oz sugar
1 egg white
1 teaspoon caster sugar

Scoop the flesh out of the passionfruit and blend in a liquidiser or food processor with the lime juice and 100 ml/4 fl oz of the water. Strain and save the juice. Place the sugar and remaining water in a pan. Heat to boiling point, stirring continuously to dissolve the sugar. Combine with the juice and pour into a rigid freezerproof container. Freeze for 2-3 hours or until almost solid. Whisk the egg white and caster sugar until stiff, then whisk into the sorbet and return to the freezer for 1-2 hours or until set.

If the sorbet has been in the freezer for 24 hours or longer, transfer to the refrigerator 15 minutes before serving to soften slightly.

## Cook's Tip

*If you are whisking only one egg white for a pastry glaze, for example, whisk it on a flat plate with a knife. It saves on washing-up.*

# 254 | Chocolate Meringue Layer

**Preparation time**
30 minutes, plus 4 hours to chill

**Cooking time**
1½-2 hours

**Oven temperature**
150C, 300F, gas 2

**Serves 6-8**

**Calories**
582 per portion

**You will need**
120 g/4½ oz icing sugar
2 egg whites
1 teaspoon vanilla essence

For the filling
150 g/5 oz plain chocolate, broken into pieces
275 ml/9 fl oz double cream
100 g/4 oz almonds, finely chopped and toasted
1 teaspoon instant coffee powder
1 tablespoon boiling water
2 tablespoons Cointreau or rum
chocolate curls to decorate

Draw an 18 cm/7 inch circle on three sheets of non-stick silicone paper. Whisk the icing sugar, egg whites and vanilla essence in a bowl over a pan of hot water until thick. Remove from the heat and beat until cool. Divide the mixture between the three circles. Place on two baking trays and bake in two batches for about 1½ hours, until crisp and dried out. Cool on a wire rack.

To make the filling, melt the chocolate over a pan of hot water. Bring 85 ml/3 fl oz of the cream to the boil, then pour into the chocolate. Stir until smooth, then add the almonds. Blend the coffee with the water and beat into the mixture with the alcohol. Chill for 4 hours. Beat the filling, whip 150 ml/¼ pint of the cream, fold it into the filling. Sandwich the meringues with the filling. Decorate with chocolate curls and the remaining whipped cream.

## Cook's Tip

*Rubbing the bowl with a cut lemon before whisking egg whites increases their volume and keeps them firm.*

# 255 | Tipsy Torten

**Preparation time**
35 minutes, plus 1 hour
10 minutes to cool and
to soak

**Cooking time**
15-20 minutes

**Oven temperature**
200C, 400F, gas 6

**Serves 12**

**Calories**
291 per portion

**You will need**
2 tablespoons Grand Marnier
1 tablespoon tangerine or mild
    orange marmalade
284 ml/10 fl oz whipped cream
16-18 langues de chat biscuits
    (see recipe 13), trimmed
1 (312 g/11 oz) can mandarin
    segments, drained
50 g/2 oz chocolate, grated

For the cake
75 g/3 oz self-raising flour
3 tablespoons cocoa powder
4 eggs
75 g/3 oz caster sugar

Sift the flour and cocoa together twice. Whisk the eggs and sugar together in a large bowl until the whisk leaves a trail. Fold in the flour mixture.

Divide the mixture between two greased and floured 23 cm/9 in cake tins and bake for 15-20 minutes or until springy to the touch. Cool on a wire rack.

Place one cake on a serving plate and drizzle over half the liqueur. Leave for 10 minutes, then spread with the marmalade and about one-third of the cream. Place the other sponge on top and drizzle over the remaining liqueur. Leave for 10 minutes. Cover the cake with the remaining cream. Chill for 30 minutes. Lightly mark the top into twelve sections. Press the biscuits around the sides of the cake. Decorate with the mandarins and grated chocolate.

# 256 | Summer Puddings

**Preparation time**
20 minutes, plus
overnight chilling

**Cooking time**
10 minutes

**Serves 8**

**Calories**
252 per portion

**You will need**
500 g/1 lb mixed blackberries,
    blackcurrants and redcurrants
75 g/3 oz caster sugar
4 tablespoons water
100 g/4 oz strawberries, sliced
100 g/4 oz raspberries
16 slices white bread, crusts
    removed

To decorate
8 tablespoons double cream,
    whipped
few sprigs of redcurrants or
    blackcurrants (optional)

Place the blackberries and currants in a heavy pan with the sugar and water. Cook gently, stirring occasionally, for 10 minutes, until tender. Add the strawberries and raspberries and leave to cool. Strain, reserving the juice.

Cut out sixteen 7.5 cm/3 in circles of bread. Cut the remaining bread into strips 2.5 cm/1 in wide. Soak in the reserve juice. Line the bases of eight ramekin dishes with the circles of bread. Arrange the strips to fit around the sides. Divide the fruit between the dishes and place the remaining circles of bread on top.

Cover each dish with greaseproof paper and stand one on top of another on two saucers. Place a cup containing a 250 g/8 oz weight on a saucer on top of each pile. Leave overnight in the refrigerator. Turn out on to plates and decorate with whipped cream and currants, if using.

## Cook's Tip

*Marmalade is a very versatile ingredient. For a special occasion, flavour dark seville marmalade with a dash of whisky and serve warm with hot pancakes and vanilla ice cream.*

## Cook's Tip

*As the season for berries and currants is very short, you can easily substitute canned fruit for this dessert if you wish.*

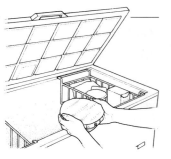

# 257 | Rum and Blackcurrant Torten

**Preparation time**
35 minutes, plus 1 hour 10 minutes to cool and to soak

**Cooking time**
15-20 minutes

**Oven temperature**
200C, 400F, gas 6

**Serves 12**

**Calories**
205 per portion

**You will need**
2 tablespoons dark rum
4 tablespoons blackcurrant jam
284 ml/10 fl oz whipped cream
50 g/2 oz flaked almonds, toasted
2-3 teaspoons cocoa powder, sifted, for sprinkling

For the cake
75 g/3 oz self-raising flour
3 tablespoons cocoa powder
4 eggs
75 g/3 oz caster sugar

Make two 23 cm/9 in cakes as instructed in recipe 255. Cool on a wire rack.

Place one cake on a cake board and drizzle over half the rum. Leave for about 10 minutes then spread with 3 tablespoons of the jam and one-third of the cream. Place the other sponge on top and drizzle over the remaining rum. Leave for 10 minutes. Reserve 3 tablespoons of the remaining cream for decoration; use the rest to coat the top and sides of the cake. Press the almonds on to the side of the cake. Chill for 30 minutes. Mark the top into 12 sections. Using a star nozzle, pipe a rosette of cream on each portion and fill with the remaining jam. Dust the centre of the cake with the cocoa powder.

## Cook's Tip

**Chop almonds when they are warm: after blanching or toasting, for example. They tend to break up if you try to do it when they are cold.**

# 258 | Raspberry Bombe

**Preparation time**
10 minutes, plus 2-3 hours to freeze

**Serves 6**

**Calories**
351 per portion

**You will need**
225 g/8 oz raspberries
3 tablespoons icing sugar
300 ml/½ pint double cream
150 ml/¼ pint single cream
100 g/4 oz meringues
raspberries to decorate (optional)

Blend the raspberries and icing sugar in a liquidiser or food processor until smooth. Sieve to remove the seeds.

Whip the double and single creams together until they form soft peaks. Break the meringues into pieces and fold into the cream. Very lightly fold half the raspberry purée into the cream mixture to give a marbled effect. Turn into a 1 litre/2 pint pudding basin, cover with foil, seal and freeze until firm.

Carefully turn out on to a serving plate and place in the refrigerator 40 minutes before serving to soften. Pour the remaining purée over the bombe to serve. Decorate with fresh raspberries, if desired.

## Cook's Tip

**Save time by making two of these special desserts. The one you do not use will keep for up to a month in the freezer.**

# 259 | Strawberry Brûlée

**Preparation time**
10 minutes, plus 2 hours to freeze and to chill

**Serves 6**

**Calories**
306 per portion

**You will need**
225 g/8 oz strawberries, halved
2 tablespoons Grand Marnier or Kirsch
300 ml/½ pint double cream, whipped
100 g/4 oz soft brown sugar

Place the strawberries in six freezerproof ramekin dishes and sprinkle with the liqueur. Divide the cream between the ramekins, smoothing to the edges. Cover, seal and freeze for 30 minutes.

Sprinkle with the sugar and place under a grill for 1 minute or until the sugar has caramelised. Cool and chill before serving.

# 260 | Crêpes Suzette

**Preparation time**
25 minutes, plus 30 minutes to rest

**Cooking time**
20 minutes

**Serves 4**

**Calories**
572 per portion

**You will need**
100 g/4 oz plain flour
pinch of salt
2 eggs, beaten
300 ml/½ pint milk
2 teaspoons corn oil
oil and butter for frying
2 tablespoons brandy, warmed

For the sauce
100 g/4 oz butter
100 g/4 oz caster sugar
grated rind of 1 orange
175 ml/6 fl oz fresh orange juice
2 tablespoons lemon juice
2 tablespoons brandy
1 tablespoon Curaçao

Make the batter as recipe 128, adding the oil to make a smooth batter. Cover and rest for 30 minutes. Heat a little oil and butter in a 15 cm/6 inch frying pan. Add 2 tablespoons of the batter and swirl around until the base is covered. Cook until golden, then turn and cook underneath. Repeat until all the batter is used, stacking the crêpes with greaseproof paper between each one.

For the sauce, place the butter, sugar, orange rind and juice and lemon juice in a frying pan and stir until the butter is melted and the sugar dissolved. Simmer for 5 minutes, then add brandy and Curaçao. Fold the crêpes to form triangles. Place in the sauce, spooning it over so that they are well coated. To serve, transfer the crêpes and any remaining sauce to a dish. Pour over the warm brandy and set alight. Serve when the flames subside.

## Cook's Tip

To wash strawberries, rinse quickly, then drain well before removing the hulls otherwise they can become very soft.

## Cook's Tip

Butter burns at a lower temperature than oil and salted butter burns faster than unsalted. Take care when cooking in butter that you don't impair the flavour by burning it.

## 261 | Hazelnut Parfait

**Preparation time**
50 minutes plus 5-6
hours to cool and
freeze

**Cooking time**
15 minutes

**Oven temperature**
200C, 400F, gas 6

**Serves 4-6**

**Calories**
438 per portion

**You will need**

For the praline
75 g/3 oz hazelnuts, roasted
75 g/3 oz sugar

For the parfait
3 egg yolks
75 g/3 oz caster sugar
300 ml/½ pint double cream

For the caramel sauce
75 g/3 oz sugar
120 ml/4 fl oz double cream

Make the praline as instructed in recipe 22, substituting the hazelnuts for the almonds.

Whisk the egg yolks, then add the caster sugar and whisk until the mixture thickens. In a separate bowl, whisk the cream until it holds its shape. Fold the yolks and sugar into the cream, then fold in half the praline. Transfer the mixture to a rigid freezerproof container and freeze for 2-3 hours until almost set. Beat well and return to the freezer for 1-2 hours or until completely firm.

For the sauce, place the sugar in a pan with sufficient water to moisten. Boil to a mid-amber caramel. Remove from the heat. Bring the cream to the boil quickly and whisk into the hot caramel. Cool until just warm.

If the parfait has been in the freezer for 24 hours or longer, transfer to the refrigerator 15 minutes before serving to soften. Pour the caramel sauce over the scoops of parfait and sprinkle with the remaining praline.

### Cook's Tip

**Praline, when homemade, spoils very quickly and will only keep for a day or two if stored in an airtight jar.**

## 262 | Chocolate Muesli Delight

**Preparation time**
20 minutes, plus 1 hour
to chill

**Serves 4**

**Calories**
575 per portion

**You will need**
1 450 g/1 lb carton natural yogurt
50 g/2 oz unsweetened muesli base
50 g/2 oz hazelnuts, finely chopped and toasted
50 g/2 oz plain chocolate digestive biscuits, finely crushed
225 g/8 oz dried apricots
2 tablespoons clear honey
100 g/4 oz plain chocolate
25 g/1 oz butter
chocolate curls to decorate

Tip the yogurt into a bowl and stir in the muesli, hazelnuts and biscuits. Roughly chop the apricots, then add to the yogurt mixture with the honey. Stir until evenly blended.

Melt the chocolate with the butter in a heatproof bowl set over hot water. Stir vigorously until smooth.

Spoon one tablespoon of the yogurt mixture into the bottom of four tall, sundae glasses. On top, spoon two teaspoons of the chocolate mixture, swirling the mixture to the sides of the glass, without stirring it into the yogurt. Continue spooning the yogurt and chocolate mixtures alternately, finishing with a spoonful of chocolate mixture. Allow to chill and then decorate with chocolate curls.

### Cook's Tip

**Make biscuit crumbs in a blender or food processor. Chill chocolate biscuits and all utensils before crushing to keep mess to a minimum.**

# 263 | Raspberry Charlotte

**Preparation time**
30 minutes, plus 1½
hours to set

**Serves 8**

**Calories**
355 per portion

**You will need**
350 g/12 oz raspberries
2 eggs
1 egg yolk
75 g/3 oz caster sugar
15 g/½ oz gelatine
3 tablespoons hot water
300 ml/½ pint double cream,
   lightly whipped
30 langues de chat biscuits (recipe
   13)

Set aside about 8 raspberries for decoration. Purée the remainder in a liquidiser or food processor, then sieve to remove the seeds. Place the eggs, egg yolk and sugar in a bowl and whisk until thick and mousse-like. Dissolve the gelatine in the hot water over a pan of simmering water, then mix into the purée. Cool slightly, then carefully fold the purée and two-thirds of the cream into the mousse. Stir over a bowl of iced water until beginning to set, then turn into a greased 18 cm/7 in loose-bottomed cake tin. Chill until set.

Turn out on to a serving dish. Spread a little of the remaining cream round the sides and press on the biscuits, overlapping slightly. Decorate with the remaining cream and raspberries.

# 264 | Strawberries Cocteau

**Preparation time**
15 minutes

**Serves 4**

**Calories**
548 per portion

**You will need**
4 macaroons
2 tablespoons Kirsch
225 g/8 oz alpine or common
   strawberries
4 scoops vanilla ice cream
1 quantity crème chantilly (recipe
   118)
candied violets (Cook's Tip 98)

Dip the macaroons in the Kirsch and place them in four dessert bowls or glass coupes. Cover them with a layer of strawberries and place a scoop of ice cream on top. Arrange more strawberries on top, reserving a few for decoration.

Make the crème chantilly as instructed in recipe 118 and pile it on top of the ice cream and strawberries. Decorate with candied violets and the reserved strawberries. Serve immediately.

## Cook's Tip

**Soft fruits such as strawberries and raspberries do not freeze successfully if frozen whole, but if you purée them raw, sweeten them and add a little lemon juice to prevent discoloration, the results are fine.**

## Cook's Tip

**If alpine strawberries are available, they will make this a very special pudding. The berries are small and tasty, and one other good point is that they do not need hulling.**

# 265 | *Orange and Rum Soufflé Omelette*

**Preparation time**
20 minutes

**Cooking time**
5 minutes

**Oven temperature**
200C, 400F, gas 6

**Serves 2**

**Calories**
343 per portion

**You will need**
4 eggs, separated
1 tablespoon caster sugar
1 tablespoon rum
15 g/½ oz butter

For the filling
1 orange, peeled, pith removed,
    and divided into segments
2 tablespoons orange marmalade
3 tablespoons rum to flambé

Prepare the omelette as instructed in recipe 73, but substituting the rum for the water and vanilla essence.

To make the filling, mix the orange segments with the marmalade. Spread on to the cooked omelette, fold it in half and turn out on to a warmed serving dish. Warm the rum in a ladle and ignite it. Pour the rum, still flaming, over the omelette and serve immediately.

---

## Cook's Tip

**Do not pour the spirit straight out of the bottle over any food to be flamed: the flame can blow back.**

# 266 | *Coffee and Walnut Cake*

**Preparation time**
25 minutes

**Cooking time**
about 30 minutes

**Oven temperature**
180C, 350F, gas 4

**Serves 6**

**Calories**
600 per portion

**You will need**
100 g/4 oz butter
100 g/4 oz caster sugar
2 eggs, beaten
100 g/4 oz self-raising flour
50 g/2 oz walnuts, chopped
1 tablespoon coffee essence

For the filling
3 egg yolks
75 g/3 oz sugar
50 ml/2 fl oz water
100 g/4 oz butter, softened
2 teaspoons coffee essence
icing sugar and walnut halves to
    decorate

Grease and flour two 18 cm/7 in sandwich tins. Cream the butter and the sugar until light and fluffy. Gradually beat in the eggs, fold in the flour and walnuts and add the coffee essence. Divide the mixture equally between the two tins, and bake for 30 minutes or until risen and springy to the touch. Turn out on to wire racks to cool.

For the filling, whisk the egg yolks until thick. Put the sugar in a pan with the water and boil, stirring constantly to dissolve the sugar. Boil to 107C, 225F on a sugar thermometer. Pour on to the egg yolks and whisk well. Beat in the butter until smooth, then stir in the coffee essence.

Sandwich the cakes together with half the filling, and use the remaining filling to decorate the cake. Lightly dust with icing sugar, then decorate with walnut halves.

---

## Cook's Tip

**To test for thread stage, remove a little of the syrup with a small spoon or fork. It should form a fine, thin thread as it falls.**

# 267 | Praline Charlotte

**Preparation time**
15 minutes, plus 2-3 hours to cool and chill

**Cooking time**
15-20 minutes

**Serves 6**

**Calories**
609 per portion

**You will need**
100 g/4 oz almonds in their skins
100 g/4 oz caster sugar

For the charlotte
3 egg yolks
75 g/3 oz caster sugar
250 ml/8 fl oz milk
15 g/½ oz gelatine
2 tablespoons hot water
250 ml/8 fl oz double cream
20 trifle sponge finger biscuits roughly broken
150 ml/¼ pint whipped cream

Grease and line a 15 cm/6 in charlotte mould. Make the praline as recipe 22. Cream the egg yolks and sugar until thick. Heat the milk until almost simmering, pour on to the egg mixture and stir. Strain into a double boiler or pan, and cook slowly, until the custard thickens enough to coat the back of a spoon. Remove from the heat.

Dissolve the gelatine in the hot water over a pan of simmering water and stir well into the custard with the praline. Pour into a large bowl and leave in a cool place, stirring occasionally until the mixture is just beginning to set. Lightly whisk the cream and fold into the custard.

Place the mould in a bowl containing ice cubes. Pour a layer of the custard into the base, then cover with a layer of the biscuits. When the first layer has set, pour in another layer of custard. Continue until the mould is full. The ice causes the custard to set almost immediately. Cover with cling film and chill for at least 2 hours. Unmould on to a plate and decorate with whipped cream.

## Cook's Tip

**The finished pudding may be wrapped and frozen in its mould for up to 4 weeks. Allow at least 3 hours for defrosting before turning out and decorating.**

# 268 | Caramel Flan

**Preparation time**
20-25 minutes, plus 1½ hours to chill

**Cooking time**
20 minutes

**Oven temperature**
220C, 425F, gas 7

**Serves 6-8**

**Calories**
171 per portion

**You will need**
2 eggs
50 g/2 oz caster sugar
50 g/2 oz plain flour
2 tablespoons cornflour
300 ml/½ pint milk
25 g/1 oz margarine or butter
25 g/1 oz walnuts, chopped
1 (410 g/14½ oz) can pear halves, drained
extra chopped walnuts and angelica diamonds to decorate

Grease a 21.5 cm/8½ inch sponge flan tin and dust with flour. Place a circle of greaseproof paper on the raised part of the tin. Whisk the eggs and half the sugar in a bowl set over a pan of hot water until thick. Remove from the heat and whisk until cool. Sift half the flour over the mixture and fold in. Add the remaining flour. Pour into the tin and bake for about 10 minutes until firm to touch.

To make the filling, blend the cornflour with a little of the milk. Melt the margarine in a large pan with the remaining sugar. Boil without stirring until caramelised and golden-brown. Heat the remaining milk to just below boiling point, pour on to the caramelised mixture and stir until dissolved. Pour the flavoured milk on to the cornflour mixture, stir well and return to the pan. Bring to the boil, stirring constantly, lower the heat and simmer for 2 minutes. Cool. Pour the mixture into the flan case and sprinkle with walnuts. Cool. Arrange the pears, then chill. Decorate with chopped walnuts and angelica.

## Cook's Tip

**Keep any odd pieces of angelica from shaping and use in any fruit cake recipe.**

# 269 | Brown Bread Ice Cream

**Preparation time**
25 minutes, plus 5-6 hours to freeze

**Serves 6-8**

**Calories**
423 per portion

**You will need**
75 g/3 oz wholemeal breadcrumbs
50 g/2 oz demerara sugar
50 g/2 oz hazelnuts, skinned and
    ground
3 egg whites
100 g/4 oz caster sugar
400 ml/14 fl oz double cream,
    lightly whipped
18 hazelnuts to decorate

Combine the breadcrumbs, demerara sugar and hazelnuts on a heatproof plate. Place under a grill until golden-brown, stirring occasionally. Leave to cool.

Whisk the egg whites until stiff, then gradually whisk in the caster sugar. Carefully fold two-thirds of the cream into the meringue with the breadcrumb mixture. Turn the mixture into a 1 litre/2 pint freezerproof mould. Cover, seal and freeze until solid.

Turn out on to a plate 30 minutes before serving. Decorate with the remaining cream and the hazelnuts. Leave in the refrigerator to soften until required.

# 270 | Champagne Water Ice

**Preparation time**
10 minutes, plus 5-6 hours to freeze

**Serves 6**

**Calories**
179 per portion

**You will need**
225 g/8 oz sugar
300 ml/½ pint water
300 ml/½ pint champagne
juice of 1 lemon
juice of 1 orange

Set the freezer to its coldest setting. If making the water ice without a processor or sorbetière, place a bowl and the whisk in the freezer to chill. If using a processor for the whisking, freeze the mixture in ice cube trays and, when rock-solid, process the cubes to smoothness.

Place the sugar in the water and stir until dissolved. Add the champagne and fruit juices, and pour into shallow trays. Freeze for 2-3 hours or until frozen round the edges but still soft in the centre. Tip into the chilled bowl and whisk until smooth. Return to the freezer. Repeat the whisking process at intervals until creamy, smooth and white. Scoop into chilled serving glasses or bowls and serve immediately.

## Cook's Tip

To refresh a loaf that has become a little stale, wrap it in foil and place it in the oven (200C, 400F, gas 6) for 30-40 minutes. Leave it to cool in the foil.

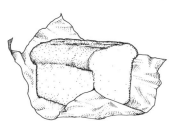

## Cook's Tip

The addition of alcohol to this water ice means that the ice will melt very quickly at room temperature, so leave it in the freezer until just before serving.

# 271 | Italian Hazelnut Ice

### Preparation time
15 minutes, plus 5-6 hours to freeze

### Serves 4-5

### Calories
387 per portion

### You will need
100 g/4 oz hazelnuts, toasted and skinned
300 ml/½ pint milk
4 egg yolks
75 g/3 oz caster sugar
3 drops vanilla essence
175 ml/6 fl oz whipping cream, whipped

Reserve a few nuts for decoration, if liked; grind the remainder coarsely.

Place the milk in a pan and bring almost to the boil. Cream the egg yolks, sugar and vanilla essence in a bowl until pale, then gradually stir in the milk. Stir in the gound nuts. Pour into a clean pan and heat gently, stirring, until the mixture is thick enough to coat the back of a spoon; do not allow to boil. Cover and leave until cold, stirring occasionally.

Fold the cream into the custard. Turn into individual freezerproof containers, cover and freeze until firm. Transfer to the refrigerator 1 hour before serving to soften. Decorate with nuts, if using.

# 272 | Rum Babas

### Preparation time
20 minutes, plus about 45 minutes to rise and prove

### Cooking time
15 minutes

### Oven temperature
200C, 400F, gas 6

### Serves 8

### Calories
264 per portion

### You will need
100 g/4 oz strong plain flour
pinch of salt
10 g/¼ oz dried instant yeast
1 teaspoon sugar
3 tablespoons milk
2 eggs, beaten
50 g/2 oz butter, softened
175 g/6 oz sugar
250 ml/8 fl oz water
strip of lemon rind
3 tablespoons dark rum

### To decorate
150 ml/¼ pint whipped cream
4 glacé cherries, cut in half
8 angelica leaves

Grease eight small ring moulds. Place the flour, salt, yeast and sugar in a warm mixing bowl. Add the milk, eggs and butter and beat for 5 minutes until the dough is smooth and elastic. Half-fill each mould with dough and cover with oiled cling film. Leave in a warm place until the dough has risen two-thirds of the way up the moulds. Bake for 15 minutes until golden-brown.

To prepare the syrup, gently heat the sugar with the water, stirring frequently until the sugar has dissolved. Add the lemon rind and boil for 5 minutes. Stir in the rum.

Turn the babas out of the moulds. When they are cool, spoon over the rum syrup until they are well saturated. Using a piping bag fitted with a rose nozzle, fill the centres with whipping cream. Top each one with half a glacé cherry and angelica leaves.

## Cook's Tip

*The flavour of this ice is so delectable that it would be a shame to mask it by overwhelming decoration. Allow it to speak for itself by keeping its accompaniment simple: perhaps meringue or plain wafers or biscuits.*

## Cook's Tip

*Instant dried yeast is available from supermarkets. It does not require pre-mixing with water, unlike other dried yeasts. If you want to use fresh yeast, double the quantity of that given for the dried kind.*

# Index